GOETHE
SELECTED POEMS

JOHANN WOLFGANG VON GOETHE

SELECTED POEMS

EDITED BY
CHRISTOPHER MIDDLETON

WITH TRANSLATIONS BY
Michael Hamburger
David Luke
Christopher Middleton
John Frederick Nims
Vernon Watkins

John Calder
LONDON

First published in Great Britain, in this translation 1983 by John Calder (Publishers) Ltd. 18 Brewer Street, London W1R 4AS by arrangement with Suhrkamp/Insel Publishers Boston, Inc. Cambridge, Massachusetts U.S.A.

British Library Cataloguing in Publication Data
Goethe, Johann Wolfgang von
 Selected poems of Johann Wolfgang von Goethe
 I. Title
 831'.6 PT2026.A3
 ISBN 0-7145-4004-8

ISBN 0-7145-4004-8 UK
ISBN 3-518-03053-1 USA

Library of Congress Cataloging in Publication Data

Goethe, Johann Wolfgang von, 1749-1832.
 Selected poems.

 English and German.
 Bibliography: p.
 Includes index.
 I. Middleton, Christopher. II. Title.
PT2026.A3 1982 831'.6 82-5492
ISBN 3-518-03053-1 AACR2

Michael Hamburger, "Found," "At Midnight," "Nearness of the Beloved," "On Originality," "Prometheus," "Roman Elegies I,V," "Anacreon's Grave," "Hegira," "Blessed Longing," "Nature and Art," "The Bridegroom," "True Enough," "Sicilian Song." Vernon Watkins, "The Godlike," "Limits of Human Nature," "A Likeness," originally appeared in *Great Writings of Goethe*, ed. by Stephen Spender. Copyright© 1958 by Stephen Spender.

Christopher Middleton, "Amor as Landscape Painter," originally appeared in *Seneca Review*, nos. 1&2, 1981. "A Winter Journey in the Harz," and "Buccaneer" originally appeared in *Great Writings of Goethe*, ed. by Stephen Spender. Copyright © 1958 by Stephen Spender. Reprinted by arrangement with New American Library.

John Frederick Nims, "The Diary" originally appeared in *Playboy* Magazine; Copyright © 1968 by Playboy. "May Song" originally appeared in the *Chicago Tribune Magazine*, May 2, 1971. Copyright © by permission of Chicago Tribune Company. "Trilogy of Passion" first appeared in *The Hudson Review*, vol. XXII, no. 1, Spring, 1969. "To Charlotte von Stein" and "Permanence in Change" first appeared in *Poetry*, Aug.-Sept. 1970. Copyright © by The Modern Poetry Association. Reprinted by permission of *Poetry*.

"Rosebud in the Heather," "To the Moon" and "The Fisherman" first appeared in *Sappho to Valéry*. Copyright © 1971 by John Frederick Nims. Reprinted by permission of Princeton University Press.

Goethe Edition: Volume 1.
© Suhrkamp/Insel Publishers Boston, Inc., 1983
ISBN 3-518-03053-1

PREFACE

This book was undertaken at the suggestion of Dr. Siegfried Unseld and completed in Spring of the 150th Goethe Centenary year 1982. To my fellow translators I am very grateful for their willingness to provide existing translations, in some cases emended, or new ones. The three translations by the Anglo-Welsh poet Vernon Watkins (1906-67) may serve as a small commemoration of his valuable work as a translator. I also wish to thank Gregor Sebba, Professor Emeritus of Emory University, for his generous guidance in several areas of selection. His incisive learning and zest articulate the tradition, passionately. Peter Green's painstaking criticism of an earlier version of the 'Euphrosyne' translation made it possible for me to revise several floundering lines. To the University of Texas at Austin I am indebted for a grant which made continuance and a timely completion of the work possible. 1832-1882-1982: fifty years after Goethe's death his *Poems in the Original Metres* appeared, with translations by various gentlemen; one hundred years later a commemoration is due, notably of E. A. Bowring, W. E. Aytoun, and Theodore Martin, whose labours have been worth rescuing.

$-$ C.M.

CONTENTS

THE POEMS

These appear in chronological sequence by year of composition. An exception is made for the five natural-scientific poems, variously dated, 'Parabasis,' 'The Metamorphosis of Plants,' 'Epirrhema,' 'Metamorphosis of Animals,' and 'Antepirrhema,' which appear on the dateline 1798. With allowance for changes in modern editions (Hamburg 1948, Artemis 1950), letters in brackets after German titles show in which group Goethe placed his poems, according to notions of genre, in the original collections of 1789, 1808, and 1830. Code: AF = Antiker Form sich nähernd (Approaching Classical Form); AP = An Personen (To Persons); B = Balladen (Ballads); CDJT = Chinesisch-Deutsche Jahres- und Tageszeiten (Chinese-German Times of Year and Day); E = Elegien (Elegies); Ep = Epigrammatisch (Epigrams); GW = Gott und Welt (God and World); K = Kunst (Art); L = Lieder (Songs); P = Parabolisch (Parabolic Poems); S = Sonette (Sonnets); Sp = Sprüche (Sayings); VG = Vermischte Gedichte (Miscellaneous Poems); ZX = Zahme Xenien (Tame Invectives). Poems from the *Diwan* appear in a section of their own (IV). Texts follow the Artemis edition.

II. THE FIRST WEIMAR YEARS

V. LATER POEMS, 1815-30

And to the wise should it be manifest
That good things and things pleasing to God
Have always been since he said Let there be Light
Also therefore preserved parchments
Which tell us how the spirit hovered
Over the deep and brought life to it
And writings enough remain to us
So that we may know
Wise men and good endeavoured
To continue God's work and imagination
To excite the activity of the spirit
And morally to shape circumstances on earth
Even if the original
Inherited crudeness always stood in their way
Giving them much to do
And much to think about.

Goethe, *Paralipomena* to *Gedichte* (Artemis II, 550)

INTRODUCTION

O que será que será
Que andam suspirando pelas alcovas
Que andam sussurrando em versos e trovas
Que andam combinando no breu das tocas . . .
— Chico Buarque

For two centuries Goethe has been the major figure in the history of German literature. During the past century (since the Age of Bismarck), he has become a principal turbine in what is now called, disparagingly, the German "culture industry." But what sort of a poet is he? Is it anomalous that a man with such massive powers of reflection should have been actually not an intellectual poet? Odd questions — if he was as great as they say, if fortune so favoured his magnitude, they might have been settled long ago. It is astonishing how many and various they were, the works of this single imagination, works that were in one breath pioneering and exemplary, whether they reconstituted a genre or broke away, like *Faust*, into the transgeneric. But did his art shape the language and temper of German writing after him beneficially. That question too should have been settled. The critical literature is profuse, also semioticians can now accurately fathom, we suppose, the workings and effects of creative genius in language. When and why did Goethe become an overwhelming "classic"? Do people still read him for pleasure, as Gottfried Keller in the 1840s did, responding wholly to the warming golden light with which Goethe's writings, or so it has been said, wash reality? Has he been a beacon for hearts and minds far afield in the civilized world, as other classics have been, or is he only a name that awakens vague prejudice, does his spectre only provoke conformingly, to quicken neither judgment nor desire? What a fatal joke the Germans played on themselves when they adopted this driven (but princely) immoralist as their Confucius, their Great Educator! Worse, what features of Goethe's writings did his devotee Nietzsche overlook that so enraged, in the year of dejection among Surrealists and collapse in the Weimar Republic, 1932, a critic as perceptive as the radical Carl Einstein? Einstein bitterly denounced Goethe as a complacent windbag who never considered the gulfs of disorder between words and facts, a glib juggler employing "eclectically a host of incoherent platitudes," and he lambasted him as the pernicious egotistical idolater of "a conflictless, lazy unity, a roseate bat in an evolution belfry."[1]

Especially if fascination with Goethe deflects attention from a host of less comfortable older and younger writers of his time, Einstein's rage can still be shared by many. For others, Goethe has survived the petrifactions of adulation and exact scholarship alike. For sympathetic readers, his early ferocities are not empty, his middle "classicism" is not leaden, the later wisdom is neither forbidding nor vaporous. It is possible to see

Goethe at the opposite end of a tortuously long time-tunnel, as long as you can wriggle back through it, as a stark human being and as a poet whose best work is gravel in the machinery of the culture industry. At each stage in the growth of his labyrinthine individuality he was perhaps too fiercely hounded by vast imaginings to be found less than demonic. The famous later Master of Taxonomies, the tippling Privy Councillor in post-Napoleonic Weimar, in his utterances alternately Lear, Prospero, and Polonius, living finally surrounded by catalogued bibelots, lists and maps, collections of scientific and numismatic specimens, himself an imaginary museum (and easily outliving his only son, the alcoholic August), Goethe himself eludes all classification, he matches no literary or mythic archetype — unless it be the protean Magus. The questions begin with his being paradigmatic only of himself. So I shall only touch on the evergreen questions and address in this introduction chiefly matters that are central to this particular book: How does Goethe respond to English translation? What can a translator discover in the dark folds of his verse-textures? The views that follow are based solely on my own efforts to translate certain poems of his, while making a selection that matches the canon as closely as limits of translation — and of space — would allow.[2]

Translating a poem is not quite the imaginative act of writing one. All the same, the synthesis of possibilities for which a translator settles is derived from his judgment as a feature of his linguistic imagination. He tries to weigh each value singly against all the others, grading also each to each as functions of a whole consortium, much as Kurt Schwitters required of the Merz artist. In Goethe's poems, rhyme belongs somehow with linearity, and linearity somehow belongs with a fluid resolution of stark-edged form. Rhyme belongs also with an air of improvisation, in so far as the lyrical speech-act flows, to all appearances, straight from a perception of circumstance (or an "occasion"). At the same time, his poems always have a high finish. They are anything but stammered, although one or two might give the illusion of wandering (e.g., 'A Winter Journey in the Harz'). He was sensitive to the distances that can separate random from pure language. "Language," he said in an undated poem called 'Etymologie,' is "ein reiner Himmelshauch," a pure breath of heaven, but conventions clog the channels, a great makeshifting occurs, and "That which a people has stammeringly put together/Must be Eternal Law for heart and soul." He was also sensitive to the veiling by illusion that makes absurdity and paradox in art mobilize the peculiar, intense image of experience which is a work of art. Not that his poems go off into the blue, on the contrary they are almost always addressed to some recipient or other, things, persons, or figments, or the spirits. But even lyrical apostrophe is a kind of absurdity — winged words addressed to a grape, a mountain, or to one's own eyes, even to unreceptive stars. Goethe made

some apposite remarks to Eckermann on a landscape by Rubens in which the light comes from two opposed quarters, to throw impossible shadows: "A picture as beautiful as this has never been seen in nature. . . . We would search reality in vain for it. . . . The artist wants to speak to the world by means of the All, and he does not find this All in nature: it is the fruit of his own genius, or, if you like, of the breath of a divine and fecundating spirit" (1827). So I would understand rhyme, linearity, the air of improvisation and other formal traits in his poems as means, among others, by which he invites the pure to take over from the random, in radicalizing language, to "shape an image" (as he says in 'Amor as Landscape Painter').

First, then, the question of end-rhyme. Obviously the mimetic translations attempted in this book would miss the mark if they lacked rhyme entirely. But how can one invent in rhyme a "believable modern English idiom"?[3] How, for translators or poets today, can a sense of the old *harmonia mundi* be restored, if only for a little time? A tacit faith in a cosmic harmony might seem to underlie the ability of older poets — think of Keats, of Byron — to rhyme with great zest and no effort. Rhyme was closure, proof of the veracity of the lyrical disclosure. It was also secretly linked with the onward thrusting of (apparent) extempore, with the crisp definition and suavity proper to any style, as the Latin classics had taught. At least, from Keats' letter of April 1819 to George and Georgiana we learn by the correction in his "extempore" canto xii, that rhyme always urged his imagination ahead of the act of writing, one line ahead or so, in a flow that crests in rhyme after rhyme.[4] The same might be said of the interplay of rhyme and undulance in many of Goethe's poems.

Rhyme in translation, however, is likely to coarsen the effect, smell of the lamp. There is, then, a general problem: How to make rhyme sound as unprompted and as interesting as possible. This can be done, if coupled or alternate lines have sufficient flow and consonance in other phases, not over the line-breaks only, but in larger syntactical units, and in variant kinds of sound-patterning, such as assonance, whether final or inside the lines. Even then, assonance can dilute everything. For the feminine rhymes, in which English is poor and German rich, one can also substitute hidden tactful assonances with feminine endings — "bedroom"/"zestful," "kisses"/"shivers," in 'Wedding Night.' I also found that a phonetic shift (from feminine to masculine rhymes) might secure the tonal consistency of a translation, if the masculine ending had an open final vowel, not closing the word with a stop consonant, either. The point is, of course, to rhyme not because the original does, but because rhyming is proper to this English tonal mimesis of the original poem's *decorum*. The mimesis crumbles, if there is no rhyme or if the assonance is inept, or inconspicuous, or random. The other point is to use no hackneyed rhymes, or *nolens volens*, to rhyme interestingly on different parts of speech (something at which

Alexander Pope was so deft). Verse-design is also a linguistic event in which rhyme relates closely to metric and its rhythmical fluctuations. It was necessary, for instance, in 'One and All,' to lengthen the line by one measure from four to five beats, in order to make room for grammatical negotiations that would accommodate rhymes. This meant that the two poems 'One and All' and 'Testament' came to be translated into different metres, although the originals match, the latter picking up and modifying the theme of the former poem. Translations otherwise do observe the original metres, and only 'Pain, Dumb' breaks experimentally away.

Inevitably, the substitution of masculine for feminine rhyme, as in 'Universal Soul,' modifies the tonal shape of the original. For that change to be made positive (mimesis being anything but replication) the translation ought to have its own tonal coherence and be, as regards rhyme, consistent. In 'Universal Soul' there is an inconsistency — one set of feminine rhymes (assonances) intrudes. Another translation with traces of the desirable intrinsic tonal coherence was the 'Night Song' of 1804. The original is a glossolalian rondeau with feminine endings. The translation with masculine endings sounds more clipped. But the insistent low pitches of the English rhymes are meant to capture the original's dreamy murmur. To an attempt at translating acoustically the tiny arch-lyric 'Über allen Gipfeln' I was eventually taunted by Haroldo de Campos' Portuguese version (of 1966):

> Sobre os picos
> Paz.
> Nos cimos
> Quase
> Nenhum sopro.
> Calam aves nos ramos.
> Logo — vamos —
> Virá o repouso.

Goethe's poems do comprise, and not just sporadically, figures of sound (rather than "figures of speech"). In 'Über allen Gipfeln,' for instance, between the *u* of "du" (line 3) and the next sound, the *k* of "kaum," a tiny voiceless breath has to be breathed (and the poem is also saying "hardly a breath"). The poem is not only *about* the "Hauch," or about its mood or subject: it enacts mood pneumatically. In 'Wiederfinden' another such moment occurs, at the end of strophe 2: here the cosmogonic Alpha is kept in translation, but spliced with an apocalyptic Omega absent from the original:

> As he spoke the word "Become!"
> An anguished "Ah!" rang out, the All
> Exploded with a motion vast
> Into being actual.

Here the eschatological note may pass unheard; but to Goethe, versed as

he was in the esoteric, the splicing would have signalled, aptly, Judgment Day, *apokatastasis*, the Restitution, in the End, of the Beginning.

Always end-rhyme is a cresting of sound-waves that move through other phases of the lines. If a rhyme scheme was changed, as in 'Primal Words. Orphic,' or in 'Mignon,' I still did what I could to get the right melodic clarity in the word-attunements interior to the lines, so as to recreate patterns of vocal quality (cf. the early 'Autumn Feeling'). Sometimes I had in mind Jean-Paul Richter's description of Goethe's voice in 1796: "His reading is like deep-toned thunder, blended with soft, whispering raindrops."[5] Charming, but not unhelpful. Goethe certainly liked words to roll. Homer was an open book to him, once he had read him in earshot of the sea near Naples. But he does also singularize sounds. Ezra Pound, in his 'A Few Don'ts' of 1913, when he tells "the candidate" to "dissect the lyrics of Goethe coldly into their component sound values," was actually inviting him to notice the graduations of the shine on what Jean-Paul, as ear-witness, called "raindrops."[6] Goethe is also the poet with a hundred voices, each with inflections of its own, and several are feminine ('The Spinner,' 'Mignon,' 'In Court,' 'Nearness of the Beloved,' and of course Gretchen). This polyphony was instrumental in his becoming such a popular poet in some ways. Like the fifteenth century Florentine artists under Lorenzo de' Medici, he so revised relations between popular (and oral) literature and humanistic culture, as to break down some of the barriers that separated them. People in his time also liked rhyme and they expected it, not as a jingle, not as décor, but as a voicing of the *harmonia mundi*, of which poets were supposed to be the singing messengers.

Linearity is another feature of Goethe's poems which some readers might now find old-fangled. The verse-line is felt and delivered as a unit. This is not so noticeable in the quasi-Pindaric or proto-Expressionist poems of 1773-4, where a phrasing in clusters, or bursts, replaced linear design to some extent. But even in the earlier Sesenheim lyrics, and throughout the middle and later periods, the line is the backbone of the verse-design, even in such a strange song as 'Mignon.' This line-by-line, step-by-step progression of the poem is counterpointed, even in the hexameters and elegiac distichs, by Goethe's characteristic vocal undulation, which flows from the poem's imaginative matrix and "organizes" everything. Now the original semantic of lines in sequence had to be kept. Transposition of words into different lines might be feasible, I thought, if it facilitated navigation of the straits of rhyme, or so long as it would make the undulation of the poetic logic more distinct. In practice, I found that any displacement of a word from its original line led to a slide, if not in the logic, then in the verse-texture itself. At the same time, adherence to the original linear sequence could lead, if one trod carelessly, to a loss of animation: the translation lacked the original's buoyancy. What I aimed

at, then, was a balance between linearity and undulance — in Walt Whitman's sense of the poetic:

> "human thought, poetry or melody, must leave dim escapes and outlets — must possess a certain fluid, aerial character, akin to space itself, obscure to those of little or no imagination, but indispensable to the highest purposes. Poetic style, when addressed to the Soul, is less definite form, outline, sculpture and becomes vista, music, half-tints, and even less than half-tints."[7]

At the same time I had to observe the line's closure, when that was distinctively marked. Linearity is what makes gnomic phrasing possible; it provides the definition and clang of a "truth," even if it may also open the door on cliché (and Goethe lent himself to quotation for all of life's occasions and ages, his gnomic lines have been embroidered into millions of samplers and mounted in bronze on many buildings). So if a rhyme scheme was changed (as the *ottava rima* was in 'Dedication'), this could mean the loss of just that rhyme in the original which marked closure, furnished the gnomic rondure. Such loss might be made up, I hoped, by some alliteration:

> Warum sucht ich den Weg so sehnsuchtsvoll,
> Wenn ich ihn nicht den Brüdern zeigen soll?

> Why did I seek the way with such a passion,
> If not to show my fellows what I found?

Eventually I was finding my way toward the nodal point at which linearity in rhyme is a dialectic of closure and disclosure. A line begins, opens up, closes (with or without rhyme); but no sooner has it closed than it is opening into the next line, in a fugitive instant, pure transition. This shutterflutter occurs even when the syntax entails complex subordination — those relative clauses, for instance, which in German promise a downward float into closure. What Goethe does is keep the shutterfluttering continuum in motion. There is an urgent forward motion, sometimes large like the roll of attacking momentum in Beethoven, sometimes microscopic, as in Goethe's handling of the word "und" ("and"). To be sure, his "und" can be a mere link between lines; but more often it is a sling from which an ensuant phrase or line is catapulted forward. In 'On the Lake,' in an outrageous way at the time, he had an "und" set off the poem's first burst. That particular "und" signals an eruptiveness for which Goethe's early writings were duly notorious.

Constantly it was a question of gauging the specific energy in a line as one event in a nexus of lines, and of capturing that energy in its proper formal diffusion. This might require a transformation of grammatical types. For instance, the first line in 'Mignon': the original has a relative clause ("wo die Zitronen blühn"), but I substituted a straight English genitive with present participle ("of flowering lemon trees"). In other translations too a present participial clause replaces the original relative,

without loss, I think, of the dynamic of the relative. These are small points, but a translator has to work like a pointillist. Goethe's celebrated dynamism (absent from so many translations, including French ones) can only be preserved by being punctiliously re-enacted. That re-enaction requires transformations which fly apart unless they are carefully controlled by respect for the channels, straight or twisting, through which the original line-energy came to be generated.

My next point, enhancement, also entailed a showing of respect. Translation into a believable modern English idiom, without the usual archaisms, requires a certain amount of judicious enhancement. One goes to work as a salvage archaeologist, or as a restorer of old paintings. Nothing may be distorted, but the treasure has to be raised in the nick of time. Thus it may be an enhancement, in 'Ganymede,' when I make an appropriately mimetic triple rhyme undulate across the two lines

> Withal the nightingale lovingly
> Calls from the misty vale to me

— for which there is no phonetic match in the original. Again, in 'The Bride of Corinth,' where I was adapting the Aytoun-Martin Victorian version, the original strophe 16 does not speak of "muscle from the thrill of love." It says "youthful strength of love." Here I felt that the change was due, the tissue of the line had to be fortified, and the "muscle" phrase seemed to bring out, chastely enough, what the original implies, with the young man so amorous and "durchmannt." In 'Primal Words. Orphic,' finding it impossible to recreate the original daisy-chain of feminine rhymes, I chose to toughen the phrasing here and there, in order to achieve a denser consistency on the semantic level. In strophe 2, line 4, the original says, literally: "Likely you'll act as any other does;" "other" is weak here, so I enhanced with "manjack," which is a touch more robust (though little known in America). In strophe 3, line 8, the original says: "The noblest, yet, themselves to one devote;" here again I wanted to avoid the colourless "themselves," so I wrote, finally: " . . . their all to one devote," which is more clinching, yet fully consonant with the urbane wit which organizes the architecture of these monumental strophes. Seldom did I consciously intensify effects or meanings in ways that could be thought excessive. In 'Legend' I added a joke ("Or open it? For kicks?"), and in 'Shopping' I sharpened and modernized the anger. But that is all, I think. John Frederick Nims' irresistible translation 'The Diary,' on the other hand, involves a quite radical change of tone, of character: his speaker is much more of a madcap Casanova, more seventeenth century perhaps, than Goethe was in his original of 1810.

By and large my "transcreations" (the term Haroldo de Campos applied to those he has seen)[8] are context-controlled. For instance, in 'Twilight Down From Heaven' the oscillating stress on "unsteady" in line 14 brings out the shimmering by enacting it rhythmically, although the original shimmering is on the semantic level. In the same translation, "a silver

glow" is not quite "Mondenglanz und -glut," accenting semantically as it does the colour, silver. The silver is proper, all the same, to the phanopoeia of these lines, and it is consistent with Goethe's feeling for that kind of light-effect elsewhere: in *Faust I*, Faust speaks of "the silver figures of the ancestral world," and in *Faust II* there are the miraculous lines "And in rolling waves of silver,/Seed to harvest urges on." Another aspect of this area is *antiquing*. Generally, I resisted it, as something adverse to enhancement, if not downright dilution. The last thing a translator must do is mistake turns of speech that became archaic after (or because of) his author's practices for any archaism or poeticism which might be embedded in the original. Yet that is the mistake made even by quite recent translators of Goethe. It is a curious situation: there was no English idiom comparable to Goethe's in his own time, yet he has been translated till now in ways that simulate a "period" style trashy in any age. Certainly his work became a mine for cliché-mongers, and he is not averse to mongering a little on the side himself. In principle all the translations I was making had to be free from outright archaism; but inevitably, even those that have some flourish in phrasing and sentiment shrink the force of their originals by containing it in a confoundedly unmodern idiom. Some lyrics, too, notably others from the novel *Wilhelm Meisters Lehrjahre* and several from the *Diwan* were not to be retrieved and are thus omitted. In only a few poems did I risk a "tis" or a "thou," when such wording seemed both apt and inescapable. (It must be recalled that the German "thou" is not archaic, but simply familiar.) 'On the Lake' was typical of another such difficulty. How to make outdated sentiment credible and strip archaism away? Who would now speak, as Goethe does here, and so anxiously, to his own eyes? Some readers will find a distinct change in 'Mignon' rather steep, perhaps. Her "Dahin!" became "Aiee!" Yet this (non-semantic, surface-phonetic) transposition into Flamenco Romany was carefully weighed against alternatives. One cannot ask Mignon to exclaim "Thither!" "Aiee" suits her zither, and it is her cry, her sigh, her primal sorrow fully voiced in what they call, I believe, a "phatic morpheme."

Contextual control in the act of transcreation is what I was striving for. This was not only a question of rightness in texture, consistency, shape, or energy, to be regenerated. It was also a question of honesty toward the quality, mass, and measure (*tempi*) of the perceptual experience which lines and rhymes and syntax unmistakeably voice. 'Mignon,' again, is an instance. I modified the rhyme scheme, true, but the English scheme does not blur the deep, symmetrical, intuitive design in the perceptual and imaginative scene which the poem tracks, line by line. There are three layers, or stages, of ubiquitous perception in this scene, in the three strophes: nature, culture, and myth (Goethe was at one time most receptive to Rousseau). With uncanny nonchalance Goethe may implant

such deep designs in the lightest of his poems. The designs appear to have arisen out of his exceptionally clear and steady eidetic imagination. Another triangulation figures cryptically in the great "floating buzzard" poem 'A Winter Journey in the Harz,' and it is traceable in 'Über allen Gipfeln' ('Another Night Song'). When the nonchalance drifts toward cliché, the translator must be doubly careful to salvage the original dynamic from the cosmetic décor. He can do this by attending to the vocal values of the poems. Even in a single poem, those values may be versatile: naive, sly, jocose, pontifical, ironic notes conspire, but do not become bloated or slack. Did Goethe privilege a grand-bourgeois outlook and combine it with an art which cosmetically screens the wrinkles out of reality? Was there to be nothing nasty in the poetry of everyday? Yet he also knew of imagination as a "violence within that protects us from a violence without . . . pressing back against the pressure of reality."[9] In his time, the lyric poet, by definition, spoke to sublimate such violences; ugliness was outside his art's domain, even if he loathed or liked it as a human being.

Open and sensuous as Goethe's poems usually are, too, he seems to have quietly suspected that a poetic gnosis discloses a truth that is *sui generis*. Poetry in the last analysis was as different from other modes of speech or writing as the visual knowledge presented in a painting differs from linguistic or mathematical kinds of cognition. For Goethe, poetry and its gnosis arise from a clear apprehension of formal relationships between moves in the dance of his imagination among objects of sense — with those objects as partners in the dance. He glorifies the palpable. Yet discursive components of speech are not burned away in the process. When such components become "poeticism," they inhibit the process, of course. But even an apparent cliché can be saturated with the formal-aesthetic patterning dynamism that informs the text as it unfolds. The cosmetic can condense the dew of cogitation and turn it into a nutrient for the inexcogitable inner thing. That thing is the patterning which is first and last in the process.

For all the ultimacy to be found in his work, Goethe is little known as a poet today. There are hardly any good translations into European languages. The English record is forlorn, but not unique. A false tone was set early on, by flummery translations from the great gossips Walter Scott and Thomas Carlyle. (In adopting some older translations, I revised them, for the most part.)[10] So the rebuffal of Goethe has been due, perhaps, to failure in translation. It might also be due to the fact that his *Lebensphilosophie* was too transcendental to interest ordinary people who have no patience with the vagaries, and with the lumberings, of the *mens teutonica* (as Balzac called it).[11] Besides, Goethe wrote so many other things. From every phase in his continuous work as a lyric poet came plays, narratives, memoirs, reflections, not to mention studies in

natural science (from about the early 1790s). The rebuffal from the English-language side might have been due to something else also. Generally, readers have responded favorably, if slowly, to non-English European poets whose work has a dense and subtle intellectual foreground: Dante, Leopardi, recently Mandelstam. Rilke is somewhat of an anomaly. Even then, his Sonnets and Elegies have spellbound readers (of inadequate translations) with their uniquely sensuous intelligence, their intellectually pregnant metaphors. Likewise the Hölderlin to whom readers now defer is the later one, whose "intellectualism" has a rigorous dialectical character, even when it is rhapsodic. Goethe seems to have missed the boat, on the other hand, because he is not critically argumentative, even though he may be dialectical, or prosy, in other ways. He is a sensuous, demonstrative, exploratory, divinatory poet. Hardly a poem of his presents an arguing poetic intellect in immediate action (as in Dante, Donne, Marvell, Browning). It is as if his poems, of whatever genre, unfold in some pre- or post-cognitive region of the mind. They deliver, enshrine, and codify ideas; but they do not enact ideas in the moment of collision with other ideas. This great transformer, this monarch, of German *Gedankenlyrik* (poetry of ideas) may have set his mark on its idiom so powerfully that it has remained to this day more apt for doctrinal than for witty critical thinking. Even Brecht hardly broke the pattern.

So much presence of mind, such a powerful emotional dynamic, such decorum, melodic rondure, wholeness, consonance, even such wisdom: yet he is nothing remotely like other "classics," least of all like Góngora — because he never ceases to be an accessible poet, even a folk-minded one. His poems established, I venture to say, an uncommon linguistic ground, which may no longer be home ground, even for honest-to-goodness German loyalists. This ground oscillates at various frequencies, between directness and remoteness, immediacy and sublimity, folk-mode and high-mindedness; but, for all the intimacy that he carved out room for in German poetry, he is never savage or vulgar in his worldliness. And he writes his poem, it would seem, after the fecundating conflicts have been adjudicated by his steady imagination, but without ever becoming a mere "fair-weather" poet. In some later doctrinal poems, 'Urworte. Orphisch,' for instance, just when we might expect a poet to interrogate his vision, he indulges a fatalism that might seem trite, were it not so grim, and still seems to beg the questions of free will, justice, and choice which Aquinas and Dante addressed with such realism and acumen. [12] The one poem in which an argumentative foreground might be discerned, densely composed (at a first shot) in *terza rima*, is the late one about contemplating Schiller's skull. Here he might come close to the old Yeats, but that would be because Yeats had learned how to cry in the teeth of philosophy, coming full circle from "abstract dark" to a vision of the world as a symbolic construct of man's "bitter soul." Even in this late poem of Goethe's

there are traces of an immediate circumstance in which the utterance occurs, and there is the characteristic address to the *object* in question. The "occasion" as such is perhaps not so distinct as in many poems, but there is still the contour of the given, an aerial contour. Translating Goethe showed me, even then, something seldom noticed. This contour of the given is delicate and mobile, because it frames the fundamental experience voiced in most of his more celebrated poems: the experience of crossing back and forth across limits, a transition of thresholds. It is the real stuff of rituals: the liminal experience. Whether its dimensions are miniature or cosmic, light or dark, deadly or redemptive, that is perhaps the core of lyric experience, and not in Goethe's work alone.

Here, too, is the mobile point amid known bounds and clear proportions from which Goethe fills his world far or near with metaphors, ideas, feelings, analogies, to create a living texture of meaning. He was one of the last poets of the old projective imagination. Poetic creation here is one leap away from the kind which Mallarmé later came to view as the unique poetic world: a world of purest "conjecture." Soon after Goethe, all such totalizations were to become suspect. He lived in apocalyptic times. Forty when the French Revolution began, he eyed the upheavals of the next quarter-century with curiosity, much doubt, some dismay, and (later) considerable disdain. In history as such he watched for signs of an infinite but not inscrutable plan: and he saw symbolic events, polarized confluences of minds human and divine, rather than moves in a finite dialectic. (Not untypically of his tough outlook in this area, he is to be found rambling through the great Valmy bombardment, of September 20, 1792, studying the effects of shockwaves on eyesight, of light on dust.) For it was also a time of splendid systems: classical harmony in music, the Critical Philosophy, Hegel's Phenomenology, and the promise of a synthesis between art and the cognitive disciplines — all systems that were not totalitarian, unlike Napoleon's ubiquitous secret police. Not without anguish and rage, not in all confidence, Goethe fashioned in the recalcitrant German language a living texture which might have served, if all things had ever been equal, to defend human beings against their own worst aptitudes, their Gorgons, and against the voids that fill with demons when the positive projections are withdrawn. Small wonder if the attempt to capture in translation some fragments of that enterprise might seem like an absurd signal, sent into the past, but saying that the enterprise continues, here and there, in other ways.

By way of conclusion, some remarks on a vignette of Goethe by the old Rococo poet J. W. Gleim. Gleim described a reading that took place in 1777, in the apartments of the Duchess Anna Amalia of Saxe-Weimar. He has brought the latest issue of a well-known poetry journal, the *Göttinger Musenalmanach*, and a "young man" has just come in, booted and spurred, wearing an unbuttoned green hunting coat. This "huntsman" sits

opposite Gleim and listens carefully, although "apart from his gleaming dark Italian eyes I hardly noticed anything about him." During a short pause, he borrows the journal from Gleim, very politely, and asks if he might read too. Gleim condescends — even though the stranger is only a huntsman. The stranger reads some poems that are typical of the time, by Voss, Stollberg, and Bürger. Then something happens:

> "Suddenly it was as if Satan had the reader by the short hairs, and I thought I was seeing with my own eyes the Devil's Huntsman. He was reading poems that were not in the journal at all, he was modulating into all possible vocal sounds and melodies, in hexameters, iambic lines, doggerel, anything and everything, all mixed up, as if he were shaking it out of his sleeves . . . With what humour he brought all his fantasies together that evening! Sometimes such splendid thoughts came out of it, however fugitive, in fragments, that the authors to whom he ascribed them should have thanked God on their knees, if ever those thoughts had come to them at their desks. And for every person present he had something to offer . . ."[13]

Goethe's virtuosity depicted here has a history in Renaissance beliefs about the ordering and creative power of the word, a power that "bespeaks a great confidence in the mind's authority over nature."[14] Romantic and post-Romantic poetry, on the other hand, reflects a momentous shift away from that confidence. Poets perceive varieties of agonizing separation between mind and nature, words and things: a gulf has to be bridged, or closed. Goethe's poems span the epochs and are remarkable for the ways in which the conduct of poetic language and the spectacle of the world coalesce effortlessly in them. He was a master of that kind of supreme fiction by which the poem becomes "part of the *res* itself, and not about it" (Wallace Stevens).

Yet this is the crux, at which contemporary readers of his poems, at least, might find his sanguine temperament too beaming, his confidence too easy, his reality too unresistant. Unlike Auden's "governess," who gives the universe nought for behaviour, Goethe offends us by giving it a sort of placating A. Not that his language overwhelms the real; rather, it can seem to be remote from those realities which we experience without mediation, without help from any ordering forms or formalities. Hence the decorum of his poems is strange to us. We may be averse to his rhetoric, as "old hat." Inside the rhetoric, however, and not so far inside it either, there is a body of vital lyric experience which a reader can feel on his own skin, once he has made the imaginative effort, the effort that translation may or may not provoke. That experience is coherent and intact. It is partly the experience of an undulatory relationship, mediated by countless sensory and linguistic correspondences, metaphoric or not, between the act of speech and the whole scope of finite existence, from luminous spirits to deadly darkness, from psychic liberation to confine-

ment in a body of fate. To that extent, Goethe's fictions of concord, born of this undulatory experience, should not so much tax our patience as train it. The supposed "power" of speech to order real experience is here not a violence. Rather it is a kind of ductile vigilance in tune with an unshaken sense of the interrelatedness of things, with humanity as "part of the natural continuum, and all nature indivisibly divine."[15] One of the themes which Goethe modulates, largely or in miniature, is thus the integration of opposites, the consorting of Yin and Yang. Another is the momentum of flowering (in the very motion of the poem), the unfolding of being, in and out of mind, which is generated by such instants of integration. The pneumatic power of the word gives access to the Law, it is the "Gate" to the Law, in so far as the word is the Now, fully articulated. It is this Now about which Kafka's country simpleton asks, in the famous parable, even though the simpleton is not really conscious of what he is asking about. To this Now he can gain no access, stupefied as he is by the answers of the Gate-Keeper. Because of the latter's Authority, the simpleton cannot even risk a glimpse into the interior of the literal.

For us, too, Goethe is strange because he fathered something we simply take for granted: the interiority of modern German lyric language. He also made intimacy over to the public world — for every person, as Gleim said, he had something to offer. There were notable antecedents, to be sure, but Goethe enriched and subtilized the emotional, tonal, and semantic range of German poetry in ways that were unheard-of. (A century later, Debussy was to conjure likewise an otherworld of tonalities from the piano.) How then is one to perceive the enduring *Gestalt* of his poetry? — not forgetting that the *Gestalt* concept of today was shaped by his manner of thinking. Nineteenth-century positivist critics invited readers to interpret the poems as confessional works. Goethe had prompted this, calling his poems "fragments of a great confession;" and he was a godsend for both positivist scholars and readers pursuing vicarious experience in lieu of none at all. Every poem sprang from a vital occasion, it was thought, and so he was celebrated as the founder of *Erlebnislyrik*, the poetry of experience. We now insist that a poem is a distinct linguistic event, a transformation of whatever elements may have ignited it. We care far less for biographical ingredients that for the semiotic process of the poem itself. I would simply hope that a reader will come to intuit the *Gestalt* by enjoying some poems as a feast: if the feast is translated, still it is not just leftovers or the menu-card.

I say "feast" with specific emphasis. Inherent in language there is a pneumatic and festive power, or a joy, which, like Aristotle's Infinite, initiates variety, as it orders development, and which links the dissimilar logics of civil liberty and art. The play of Goethe's verse-textures testifies to the latencies and activities of that power, whether or not it is "god-given" (as Goethe's Tasso claimed). Currently there is much talk about language as a "ritual event" having effects that are "repressive" or

occlusive. Such talk can be salutary, if it disposes of the brouhaha, and if it reflects a strict philosophical delight in the integrity of the translinguistic, if it makes recognizable the pristine values of beings and things neither tainted nor falsified by our linguistic ways of rendering them to ourselves. The talk is otiose if it only parrots fashionable theories, of course; it is thoughtless if it ignores the existential (historic) experience upon which those theories are predicated. For there are two historic moments. First, the majesty and joy of the creative word engages human communities in the awesome task of civilization. Second, a disenchantment occurs, oddly shared at the start of this century by Alfred Jarry's King Ubu and Hugo von Hofmannsthal's Lord Chandos: the pneumatic and festive power of the word has withdrawn, it withdrew long ago, from our not-so-civilized midst, we are immobilized, and only *now* do we know it.

What is the festive power of the first moment? It enables its vehicles to return to a virgin condition, to be renewed, and it dwells in words, just as it dwells in aquifers, so long as the words and the water are left to themselves for long enough. To dismiss language *in toto* as an oppressive ritual is to deny that feasts of refreshment are there for the eating, and for the cooking. It is to puncture with a sort of puritanic acid — let us call it the Savonarola Solution — the very eyes upon which the rainbow of being depends. It is to *ob-literate* the "Event," which in authentic feasts like those of the Pueblo or of the Kannapuram spirit-dancers in South Asia configures commonplace life with what is variously called The Time of Beginning, The Dawn of Becoming, the Originative Now. More topically, it is to recommend that we become like the Americanized Poles in *The Deerhunter*, a film that so incisively diagnosed the last years: slaves of the inarticulate, delivered up to existence as a gamble complete and militarized, a game of Russian roulette. The bullet waiting in the chamber of that pistol is rather different from the one that was waiting for Goethe's Werther.

REFERENCES

1. Carl Einstein, 'Obituary: 1832-1932,' in *Transition* (Paris), 21, 1932. Eugene Jolas' English translation from the German is the only extant version of this text.

2. The reader without German can still refer with profit to studies in English by Barker Fairley (1947), Karl Viëtor (1949), and Richard Friedenthal (1965), also to Stephen Spender's introduction to *Great Writings of Goethe* (Mentor 1948, recently reprinted) and to David Luke's to Goethe, *Selected Verse* (Penguin 1964). Two other special books are W.H. Bruford, *Culture and Society in Classical Wiemar* (1962), and Wolfgang Leppmann, *The German Image of Goethe* (1961).

3. See Donald Carne-Ross's incisive remarks on modern translations of old classic poets, especially Góngora, in his essay 'Dark With Excessive Bright,' in *Instaurations*, Berkeley, University of California Press 1979.

4. John Keats, *Complete Works*, edited by H. Buxton Forman, Glasgow 1901, Vol. V, p.43.

5. Eliza Buckminster Lee, *The Life of Jean Paul Frederic Richter, Preceded By His Autobiography*, Boston 1864, p.249.

6. *Make It New*, London, Faber and Faber, 1934, p. 338.

7. 'Preface 1876,' in *Complete Poetry and Selected Prose*, ed. James E. Miller, Boston, Houghton Mifflin 1959, p.440.

8. See 'Post Scriptum' to his book of remarkable Portuguese translations from Faust, and essays: *Deus e o Diabo: No Fausto de Goethe*, São Paulo, Editora Perspectiva 1981.

9. Wallace Stevens, *The Necessary Angel*, New York, Vintage 1951, p.7. and p.36. One is touching here on the *oneiric* domain of his work, profoundly respected by Surrealists and depth-psychologists.

10. Source: *Poems of Goethe Translated in the Original Metres*, 1882 (earlier editions go back to the 1850s), with versions by E.A. Bowring, Theodore Martin, W.E. Aytoun, and others. My revisions have been slight emendations in some cases, but 'Dedication' and 'The Bride of Corinth' needed some heavy restoration. Henri-Frédéric Amiel (*Les Etrangères*, Paris 1876) and O.V. De L.Milosz (*Chefs d'Oeuvre Lyriques du Nord*, Paris 1968) achieved a few striking, poetic, and largely ignored successes in French. Amiel's version of 'Song of the Spirits Over the Waters' is unique for its rendition of the *phonic* character of the original.

11. In *Cousin Pons* (1848), Penguin 1968, trans. by H.J. Hunt, and in a passage that speaks volumes, e.g., ". . . the urge to find psychic meaning in material trifles which is responsible for the uninterpretable works of Jean-Paul Richter, the tipsy fantasies which Hoffmann has put into print and the folio volumes which, in Germany, ward off access to the simplest questions and delve down into unfathomable depths, only to reveal a *mens teutonica* at the bottom" (p.34).

12. Cf. Chapter 7 of Philip Wicksteed's brilliant, stylish, and forgotten lectures, *Dante and Aquinas*, London 1913.

13. Max von Boehn, *Deutschland im 18.Jahrhundert*, Berlin 1927, Vol. 1, pp.494-5. Boehn misdates the event; I am grateful to Gregor Sebba for referring me to the source for the correct date (1777, cf. Biedermann, *Goethes Gespräche*, 1909-11).

14. Carne-Ross, *Instaurations (cit.)*, p.140.

15. David Luke, in his introduction to Goethe, *Selected Verse (cit.)*, p.xxx.

I
Frühe Gedichte
Early Poems
1768–75

Scheintod

Weint, Mädchen, hier bei Amors Grabe; hier
Sank er von nichts, von ohngefähr danieder.
Doch ist er wirklich tot? Ich schwöre nicht dafür:
Ein Nichts, ein Ohngefähr erweckt ihn öfters wieder.

Suspended Animation (1767–68)

Weep, pretty maids, at Amor's tomb; the merest
Fluke, a hint, has brought him his demise.
But is he truly dead? I would not swear it.
Oft at the merest hint again he'll rise.

Wechsel

Auf Kieseln im Bache da lieg ich, wie helle!
Verbreite die Arme der kommenden Welle,
Und buhlerisch drückt sie die sehnende Brust;
Dann führt sie der Leichtsinn im Strome danieder,
Es naht sich die zweite, sie streichelt mich wieder:
So fühl ich die Freuden der wechselnden Lust.

Und doch, und so traurig, verschleifst du vergebens
Die köstlichen Stunden des eilenden Lebens,
Weil dich das geliebteste Mädchen vergißt!
O ruf sie zurücke, die vorigen Zeiten!
Es küßt sich so süße die Lippe der Zweiten,
Als kaum sich die Lippe der Ersten geküßt.

Brautnacht

Im Schlafgemach, entfernt vom Feste,
Sitzt Amor dir getreu und bebt,
Daß nicht die List mutwillger Gäste
Des Brautbetts Frieden untergräbt.
Es blinkt mit mystisch heilgem Schimmer
Vor ihm der Flammen blasses Gold,
Ein Weihrauchswirbel füllt das Zimmer,
Damit ihr recht genießen sollt.

Wie schlägt dein Herz beim Schlag der Stunde,
Der deiner Gäste Lärm verjagt,
Wie glühst du nach dem schönen Munde,
Der bald verstummt und nichts versagt.
Du eilst, um alles zu vollenden,
Mit ihr ins Heiligtum hinein;
Das Feuer in des Wächters Händen
Wird wie ein Nachtlicht still und klein.

Exchange (1767–68)

The stones in the torrent I make my light pillow,
Open my arms to the oncoming billow,
It rushes coquettish to lie on my breast.
Then levity soon makes it onward be flowing,
A second one comes, its caresses bestowing:
And so by the changes of pleasure I'm blest.

And yet it's in vain that you drag out in sadness
The moments that fugitive life made for gladness,
Because of a charmer who showed you the door.
O call back to mind bygone days and their blisses!
The lips of another will give such sweet kisses
As any the lips of the one gave before.

Wedding Night (c. 1768)

Far from the feasting, in the bedroom
Sits loyal Amor and quakes with dread:
What if the guests become too zestful,
Break the peace of the bridal bed?
A mystical and holy shimmer
Flows from his pale flames of gold;
For you both a whirl of incense
Readies pleasures manifold.

How throbs your heart as chiming timepiece
Chases noisy guests away;
Any moment, lips you burn for
Nought will utter, nought gainsay.
You hasten with her to the temple,
There to consummate your bliss;
The guardian holds aloft his flambeau,
Still and small as a taper is.

Wie bebt vor deiner Küsse Menge
Ihr Busen und ihr voll Gesicht;
Zum Zittern wird nun ihre Strenge,
Denn deine Kühnheit wird zur Pflicht.
Schnell hilft dir Amor sie entkleiden
Und ist nicht halb so schnell als du;
Dann hält er schalkhaft und bescheiden
Sich fest die beiden Augen zu.

An Luna

Schwester von dem ersten Licht,
Bild der Zärtlichkeit in Trauer!
Nebel schwimmt mit Silberschauer
Um dein reizendes Gesicht;
Deines leisen Fußes Lauf
Weckt aus tagverschloßnen Höhlen
Traurig abgeschiedne Seelen,
Mich und nächtge Vögel auf.

Forschend übersieht dein Blick
Eine großgemeßne Weite.
Hebe mich an deine Seite!
Gib der Schwärmerei dies Glück,
Und in wollustvoller Ruh
Säh der weitverschlagne Ritter
Durch das gläserne Gegitter
Seines Mädchens Nächten zu.

How she trembles with your kisses,
Bosom, lips, and cheeks, and brow;
He severities are shivers,
Your derring-do is duty now.
Quick, Amor helps you undress her,
He has half your enterprise;
Roguish, then, but also modest,
He'll be closing both his eyes.

To Luna (1768)

Sister of Creation's light,
Image of tenderness in sorrow,
Silver mists thy radiance borrow
As they swim across thy sight.
At thy footfall through the sky
In their dusky hollows waken
Souls that sadly died forsaken,
Birds that shun the day, and I.

Looking downward far and wide
Hidden things thou dost discover,
Luna! help a pining lover,
Lift me upward to thy side,
And with peace in pleasure show
This errant knight his maiden sleeping,
Through the glassy lattice peeping
Let him see her there below.

Des Beschauens holdes Glück
Mildert solcher Ferne Qualen,
Und ich sammle deine Strahlen,
Und ich schärfe meinen Blick;
Hell und heller wird es schon
Um die unverhüllten Glieder,
Und nun zieht sie mich hernieder,
Wie dich einst Endymion.

Willkommen und Abschied

Es schlug mein Herz, geschwind zu Pferde!
Es war getan fast eh gedacht.
Der Abend wiegte schon die Erde,
Und an den Bergen hing die Nacht;
Schon stand im Nebelkleid die Eiche,
Ein aufgetürmter Riese, da,
Wo Finsternis aus dem Gesträuche
Mit hundert schwarzen Augen sah.

Der Mond von einem Wolkenhügel
Sah kläglich aus dem Duft hervor,
Die Winde schwangen leise Flügel,
Umsausten schauerlich mein Ohr;
Die Nacht schuf tausend Ungeheuer,
Doch frisch und fröhlich war mein Mut:
In meinen Adern welches Feuer!
In meinem Herzen welche Glut!

Dich sah ich, und die milde Freude
Floß von dem süßen Blick auf mich;
Ganz war mein Herz an deiner Seite
Und jeder Atemzug für dich.
Ein rosenfarbnes Frühlingswetter
Umgab das liebliche Gesicht,
Und Zärtlichkeit für mich—ihr Götter!
Ich hofft es, ich verdient es nicht!

Sight of her with bliss allays
Agonies of being other,
And I bring thy beams together,
And I sharpen now my gaze;
Now a brightening I see
Round the limbs no robes encumber,
And she draws me to her slumber
As Endymion once drew thee.

Welcome and Farewell (1771; 1789)

My heart beat fast, a horse! away!
Quicker than thought I am astride,
Earth now lulled by end of day,
Night hovering on the mountainside.
A robe of mist around him flung,
The oak a towering giant stood,
A hundred eyes of jet had sprung
From darkness in the bushy wood.

Atop a hill of cloud the moon
Shed piteous glimmers through the mist,
Softly the wind took flight, and soon
With horrible wings around me hissed.
Night made a thousand ghouls respire,
Of what I felt, a thousandth part—
My mind, what a consuming fire!
What a glow was in my heart!

You I saw, your look replied,
Your sweet felicity, my own,
My heart was with you, at your side,
I breathed for you, for you alone.
A blush was there, as if your face
A rosy hue of Spring had caught,
For me—ye gods!—this tenderness!
I hoped, and I deserved it not.

Doch ach, schon mit der Morgensonne
Verengt der Abschied mir das Herz:
In deinen Küssen welche Wonne!
In deinem Auge welcher Schmerz!
Ich ging, du standst und sahst zur Erden,
Und sahst mir nach mit nassem Blick:
Und doch, welch Glück, geliebt zu werden!
Und lieben, Götter, welch ein Glück!

Mailied

Wie herrlich leuchtet
Mir die Natur!
Wie glänzt die Sonne!
Wie lacht die Flur!

Es dringen Blüten
Aus jedem Zweig
Und tausend Stimmen
Aus dem Gesträuch

Und Freud und Wonne
Aus jeder Brust.
O Erd, o Sonne!
O Glück, o Lust!

O Lieb, o Liebe!
So golden schön,
Wie Morgenwolken
Auf jenen Höhn!

Du segnest herrlich
Das frische Feld,
Im Blütendampfe
Die volle Welt.

Yet soon the morning sun was there,
My heart, ah, shrank as leave I took:
How rapturous your kisses were,
What anguish then was in your look!
I left, you stood with downcast eyes,
In tears you saw me riding off:
Yet, to be loved, what happiness!
What happiness, ye gods, to love!

May Song (1771)

How fine a light on
Nature today!
The sun's in glory!
The fields at play!

Marvellous Nature
Shining on me!
Glorious sunlight,
Field shaking with glee!

What feats of blossom
A twig achieves!
A thousand voices
Delight the leaves!

From all the branches
Flowerlets rush,
A thousand voices
Out of the bush,

And every pleasure
For girl, for boy!
The sun-warm country
Of joy on joy!

And gladness, rapture
From every breast:
O sun, what pleasure!
O earth, how blest!

O love! O lovely!
My golden girl!
Like clouds at morning
Your rose and pearl!

O love, with a golden
Glow you adorn
The hilltops yonder
Like mist in the morn,

You lean in blessing
On earth's cool bloom,
The world a richness of
Dense perfume!

Splendidly blessing
The meadow trim,
In a haze of blossom,
World full to the brim.

O Mädchen, Mädchen,
Wie lieb ich dich!
Wie blickt dein Auge!
Wie liebst du mich!

So liebt die Lerche
Gesang und Luft,
Und Morgenblumen
Den Himmelsduft,

Wie ich dich liebe
Mit warmem Blut,
Die du mir Jugend
Und Freud und Mut

Zu neuen Liedern
Und Tänzen gibst.
Sei ewig glücklich,
Wie du mich liebst!

Der Neue Amadis

Als ich noch ein Knabe war,
Sperrte man mich ein,
Und so saß ich manches Jahr
Über mir allein
Wie in Mutterleib.

Doch du warst mein Zeitvertreib
Goldne Phantasie,
Und ich ward ein warmer Held,
Wie der Prinz Pipi,
Und durchzog die Welt.

Baute manch kristallen Schloß
Und zerstört' es auch,

O darling, darling!
I'm wild for you!
Your lashes dazzle:
You love me too!

Sweetheart, I love you,
Your glances tell,
Sweet, how you love me,
Love me as well,

The lark loves singing
Away up there;
The flowers at morning
Delight in air,

So does the lark love
Song and the blue,
And morning flowers
The heavenly dew,

As I adore you, with
Blood a-thrill!
It's youth you give me,
Ecstatic will

So do I love you,
With hottest blood,
Who give me youth's gladness
And brace my mood

For newer music
And dancing! Be
In bliss forever,
As you love me!

New songs to be making,
New dances to know:
Be happy for ever
In loving me so.

(JFN)

(CM)

The New Amadis (between 1771 and 1774)

When I was a little lad
They shut me in a room,
So for many a year I had
To sit there all alone,
As in my mother's womb.

Golden fantasy, you spent
Yet the time for me!
Out into the world I went
Like young Prince Pipi,
On adventure bent.

Palaces of crystal built
And destroyed again,

Warf mein blinkendes Geschoß
Drachen durch den Bauch,
Ja, ich war ein Mann!

Ritterlich befreit' ich dann
Die Prinzessin Fisch;
Sie war gar zu obligeant,
Führte mich zu Tisch,
Und ich war galant.

Und ihr Kuß war Götterbrot,
Glühend wie der Wein.
Ach! ich liebte fast mich tot!
Rings mit Sonnenschein
War sie emailliert.

Ach! wer hat sie mir entführt?
Hielt kein Zauberband
Sie zurück vom schnellen Fliehn?
Sagt, wo ist ihr Land?
Wo der Weg dahin?

Drove into the dragon's gut
My shining javelin.
What a man I was!

Like a cavalier then
Princess Fish I freed,
Très comme il faut she asked me in
To sup, and I agreed:
I was most *galant*.

And her kiss was heavenly bread,
Spiced like glowing wine.
Loved I my love till nearly dead!
Her painted scales were sunshine
From dainty foot to head.

Who has rapt her from me now?
Could no magic spell
A moment stay her flight?
Where is her country, tell!
Where the way to it?

Heidenröslein

Sah ein Knab ein Röslein stehn,
Röslein auf der Heiden,
War so jung und morgenschön,
Lief er schnell, es nah zu sehn,
Sahs mit vielen Freuden.
Röslein, Röslein, Röslein rot,
Röslein auf der Heiden.

Knabe sprach: Ich breche dich,
Röslein auf der Heiden!
Röslein sprach: Ich steche dich,
Daß du ewig denkst an mich,
Und ich wills nicht leiden.
Röslein, Röslein, Röslein rot,
Röslein auf der Heiden.

Und der wilde Knabe brach
's Röslein auf der Heiden;
Röslein wehrte sich und stach,
Half ihm doch kein Weh und Ach,
Mußt es eben leiden.
Röslein, Röslein, Röslein rot,
Röslein auf der Heiden.

Wandrers Sturmlied

Wen du nicht verlässest, Genius,
Nicht der Regen, nicht der Sturm
Haucht ihm Schauer übers Herz.
Wen du nicht verlässest, Genius,
Wird dem Regengewölk,
Wird dem Schloßensturm
Entgegensingen,
Wie die Lerche,
Du da droben.

Den du nicht verlässest, Genius,
Wirst ihn heben übern Schlammpfad

Rosebud in the Heather (1771)

Urchin saw a rose—a dear
Rosebud in the heather.
Fresh as dawn and morning-clear;
Ran up quick and stooped to peer,
Took his fill of pleasure,
Rosebud, rosebud, rosebud red,
Rosebud in the heather.

Urchin blurts: "I'll pick you, though,
Rosebud in the heather!"
Rosebud: "Then I'll stick you so
That there's no forgetting, no!
I'll not stand it, ever!"
Rosebud, rosebud, rosebud red,
Rosebud in the heather.

But the wild young fellow's torn
Rosebud from the heather.
Rose, she pricks him with her thorn;
Should she plead, or cry forlorn?
Makes no difference whether.
Rosebud, rosebud, rosebud red,
Rosebud in the heather.

Wanderer's Storm-Song (1772)

Spirit, he whom you do not forsake,
Rain does not, nor tempest,
Breathe across his heart the horrors.
Spirit, he whom you do not forsake,
Will to the raincloud,
Will to the hailstorm
Sing out
Like the lark,
You lark aloft there.

Spirit, not forsaking him,
Above the mud path you lift him,

Mit den Feuerflügeln.
Wandeln wird er
Wie mit Blumenfüßen
Über Deukalions Flutschlamm,
Python tötend, leicht, groß,
Pythius Apollo.

Den du nicht verlässest, Genius,
Wirst die wollnen Flügel unterspreiten,
Wenn er auf dem Felsen schläft,
Wirst mit Hüterfittichen ihn decken
In des Haines Mitternacht.

Wen du nicht verlässest, Genius,
Wirst im Schneegestöber
Wärmumhüllen;
Nach der Wärme ziehn sich Musen,
Nach der Wärme Charitinnen.

Umschwebet mich, ihr Musen,
Ihr Charitinnen!
Das ist Wasser, das ist Erde,
Und der Sohn des Wassers und der Erde,
Über den ich wandle
Göttergleich.

Ihr seid rein, wie das Herz der Wasser,
Ihr seid rein, wie das Mark der Erde,
Ihr umschwebt mich, und ich schwebe
Über Wasser, über Erde,
Göttergleich.

Soll der zurückkehren,
Der kleine, schwarze, feurige Bauer?
Soll der zurückkehren, erwartend
Nur deine Gaben, Vater Bromius,
Und helleuchtend umwärmend Feuer?
Der kehren mutig?
Und ich, den ihr begleitet,
Musen und Charitinnen alle,
Den alles erwartet, was ihr,
Musen und Charitinnen,
Umkränzende Seligkeit,
Rings ums Leben verherrlicht habt,
Soll mutlos kehren?

With wings of fire
He will walk
As on feet of flowers
Over Deucalion's flood ooze,
Killing Python, light, large,
A Pythian Apollo.

Spirit, he whom you do not forsake,
Woollen wings you'll spread beneath him
When he sleeps on rock,
With guardian pinions deck him
In the midnight bosk.

Spirit, not forsaking him,
Him you will cloak
Warm in the snow-whirl;
To warmth the Muses come,
Come the Graces.

Float round me, Muses
And you Graces!
Here is water, here is earth,
And the son of earth and water
Over whom I walk,
Godlike.

You are pure, like water's heart,
You are pure, like earth's marrow,
Round me you float and I
Float over water, over earth,
Godlike.

Shall he return,
The small dark fiery farmer?
Shall he return, in expectation
Only of your gifts, Father Bromius?
And bright shining fire's warmth around?
He return, in good heart?
And I, whom you consort with,
Muses and Graces all,
I whom all expects that you,
Muses and Graces,
All the garlanding bliss,
The glory you have ringed this earth with,
Should I return despondent?

Vater Bromius!
Du bist Genius,
Jahrhunderts Genius,
Bist, was innre Glut
Pindarn war,
Was der Welt
Phöbus Apoll ist.

Weh! Weh! Innre Wärme,
Seelenwärme,
Mittelpunkt!
Glüh entgegen
Phöb Apollen;
Kalt wird sonst
Sein Fürstenblick
Über dich vorübergleiten,
Neidgetroffen
Auf der Zeder Kraft verweilen,
Die zu grünen
Sein nicht harrt.

Warum nennt mein Lied dich zuletzt?
Dich, von dem es begann,
Dich, in dem es endet,
Dich, aus dem es quillt,
Jupiter Pluvius!
Dich, dich strömt mein Lied,
Und kastalischer Quell
Rinnt ein Nebenbach,
Rinnet Müßigen,
Sterblich Glücklichen
Abseits von dir,
Der du mich fassend deckst,
Jupiter Pluvius!

Nicht am Ulmenbaum
Hast du ihn besucht,
Mit dem Taubenpaar
In dem zärtlichen Arm,
Mit der freundlichen Ros umkränzt,
Tändelnden ihn, blumenglücklichen
Anakreon,
Sturmatmende Gottheit!

Father Bromius!
You the Spirit are,
Spirit of the Century,
Are what heart's glow
Was to Pindar,
What to the world
Phoebus Apollo is.

Ow! Ow! Inner warmth,
Soulwarmth,
Midpoint!
Glow toward
Phoebus Apollo;
Else coldly will
His princely gaze
Pass over you,
Panged with envy
Dwell upon the cedar's power,
Which to be green
Waits not for him.

My song, why does it name you last,
You from whom it began,
You in whom it ends,
You from whom it streams,
Jupiter Pluvius?
You, you my song pours forth,
And this Castalian spring
Runs like a trickle,
Trickles, for idlers,
Mortally fortunate men,
A tributary brook, while you
Hold and shelter me,
Jupiter Pluvius.

Not by the elm,
Him you visited not,
A pair of doves
Perched on his delicate arm,
Garlanded with friendly rose,
Titillating and flower-fortunate
Anacreon,
God who breathes the storm out.

Nicht im Pappelwald
An des Sybaris Strand,
An des Gebirgs
Sonnebeglänzter Stirn nicht
Faßtest du ihn,
Den Blumen-singenden,
Honig-lallenden,
Freundlich winkenden
Theokrit.

Wenn die Räder rasselten,
Rad an Rad rasch ums Ziel weg,
Hoch flog
Siegdurchglühter
Jünglinge Peitschenknall,
Und sich Staub wälzt',
Wie vom Gebirg herab
Kieselwetter ins Tal,
Glühte deine Seel Gefahren, Pindar,
Mut.—Glühte?—
Armes Herz!
Dort auf dem Hügel,
Himmlische Macht!
Nur so viel Glut,
Dort meine Hütte,
Dorthin zu waten!

Mahomets Gesang

Seht den Felsenquell,
Freudehell,
Wie ein Sternenblick;
Über Wolken
Nährten seine Jugend
Gute Geister
Zwischen Klippen im Gebüsch.

Jünglingfrisch
Tanzt er aus der Wolke

Not among the poplars,
On the coast of Sybaris,
On the sunlit brow
Of the mountain, not him
Did you hold,
Flower-singing,
Honey-babbling,
Amiably beckoning
Theocritus.

When the wheels rattled,
Wheel by wheel, fast to the finish,
High flew
The whipcracks
Of the lads who glowed for a win,
And dust churned like hail
Tumbling down
Into the dale from the mountain,
Did your soul glow, Pindar,
Against perils
Courage.—Glow, did it?
Poor heart,
There on the hill,
Heavenly power,
Glow enough only,
There my cabin,
To wade my way there!

A Song to Mahomet (1772–73)

See the mountain spring
Flash gladdening
Like a glance of stars;
Higher than the clouds
Kindly spirits
Fuelled his youth
In thickets twixt the crags.

Brisk as a young blade
Out of cloud he dances

Auf die Marmorfelsen nieder,
Jauchzet wieder
Nach dem Himmel.

Durch die Gipfelgänge
Jagt er bunten Kieseln nach,
Und mit frühem Führertritt
Reißt er seine Bruderquellen
Mit sich fort.

Drunten werden in dem Tal
Unter seinem Fußtritt Blumen,
Und die Wiese
Lebt von seinem Hauch.

Doch ihn hält kein Schattental,
Keine Blumen,
Die ihm seine Knie umschlingen,
Ihm mit Liebes-Augen schmeicheln:
Nach der Ebne dringt sein Lauf
Schlangenwandelnd.

Bäche schmiegen
Sich gesellig an. Nun tritt er
In die Ebne silberprangend,
Und die Ebne prangt mit ihm,
Und die Flüsse von der Ebne
Und die Bäche von den Bergen
Jauchzen ihm und rufen: Bruder!
Bruder, nimm die Brüder mit,
Mit zu deinem alten Vater,
Zu dem ewgen Ozean,
Der mit ausgespannten Armen
Unser wartet,
Die sich, ach! vergebens öffnen,
Seine Sehnenden zu fassen;
Denn uns frißt in öder Wüste
Gierger Sand; die Sonne droben
Saugt an unserm Blut; ein Hügel
Hemmet uns zum Teiche! Bruder,
Nimm die Brüder von der Ebne,
Nimm die Brüder von den Bergen
Mit, zu deinem Vater mit!

Down to marble rocks
And leaps again
Skyward exultant.

Down passages that hang from peaks
He chases pebbles many-coloured,
Early like a leader striding
Snatches up and carries onward
Brother torrents.

Flowers are born beneath his footprint
In the valley down below,
From his breathing
Pastures live.

Yet no valley of the shadows
Can contain him
And no flowers that clasp his knees,
Blandishing with looks of love;
To the lowland bursts his way,
A snake uncoiling.

Freshets nestle
Flocking to his side. He comes
Into the lowland, silver sparkling,
And with him the lowland sparkles,
And the lowland rivers call,
Mountain freshets call exultant:
Brother, take your brothers with you,
With you to your ancient father,
To the everlasting ocean,
Who with open arms awaits us,
Arms which, ah, open in vain
To clasp us who are craving for him;
Avid sand consumes us
In the desert, sun overhead
Will suck our blood, blocked by a hill
To pools we shrink! Brother, take us,
Take your lowland brothers with you,
Take your brothers of the mountains,
To your father take us all!

Kommt ihr alle!—
Und nun schwillt er
Herrlicher; ein ganz Geschlechte
Trägt den Fürsten hoch empor!
Und im rollenden Triumphe
Gibt er Ländern Namen, Städte
Werden unter seinem Fuß.

Unaufhaltsam rauscht er weiter,
Läßt der Türme Flammengipfel,
Marmorhäuser, eine Schöpfung
Seiner Fülle, hinter sich.

Zedernhäuser trägt der Atlas
Auf den Riesenschultern; sausend
Wehen über seinem Haupte
Tausend Flaggen durch die Lüfte,
Zeugen seiner Herrlichkeit.

Und so trägt er seine Brüder,
Seine Schätze, seine Kinder
Dem erwartenden Erzeuger
Freudebrausend an das Herz.

Prometheus

Bedecke deinen Himmel, Zeus,
Mit Wolkendunst
Und übe, dem Knaben gleich,
Der Disteln köpft,
An Eichen dich und Bergeshöhn;
Mußt mir meine Erde
Doch lassen stehn
Und meine Hütte, die du nicht gebaut,
Und meinen Herd,
Um dessen Glut
Du mich beneidest.

Join me then!
And now he swells
More lordly still; one single kin,
They loft the prince and bear him high
Onward as he rolls triumphant,
Naming countries, in his track
Towns and cities come to be.

On he rushes, unrelenting,
Leaves the turrets tipped with flame,
Marble palaces, creation
Of his plenitude, behind him.

Cedar houses he like Atlas
Carries on his giant shoulders;
Flags a thousand rustling flutter
In the air above his head,
Testifying to his glory.

So he bears his brothers, bears
His treasures and his children surging
In a wave of joy tumultuous
To their waiting father's heart.

Prometheus (1773)

Cover your heaven, Zeus,
With cloudy vapors
And like a boy
Beheading thistles
Practice on oaks and mountain peaks—
Still you must leave
My earth intact
And my small hovel, which you did not build,
And this my hearth
Whose glowing heat
You envy me.

Ich kenne nichts Ärmeres
Unter der Sonn als euch, Götter!
Ihr nähret kümmerlich
Von Opfersteuern
Und Gebetshauch
Eure Majestät
Und darbtet, wären
Nicht Kinder und Bettler
Hoffnungsvolle Toren.

Da ich ein Kind war,
Nicht wußte, wo aus noch ein,
Kehrt ich mein verirrtes Auge
Zur Sonne, als wenn drüber wär
Ein Ohr, zu hören meine Klage,
Ein Herz wie meins,
Sich des Bedrängten zu erbarmen.

Wer half mir
Wider der Titanen Übermut?
Wer rettete vom Tode mich,
Von Sklaverei?
Hast du nicht alles selbst vollendet,
Heilig glühend Herz?
Und glühtest jung und gut,
Betrogen, Rettungsdank
Dem Schlafenden da droben?

Ich dich ehren? Wofür?
Hast du die Schmerzen gelindert
Je des Beladenen?
Hast du die Tränen gestillet
Je des Geängsteten?
Hat nicht mich zum Manne geschmiedet
Die allmächtige Zeit
Und das ewige Schicksal,
Meine Herrn und deine?

Wähntest du etwa,
Ich sollte das Leben hassen,

I know of nothing more wretched
Under the sun than you gods!
Meagerly you nourish
Your majesty
On dues of sacrifice
And breath of prayer
And would suffer want
But for children and beggars,
Poor hopeful fools.

Once too, a child,
Not knowing where to turn,
I raised bewildered eyes
Up to the sun, as if above there were
An ear to hear my complaint,
A heart like mine
To take pity on the oppressed.

Who helped me
Against the Titans' arrogance?
Who rescued me from death,
From slavery?
Did not my holy and glowing heart,
Unaided, accomplish all?
And did it not, young and good,
Cheated, glow thankfulness
For its safety to him, to the sleeper above?

I pay homage to you? For what?
Have you ever relieved
The burdened man's anguish?
Have you ever assuaged
The frightened man's tears?
Was it not omnipotent Time
That forged me into manhood,
And eternal Fate,
My masters and yours?

Or did you think perhaps
That I should hate this life,

In Wüsten fliehen,
Weil nicht alle
Blütenträume reiften?

Hier sitz ich, forme Menschen
Nach meinem Bilde,
Ein Geschlecht, das mir gleich sei,
Zu leiden, zu weinen,
Zu genießen und zu freuen sich,
Und dein nicht zu achten,
Wie ich!

Ganymed

Wie im Morgenglanze
Du rings mich anglühst,
Frühling, Geliebter!
Mit tausendfacher Liebeswonne
Sich an mein Herz drängt
Deiner ewigen Wärme
Heilig Gefühl,
Unendliche Schöne!

Daß ich dich fassen möcht
In diesen Arm!

Ach, an deinem Busen
Lieg ich, schmachte,
Und deine Blumen, dein Gras
Drängen sich an mein Herz.
Du kühlst den brennenden
Durst meines Busens,
Lieblicher Morgenwind!
Ruft drein die Nachtigall
Liebend nach mir aus dem Nebeltal.

Ich komm, ich komme!
Wohin? Ach, wohin?

Flee into deserts
Because not all
The blossoms of dream grew ripe?

Here I sit, forming men
In my image,
A race to resemble me:
To suffer, to weep,
To enjoy, to be glad—
And never to heed you,
Like me!

Ganymede (1774)

How in the morning gleam
All around you glow at me,
Springtime, belovèd!
With joy of love a thousandfold
Rushes to my heart
Of your eternal warmth
A holy feeling,
Infinite beauty!

That in this arm I might
Hold you.

Ah, upon your breast
I stretch out, swoon,
And your flowers, your grass
Rush to my heart.
You slake the burning
Thirst in my breast,
Delicate morning wind,
Withal the nightingale lovingly
Calls from the misty vale to me.

I am coming, coming,
Where, ah where?

Hinauf! Hinauf strebts.
Es schweben die Wolken
Abwärts, die Wolken
Neigen sich der sehnenden Liebe.
Mir! Mir!
In euerm Schoße
Aufwärts!
Umfangend umfangen!
Aufwärts an deinen Busen,
Alliebender Vater!

Up, a striving upward.
The clouds are floating
Down, the clouds
Bow to love that is yearning.
Take me, take me,
Clouds, in your lap,
Upward,
Embraced embracing!
Upward to your breast,
All-loving father!

Der König in Thule

Es war ein König in Thule
Gar treu bis an das Grab,
Dem sterbend seine Buhle
Einen goldnen Becher gab.

Es ging ihm nichts darüber,
Er leert' ihn jeden Schmaus;
Die Augen gingen ihm über,
Sooft er trank daraus.

Und als er kam zu sterben,
Zählt' er seine Städt' im Reich,
Gönnt' alles seinen Erben,
Den Becher nicht zugleich.

Er saß beim Königsmahle,
Die Ritter um ihn her,
Auf hohem Vätersaale,
Dort auf dem Schloß am Meer.

Dort stand der alte Zecher,
Trank letzte Lebensglut,
Und warf den heilgen Becher
Hinunter in die Flut.

Er sah ihn stürzen, trinken
Und sinken tief ins Meer.
Die Augen täten ihm sinken;
Trank nie einen Tropfen mehr.

The King in Thule (1774)

There lived a king in Thule,
Right faithful, to the grave.
He loved a golden goblet
His dying sweetheart gave.

He loved it: nothing dearer,
Would not a-feasting go
But soon the cup was lifted
And soon the tears would flow.

His time of death approaching,
He counts his towns out, so.
Wills all away, and gladly.
But not the goblet, no.

The scene: a royal banquet,
His knights around his knee;
The lofty hall, ancestral,
High-castled by the sea.

Then rose the snowy toper;
A toast! to life's last glow!
His sainted cup he catches,
Flings to the foam below.

He watched it falling, filling;
He saw it settle, sink.
His eyelids ebb; then never
Another drop to drink.

Gretchen am Spinnrade

Meine Ruh ist hin,
Mein Herz ist schwer,
Ich finde sie nimmer
Und nimmermehr.

Wo ich ihn nicht hab,
Ist mir das Grab,
Die ganze Welt
Ist mir vergällt.

Mein armer Kopf
Ist mir verrückt,
Mein armer Sinn
Ist mir zerstückt.

Meine Ruh ist hin,
Mein Herz ist schwer,
Ich finde sie nimmer
Und nimmermehr.

Nach ihm nur schau ich
Zum Fenster hinaus,
Nach ihm nur geh ich
Aus dem Haus.

Sein hoher Gang,
Sein edle Gestalt,
Seines Mundes Lächeln,
Seiner Augen Gewalt

Und seiner Rede
Zauberfluß,
Sein Händedruck,
Und, ach, sein Kuß!

Meine Ruh ist hin,
Mein Herz ist schwer,
Ich finde sie nimmer
Und nimmermehr.

Gretchen at the Spinningwheel (from *Urfaust*, c. 1775)

No peace of mind,
Heartache and pain,
No peace I find
Ever again.

Where he is not
For me to have
Is a bitter spot,
For me a grave.

Poor head of mine
Turned upside down,
Poor heart of mine
To shreds is torn.

No peace of mind,
Heartache and pain,
No peace I find
Ever again.

Go to the window
Only to see,
Or out of doors,
If there he be.

His gracious figure,
Lofty walk,
His mouth, the smile!
That piercing look,

And speech that flows
With sorceries,
His hand, a touch,
And ah! his kiss!

No peace of mind,
Heartache and pain,
No peace I find
Ever again.

Mein Busen drängt
Sich nach ihm hin,
Ach dürft ich fassen
Und halten ihn

Und küssen ihn,
So wie ich wollt,
An seinen Küssen
Vergehen sollt!

Vor Gericht

Von wem ich es habe, das sag ich euch nicht,
Das Kind in meinem Leib.—
Pfui! speit ihr aus: die Hure da!—
Bin doch ein ehrlich Weib.

Mit wem ich mich traute, das sag ich euch nicht.
Mein Schatz ist lieb und gut,
Trägt er eine goldene Kett am Hals,
Trägt er einen strohernen Hut.

Soll Spott und Hohn getragen sein,
Trag ich allein den Hohn.
Ich kenn ihn wohl, er kennt mich wohl,
Und Gott weiß auch davon.

Herr Pfarrer und Herr Amtmann ihr,
Ich bitte, laßt mich in Ruh!
Es ist mein Kind, es bleibt mein Kind,
Ihr gebt mir ja nichts dazu.

For him I long
With all my might,
Could I but touch
And hold him tight,

And kiss him, kiss him,
Just as I may,
Under his kisses
Melt away.

In Court (c. 1774–75)

Who gave it me, I shall not tell,
The child I've got in me;
Call me a whore, if you like, and spit:
I'm an honest woman, see?

He's good and kind, I'll not say who,
My sweetheart that I wed,
A chain of gold on his neck he wears
And a straw hat on his head.

Chuckle and scorn to your heart's content,
I'll take the scorn from you;
I know him well, he knows me well,
God knows about us, too.

Lay off me, folks, you, reverend,
You, officer of the laws!
It is my child, it stays my child,
And it's no concern of yours.

Auf dem See

Und frische Nahrung, neues Blut
Saug ich aus freier Welt;
Wie ist Natur so hold und gut,
Die mich am Busen hält!
Die Welle wieget unsern Kahn
Im Rudertakt hinauf,
Und Berge, wolkig himmelan,
Begegnen unserm Lauf.

Aug, mein Aug, was sinkst du nieder?
Goldne Träume, kommt ihr wieder?
Weg, du Traum! so gold du bist;
Hier auch Lieb und Leben ist.

Auf der Welle blinken
Tausend schwebende Sterne,
Weiche Nebel trinken
Rings die türmende Ferne;
Morgenwind umflügelt
Die beschattete Bucht,
Und im See bespiegelt
Sich die reifende Frucht.

On the Lake (1775)

And fresh nourishment, new blood
I suck from a world so free;
Nature, how gracious and how good,
Her breast she gives to me.
The ripples buoying up our boat
Keep rhythm to the oars,
And mountains up to heaven float
In cloud to meet our course.

Eyes, my eyes, why abject now?
Golden dreams, are you returning?
Dream, though gold, away with you:
Life is here and loving too.

Over the ripples twinkling
Star on hovering star,
Soft mists drink the circled
Towering world afar;
Dawn wind fans the shaded
Inlet with its wing,
And in the water mirrored
The fruit is ripening.

Herbstgefühl

Fetter grüne, du Laub,
Am Rebengeländer
Hier mein Fenster herauf!
Gedrängter quellet,
Zwillingsbeeren, und reifet
Schneller und glänzend voller!
Euch brütet der Mutter Sonne
Scheideblick, euch umsäuselt
Des holden Himmels
Fruchtende Fülle;
Euch kühlet des Mondes
Freundlicher Zauberhauch,
Und euch betauen, ach!
Aus diesen Augen
Der ewig belebenden Liebe
Vollschwellende Tränen.

Autumn Feeling (1775)

More fatly greening climb
The trellis, you, vine leaf
Up to my window!
Gush, denser, berries
Twin, and ripen
Shining fuller, faster!
Last gaze of sun
Broods you, maternal;
Of tender sky the fruiting
Fullness wafts around you;
Cooled you are, by the moon
Magic, a friendly breath,
And from these eyes,
Of ever quickening Love, ah,
Upon you falls a dew, the tumid
Brimming tears.

Künstlers Abendlied

Ach, daß die innre Schöpfungskraft
Durch meinen Sinn erschölle!
Daß eine Bildung voller Saft
Aus meinen Fingern quölle!

Ich zittre nur, ich stottre nur,
Und kann es doch nicht lassen;
Ich fühl, ich kenne dich, Natur,
Und so muß ich dich fassen.

Bedenk ich dann, wie manches Jahr
Sich schon mein Sinn erschließet,
Wie er, wo dürre Heide war,
Nun Freudenquell genießet;

Wie sehn ich mich, Natur, nach dir,
Dich treu und lieb zu fühlen!
Ein lustger Springbrunn wirst du mir
Aus tausend Röhren spielen.

Wirst alle meine Kräfte mir
In meinem Sinn erheitern
Und dieses enge Dasein hier
Zur Ewigkeit erweitern.

An Artist's Evening Song (1775)

To have creation's inmost power
Resounding through my mind!
A shape of things, in vivid flower,
Issue from my hand!

My touch uncertain, stammering speech,
But new resolve beget;
I feel, I know you, in my reach,
Nature, I'll have you yet.

Still, down the years my mind has shed
Some of its trammelings;
Where once all parched a heathland spread
Flow now delightful springs;

Nature, that thought, and then I long
Truly to feel you near;
Your thousand flutes I'll be among
Your fountain I shall hear;

Lift to the light you surely will
All faculties of mine,
Out of this straitened life distil
A sense defeating time.

II

Die ersten Weimarer Jahre

The First Weimar Years

Erklärung eines alten Holzschnittes vorstellend Hans Sachsens poetische Sendung

In seiner Werkstatt Sonntags früh
Steht unser teurer Meister hie,
Sein schmutzig Schurzfell abgelegt,
Einen saubern Feierwams er trägt,
Läßt Pechdraht, Hammer und Kneipe rasten,
Die Ahl steckt an dem Arbeitskasten;
Er ruht nun auch am siebnten Tag
Von manchem Zug und manchem Schlag.

Wie er die Frühlings-Sonne spürt,
Die Ruh ihm neue Arbeit gebiert:
Er fühlt, daß er eine kleine Welt
In seinem Gehirne brütend hält,
Daß die fängt an zu wirken und leben,
Daß er sie gerne möcht von sich geben.

Er hätt ein Auge treu und klug,
Und wär auch liebevoll genug,
Zu schauen manches klar und rein,
Und wieder alles zu machen sein;
Hätt auch eine Zunge, die sich ergoß,
Und leicht und fein in Worte floß;
Des täten die Musen sich erfreun,
Wollten ihn zum Meistersänger weihn.

Da tritt herein ein junges Weib,
Mit voller Brust und rundem Leib,
Kräftig sie auf den Füßen steht,
Grad, edel vor sich hin sie geht,
Ohne mit Schlepp und Steiß zu schwänzen,
Oder mit den Augen herum zu scharlenzen.
Sie trägt einen Maßstab in ihrer Hand,
Ihr Gürtel ist ein gülden Band,
Hätt auf dem Haupt einen Kornähr-Kranz,
Ihr Auge war lichten Tages Glanz;
Man nennt sie tätig Ehrbarkeit,
Sonst auch Großmut, Rechtfertigkeit.

Die tritt mit gutem Gruß herein;
Er drob nicht mag verwundert sein,

Explanation of an Old Woodcut
Depicting Hans Sachs' Poetic Mission
(1776)

Sunday morning in his shop,
Here's our good master standing up:
He's doffed his dirty apron skin,
A festive doublet now he's in,
Gives hammer and thread and knife a rest,
His awl put back in his workchest;
Now takes he seventh day repose
From cutting up and hammer blows.

Now warms the springtime sun his mind,
Rest brings work of a different kind:
A little world he feels, our man,
Brewing up in his brainpan,
He feels it start to move and live
And that he'd like it forth to give.

He'd have a true eye, shrewd enough,
And in himself sufficient love
To see things clear and see them plain,
And make them all his own again:
A fluent tongue he'd have also
To make the light and fine words flow;
In this the Muses joy might take,
A Meistersinger of him make.

Just now a woman young has crossed
The stoop, her body round, her breast
Ample, and her stance is strong,
Noble and straight she walks along,
Not wiggling with her skirt or ass,
Not ogling eyes to make a pass.
A measure in her hand she holds,
Her girdle ribbon all of gold,
Has on her head a barley wreath,
Bright as the day her eyes beneath;
Honour, she's called, or, if you will,
Magnanimity, or Skill.

Well, with fair greeting, in she comes;
He's not the least surprised, it seems,

Denn wie sie ist, so gut und schön,
Meint er, er hätt sie lang gesehn.

Die spricht: «Ich habe dich auserlesen
Vor vielen in dem Weltwirrwesen,
Daß du sollst haben klare Sinnen,
Nichts Ungeschicklichs magst beginnen.
Wenn andre durcheinander rennen,
Sollst du's mit treuem Blick erkennen;
Wenn andre bärmlich sich beklagen,
Sollst schwankweis deine Sach fürtragen;
Sollst halten über Ehr und Recht,
In allem Ding sein schlicht und schlecht,
Frummkeit und Tugend bieder preisen,
Das Böse mit seinem Namen heißen.
Nichts verlindert und nichts verwitzelt,
Nichts verzierlicht und nichts verkritzelt;
Sondern die Welt soll vor dir stehn,
Wie Albrecht Dürer sie hat gesehn,
Ihr festes Leben und Männlichkeit,
Ihre innre Kraft und Ständigkeit.
Der Natur-Genius an der Hand
Soll dich führen durch alle Land,
Soll dir zeigen alles Leben,
Der Menschen wunderliches Weben,
Ihr Wirren, Suchen, Stoßen und Treiben,
Schieben, Reißen, Drängen und Reiben,
Wie kunterbunt die Wirtschaft tollert,
Der Ameishauf durcheinander kollert;
Mag dir aber bei allem geschehn,
Als tätst in einen Zauberkasten sehn.
Schreib das dem Menschenvolk auf Erden,
Ob's ihm möcht eine Witzung werden.»
Da macht sie ihm ein Fenster auf,
Zeigt ihm draußen viel bunten Hauf,
Unter dem Himmel allerlei Wesen,
Wie ihr's mögt in seinen Schriften lesen.

Wie nun der liebe Meister sich
An der Natur freut wunniglich,
Da seht ihr an der andern Seiten
Ein altes Weiblein zu ihm gleiten;
Man nennet sie Historia,
Mythologia, Fabula;

So good, so beautiful, for sure,
He thinks, he's seen her oft before.

Says she: "It's you that I have chosen,
From many in this world's confusion,
Clear senses and clear thoughts to have,
And nothing wicked to contrive.
When others criss and cross their ways,
You'll see all things with level gaze;
When others pitiably mope and groan,
You'll do your bit in a jesting tone;
On right and wrong you'll keep a watch,
Be plain direct in every touch,
Justice and virtue celebrate,
And naming evil name it straight.
Nothing softened or joked away,
No prettification, scribblers' play;
The world before you stand I bid
As it before Albrecht Dürer did:
Its vigorous masculinity,
Its inner strength and constancy.
Nature's genius by your hand
Will lead you then through every land,
Show you this life, just as it is,
People, their strange activities,
Muddling, questing, hitting, driving,
Pushing, pulling, crowding, chafing;
This world, its razzling dazzling leaps,
Boom and crash in its ant heaps;
May this no more affect you, though,
Than might a magic picture show.
For people on earth you'll write it down,
Then to their senses they might come."
Then opened she his window wide,
Showed him the motley throng outside,
Under the sky, such various folks
As you may read of in his books.

As our dear master now delights
In viewing Nature and her sights,
You see upon the other side
An ancient dame toward him glide;
She's called by all Historia,
Mythologia, Fabula;

Sie schleppt mit keichend-wankenden Schritten
Eine große Tafel in Holz geschnitten;
Darauf seht ihr mit weiten Ärmeln und Falten
Gott Vater Kinderlehre halten,
Adam, Eva, Paradies und Schlang,
Sodom und Gomorras Untergang,
Könnt auch die zwölf durchlauchtigen Frauen
Da in einem Ehren-Spiegel schauen;
Dann allerlei Blutdurst, Frevel und Mord,
Der zwölf Tyrannen Schandenport,
Auch allerlei Lehr und gute Weis,
Könnt sehn Sankt Peter mit der Geiß,
Über der Welt Regiment unzufrieden,
Von unserm Herrn zurecht beschieden.
Auch war bemalt der weite Raum
Ihres Kleids und Schlepps und auch der Saum
Mit weltlich Tugend- und Laster-Geschicht.

Unser Meister das all ersicht
Und freut sich dessen wundersam,
Denn es dient sehr in seinen Kram.
Von wannen er sich eignet sehr
Gut Exempel und gute Lehr,
Erzählt das eben fix und treu,
Als wär er selbst gesyn dabei.
Sein Geist war ganz dahin gebannt,
Er hätt kein Auge davon verwandt,
Hätt er nicht hinter seinem Rucken
Hören mit Klappern und Schellen spuken.

Da tät er einen Narren spüren
Mit Bocks- und Affensprüng hofieren,
Und ihm mit Schwank und Narreteiden
Ein lustig Zwischenspiel bereiten.
Schleppt hinter sich an einer Leinen
Alle Narren, groß- und kleinen,
Dick und hager, gestreckt und krumb,
All zu witzig und all zu dumb.
Mit einem großen Farrenschwanz
Regiert er sie wie ein'n Affentanz,
Bespöttet eines jeden Fürm,
Treibt sie ins Bad, schneidt ihnen die Würm,
Und führt gar bitter viel Beschwerden,
Daß ihrer doch nicht wollen wenger werden.

With rickety gasping steps she brings
An enormous board, with woodcuttings:
God the Father you see, all cuffs and folds,
As he a class in Scripture holds,
Adam and Eve, Paradise, the Snake,
Sodom and Gomorrah hit by earthquake;
The Twelve Distinguished Women see upon a
Looking Glass of Dignity and Honour;
Then bloodlust galore, murder, sacrilege,
The Tyrants Twelve on their rampage,
Instruction, too, and counsel, are descried,
You see Saint Peter, with his Goat, unsatisfied
With all the world and its regime:
You see Our Lord reproving him.
Pictures, too, adorn her dress,
On hem and train, an ample space,
Of worldly vice and virtue tales.

All this our master's sight regales,
And wonderfully pleased he is,
He makes it all his business.
Thence he will make palpable
Whatever he takes, in parable
And true instruction, telling no lies,
As if it played before his eyes.
His wits by this were so spellbound
He never would have turned around,
Had he not heard behind his back
Bells and clappers ping and clack.

Then was he of a Fool aware,
With goatish leaps amonkeying there,
Doing for him with farce and folly
An interlude, all blithe and jolly.
Behind him on a rope this fool
Drags all the others, big or small,
The tall, the crooked, the thin, the fat,
All crack-witted, and dumb at that.
With an oxtail whip he them commands
Like a troop of monkeys doing a dance:
Bids them go bathe, scoffs at their shapes,
Cuts them to see the worm escapes,
Complaining the while, with bitterness,
That never their number grows the less.

Wie er sich sieht so um und um,
Kehrt ihm das fast den Kopf herum,
Wie er wollt Worte zu allem finden?
Wie er möcht so viel Schwall verbinden?
Wie er möcht immer mutig bleiben,
So fort zu singen und zu schreiben?
Da steigt auf einer Wolke Saum
Herein zu's Oberfensters Raum
Die Muse, heilig anzuschauen,
Wie ein Bild unsrer lieben Frauen.
Die umgibt ihn mit ihrer Klarheit
Immer kräftig wirkender Wahrheit.
Sie spricht: «Ich komm um dich zu weihn,
Nimm meinen Segen und Gedeihn!
Ein heilig Feuer, das in dir ruht,
Schlag aus in hohe lichte Glut!
Doch daß das Leben, das dich treibt,
Immer bei holden Kräften bleibt,
Hab ich deinem innern Wesen
Nahrung und Balsam auserlesen,
Daß deine Seel sei wonnereich
Einer Knospe im Taue gleich.»

Da zeigt sie ihm hinter seinem Haus
Heimlich zur Hintertür hinaus,
In dem eng umzäunten Garten,
Ein holdes Mägdlein sitzend warten
Am Bächlein, beim Holunderstrauch;
Mit abgesenktem Haupt und Aug,
Sitzt unter einem Apfelbaum
Und spürt die Welt rings um sich kaum,
Hat Rosen in ihren Schoß gepflückt
Und bindet ein Kränzlein sehr geschickt,
Mit hellen Knospen und Blättern drein:
Für wen mag wohl das Kränzel sein?
So sitzt sie in sich selbst geneigt,
In Hoffnungsfülle ihr Busen steigt,
Ihr Wesen ist so ahndevoll,
Weiß nicht, was sie sich wünschen soll,
Und unter vieler Grillen Lauf
Steigt wohl einmal ein Seufzer auf.

Warum ist deine Stirn so trüb?
Das was dich dränget, süße Lieb,

Now round he looks and round, enough
Nearly to twist his noddle off:
Where should he find words for it all?
Where, to connect, the wherewithal?
How shall he keep his spirit strong
For writing of it, or for song?
Then from a fringe of cloud apace
Descends, through a top window space,
The Muse, most holy to behold,
Like Our Lady, framed in gold.
Round him now she puts a ring
Of light—truth, strong and everlasting.
"I consecrate you now," she says,
"For that I come, and you to bless.
There burns in you a holy flame:
Exalt it into light sublime.
But that the life which is your spur
May delicate remain and pure,
A balm and nourishment I have put
Into your being's very root,
So may delight your soul imbue
As does the bud the morning dew."

Then, secretly, a way she shows
Out through the back door of the house,
And in the sheltered garden sitting
A lovely girl, for someone waiting,
Near the elder, by a brook:
She hardly gives the world a look,
Her head is bowed, downcast her eye,
She sits beneath an apple tree,
And from her lap fresh roses takes,
Of bud and leaf a garland makes
With nimble fingers, skilfully.
For whom might now this garland be?
Her self-attentive curves attest
That breath of hope now swells her breast;
So many dreams in her aspire,
She does not know what to desire;
So many moods are passing by,
Sometimes she cannot help but sigh.

Wherefore, my dear, this darkish brow?
What weighs upon you is not so

Ist volle Wonn und Seligkeit,
Die dir in Einem ist bereit,
Der manches Schicksal wirrevoll
An deinem Auge sich lindern soll;
Der durch manch wunniglichen Kuß
Wiedergeboren werden muß,
Wie er den schlanken Leib umfaßt,
Von aller Mühe findet Rast,
Wie er ins liebe Ärmlein sinkt,
Neue Lebenstag und Kräfte trinkt.
Und dir kehrt neues Jugendglück,
Deine Schalkheit kehret dir zurück.
Mit Necken und manchen Schelmereien
Wirst ihn bald nagen, bald erfreuen.
So wird die Liebe nimmer alt,
Und wird der Dichter nimmer kalt!

Wie er so heimlich glücklich lebt,
Da droben in den Wolken schwebt
Ein Eichkranz, ewig jung belaubt,
Den setzt die Nachwelt ihm aufs Haupt;
In Froschpfuhl all das Volk verbannt,
Das seinen Meister je verkannt.

But full of lightsome joy and bliss
That now, for you, full ready is
In one for whom you'll mitigate,
Just with a look, the snarls of fate,
And who must needs be born anew
With every wondrous kiss from you.
Holds he your slender body tight,
From every toil he'll find respite;
Into your rounded arms he'll sink,
There freshest life and vigour drink.
Sweet youth to you will too come back
With merriness that now you lack.
Your teasing wit will sometimes bite,
Or, roguish sometimes, him delight:
So love will never then grow old
And never he, the poet, cold.

Now secret joys are his to have,
Come floating from a cloud above
Evergreen oakleaves, garlanded:
Therewith Posterity wreathes his head;
Such folks into the frog pond pitch
As gave for their master never a stitch.

Wandrers Nachtlied

Der du von dem Himmel bist,
Alles Leid und Schmerzen stillest,
Den, der doppelt elend ist,
Doppelt mit Erquickung füllest,
Ach, ich bin des Treibens müde!
Was soll all der Schmerz und Lust?
Süßer Friede,
Komm, ach komm in meine Brust!

Ein Gleiches

Über allen Gipfeln
Ist Ruh,
In allen Wipfeln
Spürest du
Kaum einen Hauch;
Die Vögelein schweigen im Walde.
Warte nur, balde
Ruhest du auch.

Wanderer's Night Song (1776)

Thou that from the heavens art,
 Every pain and sorrow stillest,
And the doubly wretched heart
 Doubly with refreshment fillest,
I am weary with contending!
 Why this rapture and unrest?
Peace descending
 Come, ah, come into my breast!

Another Night Song (1780)

O'er all the hill-tops
 Is quiet now,
In all the tree-tops
 Hearest thou
Hardly a breath;
 The birds are asleep in the trees:
 Wait, soon like these
 Thou, too, shalt rest.

(Longfellow)

Over mountains yonder,
 A stillness;
Scarce any breath, you wonder,
 Touches
The tops of all the trees.
 No forest birds now sing;
A moment, waiting—
 Then take, you too, your ease.

(CM)

An Charlotte von Stein

Warum gabst du uns die tiefen Blicke,
Unsre Zukunft ahnungsvoll zu schaun,
Unsrer Liebe, unserm Erdenglücke
Wähnend selig nimmer hinzutraun?
Warum gabst uns, Schicksal, die Gefühle,
Uns einander in das Herz zu sehn,
Um durch all die seltenen Gewühle
Unser wahr Verhältnis auszuspähn?

Ach, so viele tausend Menschen kennen,
Dumpf sich treibend, kaum ihr eigen Herz,
Schweben zwecklos hin und her und rennen
Hoffnungslos in unversehnem Schmerz;
Jauchzen wieder, wenn der schnellen Freuden
Unerwart'te Morgenröte tagt;
Nur uns armen Liebevollen beiden
Ist das wechselseitge Glück versagt,
Uns zu lieben, ohn uns zu verstehen,
In dem andern sehn, was er nie war,
Immer frisch auf Traumglück auszugehen
Und zu schwanken auch in Traumgefahr.

Glücklich, den ein leerer Traum beschäftigt,
Glücklich, dem die Ahndung eitel wär!
Jede Gegenwart und jeder Blick bekräftigt
Traum und Ahndung leider uns noch mehr.
Sag, was will das Schicksal uns bereiten?
Sag, wie band es uns so rein genau?
Ach, du warst in abgelebten Zeiten
Meine Schwester oder meine Frau.

Kanntest jeden Zug in meinem Wesen,
Spähtest wie die reinste Nerve klingt,
Konntest mich mit Einem Blicke lesen,
Den so schwer ein sterblich Aug durchdringt;
Tropftest Mäßigung dem heißen Blute,
Richtetest den wilden irren Lauf,
Und in deinen Engelsarmen ruhte
Die zerstörte Brust sich wieder auf;
Hieltest zauberleicht ihn angebunden
Und vergaukeltest ihm manchen Tag.
Welche Seligkeit glich jenen Wonnestunden,
Da er dankbar dir zu Füßen lag,

To Charlotte von Stein (1776)

Why confer on us the piercing vision:
All tomorrow vivid in our gaze?
Not a chance to build on love's illusion?
Not a glimmer of idyllic days?
Why confer on us, O fate, the feeling
Each can plumb the other's very heart?
Always, though in storms of passion reeling,
See precisely what a course we chart?

Look at all those many thousands drudging
(Knowing even their own nature less
Than we know each other), thousands trudging,
In the dark about their own distress;
Drunk on exultation, when they're treated
Suddenly to joy's magenta dawn.
Only we unlucky lovers, cheated
Of all mutual comfort, have forgone
This: to be in love, not understanding;
This; to see the other as he's not;
Off in gaudy dreams go hand-in-handing,
In appalling dreams turn cold and hot.

Happy man, a fleeting dream engages!
Happy man, no premonitions numb!
We however—! All our looks and touches
Reaffirm our fear of days to come.
Tell me, what's our destiny preparing?
Tell me, how we're bound in such a knot?
From an old existence we were sharing?
You're the wife, the sister I forgot?

Knew me then completely, every feature,
How each nerve responded and rang true;
Read me in a single glance—a nature
Others search bewildered for a clue.
To that heated blood, a cool transfusion;
To that crazy runaway, a rein;
In your clasp, what Edens of seclusion
Nursed to health that fellow, heart and brain.
Held him tightly, lightly, as enchanted;
Spirited the round of days away.
Where's a joy like this?—you'd think transplanted
At your feet the flushing lover lay;

Fühlt sein Herz an deinem Herzen schwellen,
Fühlte sich in deinem Auge gut,
Alle seine Sinnen sich erhellen
Und beruhigen sein brausend Blut!

Und von allem dem schwebt ein Erinnern
Nur noch um das ungewisse Herz,
Fühlt die alte Wahrheit ewig gleich im Innern,
Und der neue Zustand wird ihm Schmerz.
Und wir scheinen uns nur halb beseelet,
Dämmernd ist um uns der hellste Tag.
Glücklich, daß das Schicksal, das uns quälet
Uns doch nicht verändern mag!

An den Mond

Füllest wieder Busch und Tal
Still mit Nebelglanz,
Lösest endlich auch einmal
Meine Seele ganz;

Breitest über mein Gefild
Lindernd deinen Blick,
Wie des Freundes Auge mild
Über mein Geschick.

Jeden Nachklang fühlt mein Herz
Froh- und trüber Zeit,
Wandle zwischen Freud und Schmerz
In der Einsamkeit.

Fließe, fließe, lieber Fluß!
Nimmer werd ich froh,
So verrauschte Scherz und Kuß,
Und die Treue so.

Ich besaß es doch einmal,
Was so köstlich ist!

Lay and felt his heart, against you, lighten;
Felt your eye approving; *but he's good!*
Felt his murky senses clear and brighten;
On his raging blood, a quietude.

Now, of all that was, about him hovers
Just a haze of memory, hardly there.
Still the ancient truth avails: we're lovers—
Though our new condition's a despair.
Only half a mind for earth. Around us
Twilight thickens on the brightest day.
Yet we're still in luck: the fates that hound us
Couldn't wish our love away.

To the Moon
(1777; this second version published 1789)

Flooding with a brilliant mist
Valley, bush and tree,
You release me. Oh for once
Heart and soul I'm free!

Easy on the region round
Goes your wider gaze,
Like a friend's indulgent eye
Measuring my days.

Every echo from the past,
Glum or gaudy mood,
Haunts me—weighing bliss and pain
In the solitude.

River, flow and flow away;
Pleasure's dead to me:
Gone the laughing kisses, gone
Lips and loyalty.

All in my possession once!
Such a treasure yet

Daß man doch zu seiner Qual
Nimmer es vergißt!

Rausche, Fluß, das Tal entlang,»
Ohne Rast und Ruh,
Rausche, flüstre meinem Sang
Melodien zu,

Wenn du in der Winternacht
Wütend überschwillst,
Oder um die Frühlingspracht
Junger Knospen quillst.

Selig, wer sich vor der Welt
Ohne Haß verschließt,
Einen Freund am Busen hält
Und mit dem genießt,

Was, von Menschen nicht gewußt
Oder nicht bedacht,
Durch das Labyrinth der Brust
Wandelt in der Nacht.

Legende

In der Wüsten ein heiliger Mann
Zu seinem Erstaunen tät treffen an
Einen ziegenfüßigen Faun, der sprach:
«Herr, betet für mich und meine Gefährt,
Daß ich zum Himmel gelassen werd,
Zur seligen Freud; uns dürstet darnach.»
Der heilige Mann dagegen sprach:
«Es sieht mit deiner Bitte gar gefährlich,
Und gewährt wird sie dir schwerlich.
Du kommst nicht zum Englischen Gruß,
Denn du hast einen Ziegenfuß.»
Da sprach hierauf der wilde Mann:
«Was hat euch mein Ziegenfuß getan?
Sah ich doch manche strack und schön
Mit Eselsköpfen gen Himmel gehn.»

Any man would pitch in pain
Rather than forget.

Water, rush along the pass,
Never lag at ease;
Rush, and rustle to my song
Changing melodies,

How in dark December you
Roll amok in flood;
Curling, in the gala May,
Under branch and bud.

Happy man, that rancor-free
Shows the world his door;
One companion by—and both
In a glow before

Something never guessed by men
Or rejected quite:
Which, in mazes of the breast,
Wanders in the night.

Legend (1770's)

Once through the desert walking went
A saint, to his astonishment
There sprang across the road this faun,
Cloven hoofed. "Hi there! Good morn-
Ing!" the critter says, "feel free
At any time to pray for me,
Help me to go to Heaven!"—"Not
So easy," says the saint, "you've got
That cloven hoof. I estimate
The angel just might slam the gate."
Replies the faun (not one to mix
His words): "Or open it? For kicks?
What harm has ever a hoof done you?
Saint, I seen all sorts get through,
Easy as pie—and it appears
A tidy bunch had asses' ears."

Harzreise im Winter

Dem Geier gleich,
Der auf schweren Morgenwolken
Mit sanftem Fittich ruhend
Nach Beute schaut,
Schwebe mein Lied.

Denn ein Gott hat
Jedem seine Bahn
Vorgezeichnet,
Die der Glückliche
Rasch zum freudigen
Ziele rennt:
Wem aber Unglück
Das Herz zusammenzog,
Er sträubt vergebens
Sich gegen die Schranken
Des ehernen Fadens,
Den die doch bittre Schere
Nur einmal löst.

In Dickichts-Schauer
Drängt sich das rauhe Wild,
Und mit den Sperlingen
Haben längst die Reichen
In ihre Sümpfe sich gesenkt.

Leicht ists folgen dem Wagen,
Den Fortuna führt,
Wie der gemächliche Troß
Auf gebesserten Wegen
Hinter des Fürsten Einzug.

Aber abseits wer ists?
Ins Gebüsch verliert sich sein Pfad,
Hinter ihm schlagen
Die Sträuche zusammen,
Das Gras steht wieder auf,
Die Öde verschlingt ihn.

Ach, wer heilet die Schmerzen
Des, dem Balsam zu Gift ward?
Der sich Menschenhaß

A Winter Journey in the Harz (1777)

As the buzzard aloft
On heavy daybreak cloud
With easy pinion rests
Searching for prey,
May my song hover.

For a god has
Duly to each
His path prefixed,
And the fortunate man
Runs fast and joyfully
To his journey's end;
But he whose heart
Misfortune constricted
Struggles in vain
To break from the bonds
Of the brazen thread
Which the shears, so bitter still,
Cut once alone.

Into grisly thickets
The rough beasts run,
And with the sparrows
The rich long since have
Sunk in their swamps.

Easy it is to follow that car
Which Fortune steers,
Like the leisurely troop that rides
The fine highroads
Behind the array of the Prince.

But who is it stands aloof?
His path is lost in the brake,
Behind him the shrubs
Close and he's gone,
Grass grows straight again,
The emptiness swallows him.

O who shall heal his agony then
In whom each balm turned poison,
Who drank hatred of man

Aus der Fülle der Liebe trank?
Erst verachtet, nun ein Verächter,
Zehrt er heimlich auf
Seinen eignen Wert
In ungnügender Selbstsucht.

Ist auf deinem Psalter,
Vater der Liebe, ein Ton
Seinem Ohre vernehmlich,
So erquicke sein Herz!
Öffne den umwölkten Blick
Über die tausend Quellen
Neben dem Durstenden
In der Wüste.

Der du der Freuden viel schaffst,
Jedem ein überfließend Maß,
Segne die Brüder der Jagd
Auf der Fährte des Wilds
Mit jugendlichem Übermut
Fröhlicher Mordsucht,
Späte Rächer des Unbills,
Dem schon Jahre vergeblich
Wehrt mit Knütteln der Bauer.

Aber den Einsamen hüll
In deine Goldwolken!
Umgib mit Wintergrün,
Bis die Rose wieder heranreift,
Die feuchten Haare,
O Liebe, deines Dichters!

Mit der dämmernden Fackel
Leuchtest du ihm
Durch die Furten bei Nacht,
Über grundlose Wege
Auf öden Gefilden;
Mit dem tausendfarbigen Morgen
Lachst du ins Herz ihm;
Mit dem beizenden Sturm
Trägst du ihn hoch empor;
Winterströme stürzen vom Felsen
In seine Psalmen,
Und Altar des lieblichsten Danks

From the very fullness of love?
First held now holding in contempt,
In secret he consumes
His own particular good
In selfhood unsated.

 If in your book of songs
Father of love, there sounds
One note his ear can hear,
Refresh with it then his heart!
Open his clouded gaze
To the thousand fountainheads
About him as he thirsts
In the desert!

 You who give joys that are manifold,
To each his overflowing share,
Bless the companions that hunt
On the spoor of the beasts
With young exuberance
Of glad desire to kill,
Tardy avengers of outrage
For so long repelled in vain
By the cudgeling countryman.

 But hide the solitary man
In your sheer gold cloud!
Till roses flower again
Surround with winter-green
The moistened hair,
O love, of your poet!

 With your lantern glowing
You light his way
Over the fords by night,
On impassable tracks
Through the void countryside;
With daybreak thousand-hued
Into his heart you laugh;
With the mordant storm
You bear him aloft;
Winter streams plunge from the crag
Into his songs,
And his altar of sweetest thanks

Wird ihm des gefürchteten Gipfels
Schneebehangner Scheitel,
Den mit Geisterreihen
Kränzten ahnende Völker.

Du stehst mit unerforschtem Busen
Geheimnisvoll offenbar
Über der erstaunten Welt
Und schaust aus Wolken
Auf ihre Reiche und Herrlichkeit,
Die du aus den Adern deiner Brüder
Neben dir wässerst.

Gesang der Geister über den Wassern

Des Menschen Seele
Gleicht dem Wasser:
Vom Himmel kommt es,
Zum Himmel steigt es,
Und wieder nieder
Zur Erde muß es,
Ewig wechselnd.

Strömt von der hohen,
Steilen Felswand
Der reine Strahl,
Dann stäubt er lieblich
In Wolkenwellen
Zum glatten Fels,
Und leicht empfangen
Wallt er verschleiernd,
Leisrauschend
Zur Tiefe nieder.

Ragen Klippen
Dem Sturz entgegen,
Schäumt er unmutig
Stufenweise
Zum Abgrund.

Is the snow-hung brow
Of the terrible peak
People in their imaginings crowned
With spirit dances.

 You stand with heart unplumbed
Mysteriously revealed
Above the marveling world
And you look from clouds
On the kingdoms and magnificence
Which from your brothers' veins beside you
With streams you water.

Song of the Spirits over the Waters (1779)

The soul of man,
It is like water:
It comes from heaven,
It mounts to heaven,
And earthward again
Descends
Eternally changing.

If the pure jet
Streams from the high
Vertical rockface,
A powdering spray,
A wave of cloud
Splashes the smooth rock
And gathered lightly
Like a veil it rolls
Murmuring onward
To depths yonder.

If cliffs loom up
To stem its fall,
It foams petulant
Step by step
To the abyss.

Im flachen Bette
Schleicht er das Wiesental hin,
Und in dem glatten See
Weiden ihr Antlitz
Alle Gestirne.

Wind ist der Welle
Lieblicher Buhler;
Wind mischt vom Grund aus
Schäumende Wogen.

Seele des Menschen,
Wie gleichst du dem Wasser!
Schicksal des Menschen,
Wie gleichst du dem Wind!

Der Fischer

Das Wasser rauscht', das Wasser schwoll,
Ein Fischer saß daran,
Sah nach dem Angel ruhevoll,
Kühl bis ans Herz hinan.
Und wie er sitzt und wie er lauscht,
Teilt sich die Flut empor;
Aus dem bewegten Wasser rauscht
Ein feuchtes Weib hervor.

Sie sang zu ihm, sie sprach zu ihm:
Was lockst du meine Brut
Mit Menschenwitz und Menschenlist
Hinauf in Todesglut?
Ach wüßtest du, wie's Fischlein ist
So wohlig auf dem Grund,
Du stiegst herunter, wie du bist,
Und würdest erst gesund.

Labt sich die liebe Sonne nicht,
Der Mond sich nicht im Meer?
Kehrt wellenatmend ihr Gesicht

Along a level bed
Through the glen it slips,
In the lake unruffled
All the clustering stars
Turn their gaze.

Wind woos
The wave like a lover,
Wind churns from the ground up
Foaming billows.

Soul of man,
How like the water you are!
Fate of man,
How like the wind.

The Fisherman (end of 1770's)

The water washed, the water rose;
A fellow fishing sat
And watched his bobbin coolly drift,
His blood was cool as that.
A while he sits, a while he harks
— Like silk the ripples tear,
And up in swirls of foam arose
A girl with dripping hair.

She sang to him, she spoke to him:
"Cajole my minnows so
With lore of men, with lure of men,
To death's unholy glow?
If you could know my silver kin,
What cozy hours they passed,
You'd settle under, clothes and all
— A happy life at last.

"The sun, it likes to bathe and bathe;
The moon — now doesn't she?
And don't they both, to breathe the wave,

Nicht doppelt schöner her?
Lockt dich der tiefe Himmel nicht,
Das feuchtverklärte Blau?
Lockt dich dein eigen Angesicht
Nicht her in ewgen Tau?

Das Wasser rauscht', das Wasser schwoll,
Netzt' ihm den nackten Fuß;
Sein Herz wuchs ihm so sehnsuchtsvoll,
Wie bei der Liebsten Gruß.
Sie sprach zu ihm, sie sang zu ihm;
Da wars um ihn geschehn:
Halb zog sie ihn, halb sank er hin,
Und ward nicht mehr gesehn.

Meine Göttin

Welcher Unsterblichen
Soll der höchste Preis sein?
Mit niemand streit ich,
Aber ich geb ihn
Der ewig beweglichen,
Immer neuen,
Seltsamen Tochter Jovis,
Seinem Schoßkinde,
Der Phantasie.

Denn ihr hat er
Alle Launen,
Die er sonst nur allein
Sich vorbehält,
Zugestanden
Und hat seine Freude
An der Törin.

Sie mag rosenbekränzt
Mit dem Lilienstengel
Blumentäler betreten,
Sommervögeln gebieten
Und leichtnährenden Tau

Look up more brilliantly?
You're not allured by lakes of sky,
More glorious glossy blue?
Not by your very face transformed
In this eternal dew?"

The water washed, the water rose;
It lapped his naked toe,
As longing for the one he loved
He yearned to sink below.
She spoke to him, she sang to him;
The fellow, done for then,
Half yielded too as half she drew,
Was never seen again.

My Goddess (1780)

Which of the immortals
Merits the greatest praise?
I'll dispute with no one,
But I award it
To the ever-active,
Ever-new,
Bizarrest daughter of Jove,
His darling child,
Imagination.

For her he's endowed
With every caprice
That else he reserves
For himself alone,
And takes pleasure in
The girl's foolish ways.

Rose-garlanded
With her lily-stalk
She may walk
Wildflower valleys,
Command the summer birds
And with bee lips

Mit Bienenlippen
Von Blüten saugen;
Oder sie mag
Mit fliegendem Haar
Und düsterm Blicke
Im Winde sausen
Um Felsenwände,
Und tausendfarbig,
Wie Morgen und Abend
Immer wechselnd,
Wie Mondesblicke,
Den Sterblichen scheinen.

Laßt uns alle
Den Vater preisen!
Den alten, hohen,
Der solch eine schöne,
Unverwelkliche Gattin
Dem sterblichen Menschen
Gesellen mögen!

Denn uns allein
Hat er sie verbunden
Mit Himmelsband,
Und ihr geboten,
In Freud und Elend
Als treue Gattin
Nicht zu entweichen.

Alle die andern
Armen Geschlechter
Der kinderreichen,
Lebendigen Erde
Wandeln und weiden
In dunkelm Genuß
Und trüben Schmerzen
Des augenblicklichen
Beschränkten Lebens,
Gebeugt vom Joche
Der Notdurft.

Uns aber hat er
Seine gewandteste,
Verzärtelte Tochter,

From blossom sip
Lightly nourishing dew,
Or with hair flying
And glowering eyes
May ride in the wind,
Rush around rock face
And thousand-hued
Like morning and evening,
Always changing
Like moon glances
Appear to mortals.

Let us all
Praise the Father,
The ancient, exalted,
Who deigned to join
Mere mortal men
To so beautiful,
Unaging a consort.

For us alone
To her he has bound
With celestial bonds
And enjoined her
As a faithful spouse
Never to leave
The happy or wretched man.

All the other
Piteous kinds
Of our prolific
Living earth
Roam and forage
In dark enjoyment
Or murky pain
Of their momentary
Restricted lives,
Bowed under the yoke
Of immediate need.

But to us he's entrusted
His most resourceful,
His dandled daughter.

Freut euch! gegönnt.
Begegnet ihr lieblich,
Wie einer Geliebten!
Laßt ihr die Würde
Der Frauen im Haus!

Und daß die alte
Schwiegermutter Weisheit
Das zarte Seelchen
Ja nicht beleidge!

Doch kenn ich ihre Schwester,
Die ältere, gesetztere,
Meine stille Freundin:
O daß die erst
Mit dem Lichte des Lebens
Sich von mir wende,
Die edle Treiberin,
Trösterin Hoffnung!

Das Göttliche

Edel sei der Mensch,
Hilfreich und gut!
Denn das allein
Unterscheidet ihn
Von allen Wesen,
Die wir kennen.

Heil den unbekannten
Höhern Wesen,
Die wir ahnen!
Ihnen gleiche der Mensch;
Sein Beispiel lehr uns
Jene glauben.

Denn unfühlend
Ist die Natur:
Es leuchtet die Sonne

Be grateful for that!
Tenderly look on her
As you look on a mistress!
Grant her the dignity
Of a household's lady!

And, whatever you do,
Keep your mother-in-law,
Old Prudence, from ever
Slighting the delicate soul!

Yet I know her sister,
The elder, less flighty one,
My quiet friend—
O may she only turn
Away from me when
The light of this life does,
She who nobly impels
And comforts us: Hope!

The Godlike (early 1780's)

Noble let man be,
Helpful and good;
For that alone
Distinguishes him
From all beings
That we know.

Hail to the unknown,
Loftier beings
Our minds prefigure!
Let man be like them;
His example teach us
To believe those.

For unfeeling,
Numb, is nature;
The sun shines

Über Bös' und Gute,
Und dem Verbrecher
Glänzen wie dem Besten
Der Mond und die Sterne.

Wind und Ströme,
Donner und Hagel
Rauschen ihren Weg
Und ergreifen
Vorüber eilend
Einen um den andern.

Auch so das Glück
Tappt unter die Menge,
Faßt bald des Knaben
Lockige Unschuld,
Bald auch den kahlen
Schuldigen Scheitel.

Nach ewigen, ehrnen,
Großen Gesetzen
Müssen wir alle
Unseres Daseins
Kreise vollenden.

Nur allein der Mensch
Vermag das Unmögliche:
Er unterscheidet,
Wählet und richtet;
Er kann dem Augenblick
Dauer verleihen.

Er allein darf
Den Guten lohnen,
Den Bösen strafen,
Heilen und retten,
Alles Irrende, Schweifende
Nützlich verbinden.

Und wir verehren
Die Unsterblichen,
Als wären sie Menschen,
Täten im Großen,
Was der Beste im Kleinen
Tut oder möchte.

Upon bad and good,
And to the criminal
As to the best
The moon and the stars lend light.

Wind and rivers,
Thunder and hail
Rush on their way
And as they race
Headlong, take hold
One on the other.

So, too, chance
Gropes through the crowd,
And quickly snatches
The boy's curled innocence,
Quickly also
The guilty baldpate.

Following great, bronzen,
Ageless laws
All of us must
Fulfill the circles
Of our existence.

Yet man alone can
Achieve the impossible:
He distinguishes,
Chooses and judges;
He can give lasting
Life to the moment.

He alone should
Reward the good,
Punish the wicked,
Heal and save,
All erring and wandering
Usefully gather.

And we honor
Them, the immortals,
As though they were men,
Achieving in great ways
What the best in little
Achieves or longs to.

Der edle Mensch
Sei hilfreich und gut!
Unermüdet schaff er
Das Nützliche, Rechte,
Sei uns ein Vorbild
Jener geahneten Wesen!

Nachtgedanken

Euch bedaur ich, unglückselge Sterne,
Die ihr schön seid und so herrlich scheinet,
Dem bedrängten Schiffer gerne leuchtet,
Unbelohnt von Göttern und von Menschen:
Denn ihr liebt nicht, kanntet nie die Liebe!
Unaufhaltsam führen ewge Stunden
Eure Reihen durch den weiten Himmel.
Welche Reise habt ihr schon vollendet!
Seit ich weilend in dem Arm der Liebsten
Euer und der Mitternacht vergessen.

Grenzen der Menschheit

Wenn der uralte
Heilige Vater
Mit gelassener Hand
Aus rollenden Wolken
Segnende Blitze
Über die Erde sät,
Küss ich den letzten
Saum seines Kleides,
Kindliche Schauer
Treu in der Brust.

Let noble man
Be helpful and good,
Create unwearied
The useful, the just;
Be to us a pattern
Of those prefigured beings.

Night Thoughts (1781)

Stars, you are unfortunate, I pity you,
Beautiful as you are, shining in your glory,
Who guide seafaring men through stress and peril
And have no recompense from gods or mortals,
Love you do not, nor do you know what love is.
Hours that are aeons urgently conducting
Your figures in a dance through the vast heaven,
What journey have you ended in this moment,
Since lingering in the arms of my beloved
I lost all memory of you and midnight.

Limits of Human Nature (1781)

When the primeval,
Holy Father
With temperate hand
From thundering cloud forms
Over Earth scatters
Lightings of blessing,
I kiss the lowest
Hem of his garment,
Childlike awe throbbing
True in my breast.

Denn mit Göttern
Soll sich nicht messen
Irgend ein Mensch.
Hebt er sich aufwärts
Und berührt
Mit dem Scheitel die Sterne,
Nirgends haften dann
Die unsichern Sohlen,
Und mit ihm spielen
Wolken und Winde.

Steht er mit festen,
Markigen Knochen
Auf der wohlgegründeten
Dauernden Erde,
Reicht er nicht auf,
Nur mit der Eiche
Oder der Rebe
Sich zu vergleichen.

Was unterscheidet
Götter von Menschen?
Daß viele Wellen
Vor jenen wandeln,
Ein ewiger Strom:
Uns hebt die Welle,
Verschlingt die Welle,
Und wir versinken.

Ein kleiner Ring
Begrenzt unser Leben,
Und viele Geschlechter
Reihen sich dauernd
An ihres Daseins
Unendliche Kette.

For with gods
No man should ever
Dare to be measured.
If he uplifts himself
And bestirs
The stars with his cranium,
Nowhere then cleave
His uncertain footsoles,
And with him play
The clouds and the winds.

If he stands firm with
Marrowy bones
On the deep-founded,
Enduring Earth,
Then he aspires not,
Save to the oak tree
Or to the vine
Himself to liken.

What then distinguishes
Gods from men?
That many waves
Before them move,
An eternal stream:
Us the wave gathers,
Us the wave swallows,
And we sink.

A little ring
Confines our life,
And many generations
Link up, enduring
On their existence's
Endless chain.

Erlkönig

Wer reitet so spät durch Nacht und Wind?
Es ist der Vater mit seinem Kind;
Er hat den Knaben wohl in dem Arm,
Er faßt ihn sicher, er hält ihn warm.

Mein Sohn, was birgst du so bang dein Gesicht?—
Siehst, Vater, du den Erlkönig nicht?
Den Erlenkönig mit Kron und Schweif?—
Mein Sohn, es ist ein Nebelstreif.—

«Du liebes Kind, komm, geh mit mir!
Gar schöne Spiele spiel ich mit dir;
Manch bunte Blumen sind an dem Strand,
Meine Mutter hat manch gülden Gewand.»

Mein Vater, mein Vater, und hörest du nicht,
Was Erlenkönig mir leise verspricht?—
Sei ruhig, bleibe ruhig, mein Kind;
In dürren Blättern säuselt der Wind.—

«Willst, feiner Knabe, du mit mir gehn?
Meine Töchter sollen dich warten schön;
Meine Töchter führen den nächtlichen Reihn,
Und wiegen und tanzen und singen dich ein.»

Mein Vater, mein Vater, und siehst du nicht dort
Erlkönigs Töchter am düstern Ort?—
Mein Sohn, mein Sohn, ich seh es genau:
Es scheinen die alten Weiden so grau.—

«Ich liebe dich, mich reizt deine schöne Gestalt;
Und bist du nicht willig, so brauch ich Gewalt.»
Mein Vater, mein Vater, jetzt faßt er mich an!
Erlkönig hat mir ein Leids getan!—

Dem Vater grausets, er reitet geschwind,
Er hält in Armen das ächzende Kind,
Erreicht den Hof mit Mühe und Not;
In seinen Armen das Kind war tot.

Erlkönig (c. 1782)

Who rides by night in the wind so wild?
It is the father, with his child.
The boy is safe in his father's arm,
He holds him tight, he keeps him warm.

My son, what is it, why cover your face?
Father, you see him, there in that place,
The elfin king with his cloak and crown?
It is only the mist rising up, my son.

"Dear little child, will you come with me?
Beautiful games I'll play with thee;
Bright are the flowers we'll find on the shore,
My mother has golden robes fullscore."

Father, O father, and did you not hear
What the elfin king breathed into my ear?
Lie quiet, my child, now never you mind:
Dry leaves it was that click in the wind.

"Come along now, you're a fine little lad,
My daughters will serve you, see you are glad;
My daughters dance all night in a ring,
They'll cradle and dance you and lullaby sing."

Father, now look, in the gloom, do you see
The elfin daughters beckon to me?
My son, my son, I see it and say:
Those old willows, they look so gray.

"I love you, beguiled by your beauty I am,
If you are unwilling I'll force you to come!"
Father, his fingers grip me, O
The elfin king has hurt me so!

Now struck with horror the father rides fast,
His gasping child in his arm to the last,
Home through thick and thin he sped:
Locked in his arm, the child was dead.

Geweihter Platz

Wenn zu den Reihen der Nymphen, versammelt in heiliger
 Mondnacht,
Sich die Grazien heimlich herab vom Olympus gesellen:
Hier belauscht sie der Dichter und hört die schönen Gesänge,
Sieht verschwiegener Tänze geheimnisvolle Bewegung.
Was der Himmel nur Herrliches hat, was glücklich die Erde
Reizendes immer gebar, das erscheint dem wachenden Träumer.
Alles erzählt er den Musen, und daß die Götter nicht zürnen,
Lehren die Musen ihn gleich bescheiden Geheimnisse sprechen.

Anakreons Grab

Wo die Rose hier blüht, wo Reben um Lorbeer sich schlingen,
 Wo das Turtelchen lockt, wo sich das Grillchen ergetzt,
Welch ein Grab ist hier, das alle Götter mit Leben
 Schön bepflanzt und geziert? Es ist Anakreons Ruh.
Frühling, Sommer und Herbst genoß der glückliche Dichter;
 Vor dem Winter hat ihn endlich der Hügel geschützt.

Zueignung

Der Morgen kam; es scheuchten seine Tritte
Den leisen Schlaf, der mich gelind umfing,
Daß ich, erwacht, aus meiner stillen Hütte
Den Berg hinauf mit frischer Seele ging;
Ich freute mich bei einem jeden Schritte
Der neuen Blume, die voll Tropfen hing;
Der junge Tag erhob sich mit Entzücken,
Und alles war erquickt, mich zu erquicken.

Und wie ich stieg, zog von dem Fluß der Wiesen
Ein Nebel sich in Streifen sacht hervor;

Consecrated Place (1782)

When in the dance of the Nymphs, in the moonlight so holy
 assembled,
Mingle the Graces, down from Olympus in secret descending,
There the poet will hide and hear their beautiful singing;
There will he watch their silent dances' mysterious measure.
All that is glorious in heaven and all that the earth in her beauty
Brought to perfection in life, the dreamer awake sees before him;
All he repeats to the Muses, and lest the gods should be angered,
How to be telling of secrets discreetly the Muses instruct him.

Anacreon's Grave (1780's)

Where the rose is in flower, where vines interlace with the laurel,
 Where the turtle-dove calls, where the small cricket delights,
What a grave is this, which all the gods have embellished,
 Graced and planted with life? It is Anacreon's rest.
Springtime, summer, and autumn blessed the fortunate poet:
 And from winter the mound kept him secure in the end.

Dedication (1784)

The morning came, away its footfall sent
The gentle sleep that floated lightly o'er me,
So wide awake out of my hut I went
And gaily up the mountain slope before me.
At every stride I took, the flowers tender,
Brimming with dew, a pleasure were to see;
The young day sprang to life in all its splendour,
And everything seemed glad to gladden me.

And as I climbed, from off the meadow ground
A white and filmy mist began to hover;

Er wich und wechselte, mich zu umfließen,
Und wuchs geflügelt mir ums Haupt empor:
Des schönen Blicks sollt ich nicht mehr genießen,
Die Gegend deckte mir ein trüber Flor;
Bald sah ich mich von Wolken wie umgossen
Und mit mir selbst in Dämmrung eingeschlossen.

Auf einmal schien die Sonne durchzudringen,
Im Nebel ließ sich eine Klarheit sehn.
Hier sank er, leise sich hinabzuschwingen,
Hier teilt' er steigend sich um Wald und Höhn.
Wie hofft ich ihr den ersten Gruß zu bringen!
Sie hofft ich nach der Trübe doppelt schön.
Der luftge Kampf war lange nicht vollendet,
Ein Glanz umgab mich, und ich stand geblendet.

Bald machte mich, die Augen aufzuschlagen,
Ein innrer Trieb des Herzens wieder kühn,
Ich konnt es nur mit schnellen Blicken wagen,
Denn alles schien zu brennen und zu glühn.
Da schwebte, mit den Wolken hergetragen,
Ein göttlich Weib vor meinen Augen hin,
Kein schöner Bild sah ich in meinem Leben,
Sie sah mich an und blieb verweilend schweben.

Kennst du mich nicht? sprach sie mit einem Munde,
Dem aller Lieb und Treue Ton entfloß:
Erkennst du mich, die ich in manche Wunde
Des Lebens dir den reinsten Balsam goß?
Du kennst mich wohl, an die, zu ewgem Bunde,
Dein strebend Herz sich fest und fester schloß.
Sah ich dich nicht mit heißen Herzenstränen
Als Knabe schon nach mir dich eifrig sehnen?

Ja! rief ich aus, indem ich selig nieder
Zur Erde sank, lang hab ich dich gefühlt;
Du gabst mir Ruh, wenn durch die jungen Glieder
Die Leidenschaft sich rastlos durchgewühlt;
Du hast mir wie mit himmlischem Gefieder
Am heißen Tag die Stirne sanft gekühlt;
Du schenktest mir der Erde beste Gaben,
Und jedes Glück will ich durch dich nur haben!

Dich nenn ich nicht. Zwar hör ich dich von vielen
Gar oft genannt, und jeder heißt dich *sein*,

It came and went, until it hemmed me round,
Then rose above my head and drifted over.
The lovely scene I was no more beholding,
It lay beneath a colourless dark shroud;
And soon alone, the vapour round me folding,
I stood within the twilight of that cloud.

Suddenly, as if the sun were breaking through,
Inside the mist a clarity I sighted;
Downward where I stood the vapour drew,
Round the woody peaks it rose divided.
O how I hoped to welcome first the gleaming,
Made by the gloom it banished doubly bright!
The draughts of air in battle still were streaming,
When I was dazzled by a rush of light.

A moment, then I felt compelled to look
By some strange impulse of the heart's emotion,
But more than rapid glances scarcely took,
For all was burning like a molten ocean.
Then in the glory-cloud that seemed to bear her
A godlike woman drifted through the air;
I never did behold a vision fairer,
And now she gazed upon me, floating there.

"Do you not know me?"—and her voice was soft
As love, and full of confidence it sounded.
"Do you not recognize the one who oft
Gave healing balm to you when sorest wounded?
Ah, well you know her now, with whom forever
Your heart aspiring longs at one to be!
Did I not see your tears, your heart's endeavour?
Even as a boy you craved for me."

"Yes, I know you now!" fondly I cried,
And sank to earth before her, all adoring;
"You brought me peace, when passion's restless tide
Through my young veins like liquid fire was pouring.
And you have cooled with your celestial pinions
In the hot days of summertime my brow;
You gave me the best gifts of earth's dominions;
From you alone I seek my fortune now.

"I do not name you, but have heard you named,
Have heard you called their own before by many;

Ein jedes Auge glaubt auf dich zu zielen,
Fast jedem Auge wird dein Strahl zur Pein.
Ach, da ich irrte, hatt ich viel Gespielen,
Da ich dich kenne, bin ich fast allein;
Ich muß mein Glück nur mit mir selbst genießen,
Dein holdes Licht verdecken und verschließen.

Sie lächelte, sie sprach: Du siehst, wie klug,
Wie nötig wars, euch wenig zu enthüllen!
Kaum bist du sicher vor dem gröbsten Trug,
Kaum bist du Herr vom ersten Kinderwillen,
So glaubst du dich schon Übermensch genug,
Versäumst die Pflicht des Mannes zu erfüllen!
Wieviel bist du von andern unterschieden?
Erkenne dich, leb mit der Welt in Frieden!

Verzeih mir, rief ich aus, ich meint es gut;
Soll ich umsonst die Augen offen haben?
Ein froher Wille lebt in meinem Blut,
Ich kenne ganz den Wert von deinen Gaben!
Für andre wächst in mir das edle Gut,
Ich kann und will das Pfund nicht mehr vergraben!
Warum sucht ich den Weg so sehnsuchtsvoll,
Wenn ich ihn nicht den Brüdern zeigen soll?

Und wie ich sprach, sah mich das hohe Wesen
Mit einem Blick mitleidger Nachsicht an;
Ich konnte mich in ihrem Auge lesen,
Was ich verfehlt und was ich recht getan.
Sie lächelte, da war ich schon genesen,
Zu neuen Freuden stieg mein Geist heran;
Ich konnte nun mit innigem Vertrauen
Mich zu ihr nahn und ihre Nähe schauen.

Da reckte sie die Hand aus in die Streifen
Der leichten Wolken und des Dufts umher;
Wie sie ihn faßte, ließ er sich ergreifen,
Er ließ sich ziehn, es war kein Nebel mehr.
Mein Auge konnt im Tale wieder schweifen,
Gen Himmel blickt ich, er war hell und hehr.
Nur sah ich sie den reinsten Schleier halten,
Er floß um sie und schwoll in tausend Falten.

Ich kenne dich, ich kenne deine Schwächen,
Ich weiß, was Gutes in dir lebt und glimmt!

All eyes believe their glance at you is aimed,
And yet your radiance is too fierce for any.
Ah, many friends I had when, lost, I wandered;
I know you now and stand almost alone.
I veil your light, too precious to be squandered,
And share my fortune, as I must, with none."

She smiled and said: "Then it was wise of me
To have revealed but little, need fulfilling;
Of crude delusions you are scarcely free,
Scarce master of a childish kind of willing;
You think yourself so far above your brothers,
Neglect your duty as a man—but cease!
Who fixed the gulf between you and the others?
Know yourself, live with the world in peace."

"Forgive me," I exclaimed, "I meant no ill,
Never for nothing open eyes I wanted.
My blood is quickened by a joyous will—
I know the worth of everything you granted.
The good I nurse for others, in my fashion,
I can and would not bury in the ground;
Why did I seek the way with such a passion
If not to show my fellows what I found?"

And as I spoke to her, across her face
Sympathy passed like breath across a mirror;
In her attentive eye I then could trace
What good things I had done, and what in error.
She smiled, at once my heart regained its lightness,
The spirit in me leapt to rapture high;
Now without fear I could approach her brightness,
And look upon her close, with inward eye.

She reached her hand out now among the thin
Ethereal haze that round her presence hovered;
Slowly it shrank and coiled her grasp within,
And straight the scene again lay there uncovered;
Again my eye could scan the valley meadow,
And up I looked, the sky was clear and bright;
I saw her hold the veil without a shadow,
It rippled round her, folding in the light.

"I know you; all your weakness, all that yet
Is good in you and lives and glows I've measured,"

—So sagte sie, ich hör sie ewig sprechen—
Empfange hier, was ich dir lang bestimmt;
Dem Glücklichen kann es an nichts gebrechen,
Der dies Geschenk mit stiller Seele nimmt:
Aus Morgenduft gewebt und Sonnenklarheit,
Der Dichtung Schleier aus der Hand der Wahrheit.

Und wenn es dir und deinen Freunden schwüle
Am Mittag wird, so wirf ihn in die Luft!
Sogleich umsäuselt Abendwindes Kühle,
Umhaucht euch Blumen-Würzgeruch und Duft.
Es schweigt das Wehen banger Erdgefühle,
Zum Wolkenbette wandelt sich die Gruft,
Besänftiget wird jede Lebenswelle,
Der Tag wird lieblich, und die Nacht wird helle.

So kommt denn, Freunde, wenn auf euren Wegen
Des Lebens Bürde schwer und schwerer drückt,
Wenn eure Bahn ein frischerneuter Segen
Mit Blumen ziert, mit goldnen Früchten schmückt,
Wir gehn vereint dem nächsten Tag entgegen!
So leben wir, so wandeln wir beglückt.
Und dann auch soll, wenn Enkel um uns trauern,
Zu ihrer Lust noch unsre Liebe dauern.

She said—her voice I never shall forget—
"Accept the gift that long for you was treasured:
Happy the man, and strong, for he is shriven,
Who takes this gift with soul serene and true:
By Truth the veil of Poetry is given,
Woven of sunlight and the morning dew.

Throw it into the air when underneath
The blaze of noon you and your friends are glowing,
Fragrance of flowers and spices you will breathe,
Vesperal wind around you coolly blowing.
Blasts and alarms of earth will cease their riot,
The tomb will be a bed of cloud in flight,
Every wave of life will then be quiet,
The day delicious, luminous the night."

Come then, my friends, and whether with the load
Of heavy cares you struggle on, or whether
Blessing begun anew sprinkle your road
With flowers, golden fruit that does not wither,
We go as one toward one more tomorrow:
That is the way we live, in joy secure,
And when for us our children's children sorrow,
For their delight still must our love endure.

III
"Klassik" and the Turn of the Century

Amor als Landschaftsmaler

Saß ich früh auf einer Felsenspitze,
Sah mit starren Augen in den Nebel;
Wie ein grau grundiertes Tuch gespannet,
Deckt' er alles in die Breit und Höhe.

Stellt' ein Knabe sich mir an die Seite,
Sagte: Lieber Freund, wie magst du starrend
Auf das leere Tuch gelassen schauen?
Hast du denn zum Malen und zum Bilden
Alle Lust auf ewig wohl verloren?

Sah ich an das Kind, und dachte heimlich:
Will das Bübchen doch den Meister machen!

Willst du immer trüb und müßig bleiben,
Sprach der Knabe, kann nichts Kluges werden;
Sieh, ich will dir gleich ein Bildchen malen,
Dich ein hübsches Bildchen malen lehren.

Und er richtete den Zeigefinger,
Der so rötlich war wie eine Rose,
Nach dem weiten ausgespannten Teppich,
Fing mit seinem Finger an zu zeichnen.

Oben malt' er eine schöne Sonne,
Die mir in die Augen mächtig glänzte,
Und den Saum der Wolken macht' er golden,
Ließ die Strahlen durch die Wolken dringen;
Malte dann die zarten leichten Wipfel
Frisch erquickter Bäume, zog die Hügel,
Einen nach dem andern, frei dahinter;
Unten ließ ers nicht an Wasser fehlen,
Zeichnete den Fluß so ganz natürlich,
Daß er schien im Sonnenstrahl zu glitzern,
Daß er schien am hohen Rand zu rauschen.

Ach, da standen Blumen an dem Flusse,
Und da waren Farben auf der Wiese,
Gold und Schmelz und Purpur und ein Grünes,
Alles wie Smaragd und wie Karfunkel!
Hell und rein lasiert' er drauf den Himmel
Und die blauen Berge fern und ferner,

Amor as Landscape Painter (1787)

Sat upon a rocky peak at daybreak,
Staring fix-eyed through the mist before me;
Stretched like canvas primed with gray it mantled
Everything on either side and upward.

A little boy now came and stood beside me:
Friend, he said, I wonder what you're up to,
Peering, supine, at that empty canvas.
Might you have lost for now, if not for ever,
Pleasure in painting, shaping out an image?

Glancing at the child, I thought in secret:
Perhaps the boy thinks he can act the master.

If you sit there, sullen, doing nothing,
Said the boy, no good will be the outcome.
Watch, I'll paint a smidgeon of a picture
Now, for you, a pretty one to learn from.

Then he lifted up his index finger,
Which was quite as rosy as a rose is;
Pointing to the fabric stretched before him,
Now the boy began to trace a picture.

At the top a beauteous sun he painted,
I was almost blinded by the dazzle;
Borders of the clouds, he made them golden,
Rays of sun to perforate the cloud mass;
Painted then the delicate and tender
Tops of freshly quickened trees, with hillocks
Touched into place and freely grouped behind them;
Lower down—water he put, and plenty,
Drew the river, as it is in nature,
So much so, it seemed to glint with sunlight
And murmur as it rose against its edges.

Ah, beside the river flowers had sprouted,
And the meadow was a blaze of color,
Gold, enamel sheen, a green, and crimson,
All aglow like emerald and carbuncle.
Bright and clear, above, he glazed the sky in,
Mountains, blue, receding in the distance,

Daß ich, ganz entzückt und neugeboren,
Bald den Maler, bald das Bild beschaute.

Hab ich doch, so sagt' er, dir bewiesen,
Daß ich dieses Handwerk gut verstehe;
Doch es ist das Schwerste noch zurücke.

Zeichnete darnach mit spitzem Finger
Und mit großer Sorgfalt an dem Wäldchen,
Grad ans Ende, wo die Sonne kräftig
Von dem hellen Boden widerglänzte,
Zeichnete das allerliebste Mädchen,
Wohlgebildet, zierlich angekleidet,
Frische Wangen unter braunen Haaren,
Und die Wangen waren von der Farbe
Wie das Fingerchen, das sie gebildet.

O du Knabe! rief ich, welch ein Meister
Hat in seine Schule dich genommen,
Daß du so geschwind und so natürlich
Alles klug beginnst und gut vollendest?

Da ich noch so rede, sieh, da rühret
Sich ein Windchen und bewegt die Gipfel,
Kräuselt alle Wellen auf dem Flusse,
Füllt den Schleier des vollkommnen Mädchens
Und, was mich Erstaunten mehr erstaunte,
Fängt das Mädchen an den Fuß zu rühren,
Geht zu kommen, nähert sich dem Orte,
Wo ich mit dem losen Lehrer sitze.

Da nun alles, alles sich bewegte,
Bäume, Fluß und Blumen und der Schleier
Und der zarte Fuß der Allerschönsten,
Glaubt ihr wohl, ich sei auf meinem Felsen
Wie ein Felsen still und fest geblieben?

So that born anew I looked, ecstatic,
Now upon the painter, now the picture.

You'll admit, says he, I've demonstrated
This is a handiwork I have some skill in;
The hardest part is still to come, however.

Then, with pointing fingertip and very
Solicitously, by the little forest,
Right on the brink of it, where sunlight gathered
To be reflected off the shining humus,
He traced the loveliest girl you could set eyes on,
Pretty figure, and a graceful garment,
Cheeks a fresh complexion, all around them
Tawny hair, and more, the cheeks were tinted
Like the tiny finger that had shaped them.

Little boy, I now exclaimed, what master
Can it be who took you as his pupil,
That your designs should be so swift, so clever,
And finished, as by nature, to perfection?

Even as I'm speaking, look, a zephyr
Gently stirs, it agitates the treetops,
Ruffles all the river into wavelets,
Fills the filmy robe that she is wearing,
The perfect girl, amazed I am, and more so
When she starts to set her feet in motion,
And she moves, she walks, she's coming this way
To where I sit beside my wicked teacher.

Now everything, but everything was moving,
Trees, the flowers, filmy robe, the river,
Delicate feet of the girl in all her beauty—
Do you think I sat so calm and steadfast
Rocklike on my rock a moment longer?

Römische Elegien

I

Saget, Steine, mir an, o sprecht, ihr hohen Paläste!
 Straßen, redet ein Wort! Genius, regst du dich nicht?
Ja, es ist alles beseelt in deinen heiligen Mauern,
 Ewige Roma; nur mir schweiget noch alles so still.
O wer flüstert mir zu, an welchem Fenster erblick ich
 Einst das holde Geschöpf, das mich versengend erquickt?
Ahn ich die Wege noch nicht, durch die ich immer und immer,
 Zu ihr und von ihr zu gehn, opfre die köstliche Zeit?
Noch betracht ich Kirch und Palast, Ruinen und Säulen,
 Wie ein bedächtiger Mann schicklich die Reise benutzt.
Doch bald ist es vorbei; dann wird ein einziger Tempel,
 Amors Tempel, nur sein, der den Geweihten empfängt.
Eine Welt zwar bist du, o Rom; doch ohne die Liebe
 Wäre die Welt nicht die Welt, wäre denn Rom auch nicht Rom.

Ia

Mehr als ich ahndete schön, das Glück, es ist mir geworden,
 Amor führte mich klug allen Palästen vorbei.
Ihm ist es lange bekannt, auch hab ich es selbst wohl erfahren,
 Was ein goldnes Gemach hinter Tapeten verbirgt.
Nennet blind ihn und Knaben und ungezogen, ich kenne
 Kluger Amor dich wohl, nimmer bestechlicher Gott!
Uns verführten sie nicht, die majestätschen Fassaden,
 Nicht der galante Balkon, weder das ernste Kortil.
Eilig ging es vorbei, und niedre zierliche Pforte
 Nahm den Führer zugleich, nahm den Verlangenden auf.
Alles verschafft er mir da, hilft alles und alles erhalten,
 Streuet jeglichen Tag frischere Rosen mir auf.
Hab ich den Himmel nicht hier?—Was gibst du, schöne Borghese,
 Nipotina was gibst deinem Geliebten du mehr?
Tafel, Gesellschaft und Kors' und Spiel und Oper und Bälle,
 Amorn rauben sie nur oft die gelegenste Zeit.
Ekel bleibt mir Gezier und Putz, und hebet am Ende
 Sich ein brokatener Rock nicht wie ein wollener auf?
Oder will sie bequem den Freund im Busen verbergen,
 Wünscht er von alle dem Schmuck nicht schon behend sie befreit?
Müssen nicht jene Juwelen und Spitzen, Polster und Fischbein
 Alle zusammen herab, eh er die Liebliche fühlt?

Roman Elegies (c. 1788–90)

I

Deign to speak to me, stones, you high palaces, deign to address me
 Streets, now say but one word! Genius, will you not stir?
True, all is living yet within your sanctified precincts,
 Timeless Rome; only me all still in silence receives.
O, who will whisper to me, at what small window, revealing
 Her, the dear one, whose glance, searing, will quicken my blood?
Can I not guess on what roads, forever coming and going,
 Only for her sake I'll spend all my invaluable time?
Still I'm seeing the sights, the churches, the ruins, the columns,
 As a serious man ought to and does use his days.
That, however, will pass, and soon no more than one temple,
 Amor's temple alone, claim this initiate's zeal.
Rome, you remain a whole world; but without love the whole world
 would
 Always be less than the world, neither would Rome still be Rome.

Ia

Fortune beyond my loveliest daydreams fulfilled is my own now,
 Amor, my clever guide, passed all the palaces by.
Long he has known, and I too had occasion to learn by experience,
 What a richly gilt room hides behind hangings and screens.
You may call him a boy and blind and ill-mannered, but, clever
 Amor, I know you well, never corruptible god!
Us they did not take in, those façades so imposing and pompous,
 Gallant balcony here, dignified courtyard down there.
Quickly we passed them by, and a humble but delicate doorway
 Opened to guided and guide, made them both welcome within.
All he provides for me there, with his help I obtain all I ask for,
 Fresher roses each day strewn on my path by the god.
Isn't it heaven itself?—And what more could the lovely Borghese,
 Nipotina herself offer a lover than that?
Dinners, drives and dances, operas, card games and parties,
 Often merely they steal Amor's most opportune hours.
Airs and finery bore me; when all's said and done, it's the same
 thing
 Whether the skirt you lift is of brocade or of wool.
Or if the wish of a girl is to pillow her lover in comfort,
 Wouldn't he first have her put all those sharp trinkets away?
All those jewels and pads, and the lace that surrounds her, the
 whalebone,
 Don't they all have to go, if he's to feel his beloved?

Näher haben wir das! Schon fällt dein wollenes Kleidchen,
 So wie der Freund es gelöst, faltig zum Boden hinab.
Eilig trägt er das Kind, in leichter linnener Hülle,
 Wie es der Amme geziemt, scherzend aufs Lager hinan.
Ohne das seidne Gehäng und ohne gestickte Matratzen,
 Stehet es, zweien bequem, frei in dem weiten Gemach.
Nehme dann Jupiter mehr von seiner Juno, es lasse
 Wohler sich, wenn er es kann, irgend ein Sterblicher sein.
Uns ergötzen die Freuden des echten nacketen Amors
 Und des geschaukelten Betts lieblicher knarrender Ton.

IV

Fromm sind wir Liebende, still verehren wir alle Dämonen,
 Wünschen uns jeglichen Gott, jegliche Göttin geneigt.
Und so gleichen wir euch, o römische Sieger! Den Göttern
 Aller Völker der Welt bietet ihr Wohnungen an,
Habe sie schwarz und streng aus altem Basalt der Ägypter,
 Oder ein Grieche sie weiß, reizend, aus Marmor geformt.
Doch verdrießet es nicht die Ewigen, wenn wir besonders
 Weihrauch köstlicher Art Einer der Göttlichen streun.
Ja, wir bekennen euch gern: es bleiben unsre Gebete,
 Unser täglicher Dienst Einer besonders geweiht.
Schalkhaft, munter und ernst begehen wir heimliche Feste,
 Und das Schweigen geziemt allen Geweihten genau.
Eh an die Ferse lockten wir selbst durch gräßliche Taten
 Uns die Erinnyen her, wagten es eher, des Zeus
Hartes Gericht am rollenden Rad und am Felsen zu dulden,
 Als dem reizenden Dienst unser Gemüt zu entziehn.
Diese Göttin, sie heißt *Gelegenheit;* lernet sie kennen!
 Sie erscheinet euch oft, immer in andrer Gestalt.
Tochter des Proteus möchte sie sein, mit Thetis gezeuget,
 Deren verwandelte List manchen Heroen betrog.
So betriegt nun die Tochter den Unerfahrnen, den Blöden:
 Schlummernde necket sie stets, Wachende fliegt sie vorbei;
Gern ergibt sie sich nur dem raschen, tätigen Manne,
 Dieser findet sie zahm, spielend und zärtlich und hold.
Einst erschien sie auch mir, ein bräunliches Mädchen, die Haare
 Fielen ihr dunkel und reich über die Stirne herab,
Kurze Locken ringelten sich ums zierliche Hälschen,
 Ungeflochtenes Haar krauste vom Scheitel sich auf.
Und ich verkannte sie nicht, ergriff die Eilende, lieblich
 Gab sie Umarmung und Kuß bald mir gelehrig zurück.
O wie war ich beglückt!—Doch stille, die Zeit ist vorüber,
 Und umwunden bin ich, römische Flechten, von euch.

Us it gives much less trouble! Your plain woollen dress in a jiffy,
 Unfastened by me, slips down, lies in its folds on the floor.
Quickly I carry the child in her flimsy wrapping of linen
 As befits a good nurse, teasingly, into her bed.
Bare of silken drapery, mattresses richly embroidered,
 Spacious for two, it stands free in a spacious room.
Then let Jupiter get more joy from his Juno, a mortal
 Anywhere in this world know more contentment than I.
We enjoy the delights of the genuine naked god, Amor,
 And our rock-a-bye bed's rhythmic, melodious creak.

<div align="center">IV</div>

Pious we lovers are, and in silence revere all the spirits,
 Long to propitiate each, god and goddess alike.
And resemble in that you victors of Rome! To the gods of
 All the world's peoples you gave dwellings, a home far from
 home,
Whether black and severe out of ancient basalt Egyptians
 Or all white a Greek shaped it in marble that charms.
Yet no timeless one bears any grudge if by discrimination
 One amongst them receives incense more precious from us.
Freely, indeed, we confess that still, as in past times, our prayers,
 Daily service to one, one above all, we devote.
Roguish, lively and serious we celebrate rituals in secret,
 Knowing that silence behooves all who are pledged to that cult.
Sooner by horrible acts to our heels we should summon and fasten
 Vengeful Furies, or else dare the harsh judgement of Zeus,
Suffer his rolling wheel or in fetters be clamped to the rock-face,
 Than from that service of love sever our hearts and our minds.
And the goddess we serve? She is called Opportunity. Know her!
 Often to you she appears, always in different shapes.
Daughter of Proteus she'd like to think herself, mothered by Thetis,
 Hers by whose mutable guile many a hero was tricked.
So now her daughter tricks those inexperienced or timid,
 Teasing some in their sleep, flying past others who wake;
Gladly surrendering only to one who is quick, energetic.
 Gentle she is to that man, playful and tender and sweet.
Once she appeared to me too, as an olive-complexioned girl, whose
 Dark and plentiful hair, glistening, covered her brow,
Shorter ringlets curled round a neck that was graceful and slender,
 Wavy, unbraided hair rose from the top of her head.
And I recognized her; as she hurried I held her: and sweetly
 She, most willing to learn, soon paid me back each caress.
Oh, how delighted I was!—But enough, for that era is over.
 Now by you, Roman braids, tightly, all round, I'm entwined.

V

Froh empfind ich mich nun auf klassischem Boden begeistert;
 Vor- und Mitwelt spricht lauter und reizender mir.
Hier befolg ich den Rat, durchblättre die Werke der Alten
 Mit geschäftiger Hand, täglich mit neuem Genuß.
Aber die Nächte hindurch hält Amor mich anders beschäftigt;
 Werd ich auch halb nur gelehrt, bin ich doch doppelt beglückt.
Und belehr ich mich nicht, indem ich des lieblichen Busens
 Formen spähe, die Hand leite die Hüften hinab?
Dann versteh ich den Marmor erst recht; ich denk und vergleiche,
 Sehe mit fühlendem Aug, fühle mit sehender Hand.
Raubt die Liebste denn gleich mir einige Stunden des Tages,
 Gibt sie Stunden der Nacht mir zur Entschädigung hin.
Wird doch nicht immer geküßt, es wird vernünftig gesprochen;
 Überfällt sie der Schlaf, lieg ich und denke mir viel.
Oftmals hab ich auch schon in ihren Armen gedichtet
 Und des Hexameters Maß leise mit fingernder Hand
Ihr auf den Rücken gezählt. Sie atmet in lieblichem Schlummer,
 Und es durchglühet ihr Hauch mir bis ins Tiefste die Brust.
Amor schüret die Lamp indes und denket der Zeiten,
 Da er den nämlichen Dienst seinen Triumvirn getan.

VI

«Kannst du, o Grausamer! mich in solchen Worten betrüben?
 Reden so bitter und hart liebende Männer bei euch?
Wenn das Volk mich verklagt, ich muß es dulden! und bin ich
 Etwa nicht schuldig? Doch ach? schuldig nur bin ich mit dir!
Diese Kleider, sie sind der neidischen Nachbarin Zeugen,
 Daß die Witwe nicht mehr einsam den Gatten beweint.
Bist du ohne Bedacht nicht oft bei Mondschein gekommen,
 Grau, im dunkeln Surtout, hinten gerundet das Haar?
Hast du dir scherzend nicht selbst die geistliche Maske gewählet?
 Solls ein Prälate denn sein! gut, der Prälate bist du.
In dem geistlichen Rom, kaum scheint es zu glauben, doch
 schwör ich:
 Nie hat ein Geistlicher sich meiner Umarmung gefreut.
Arm war ich leider! und jung, und wohlbekannt den Verführern;
 Falconieri hat mir oft in die Augen gegafft,
Und ein Kuppler Albanis mich, mit gewichtigen Zetteln,
 Bald nach Ostia, bald nach den vier Brunnen gelockt.
Aber wer nicht kam, war das Mädchen. So hab ich von Herzen
 Rotstrumpf immer gehaßt und Violettstrumpf dazu.
Denn «ihr Mädchen bleibt am Ende doch die Betrognen»,
 Sagte der Vater, wenn auch leichter die Mutter es nahm.

V

Happy now I can feel the classical climate inspire me,
 Past and present at last clearly, more vividly speak.
Here I take their advice, perusing the works of the ancients
 With industrious care, pleasure that grows every day.
But throughout the nights by Amor I'm differently busied,
 If only half improved, doubly delighted instead.
Also, am I not learning when at the shape of her bosom,
 Graceful lines, I can glance, guide a light hand down her hips?
Only thus I appreciate marble; reflecting, comparing,
 See with an eye that can feel, feel with a hand that can see.
True, the loved one besides may claim a few hours of the daytime,
 But in night hours as well makes full amends for the loss.
For not always we're kissing, often hold sensible converse;
 When she succumbs to sleep, pondering, long I lie still.
Often too in her arms I've lain composing a poem,
 Gently with fingering hand count the hexameter's beat
Out on her back; she breathes, so lovely and calm in her sleeping
 That the glow from her lips deeply transfuses my heart.
Amor meanwhile refuels the lamp and remembers the times when
 Them, his triumvirs of verse, likewise he's served and obliged.

VI

How can you talk in that tone to me, so cruelly, crassly?
 Where you come from are all lovers as bitter and harsh?
If my name is mud, I must bear it; for am I not fallen,
 Guilty, in their eyes? But oh, fallen to no one save you!
These fine gowns are the evidence needed by envious neighbours
 That this widow has ceased mourning her husband indoors.
Rashly, didn't you come to this house many times in full moonlight,
 Gray, in your surplice-like cloak, hair in a clerical bun?
Didn't you, for a lark, make a point of selecting that costume?
 If a prelate it is, why, then that prelate is you.
In our spiritual Rome, believe it or not, but I'll swear it,
 Never a priest has received favours or solace from me.
Yes, I was poor, to my shame, and young, and well known to
 seducers.
 Falconieri, no less, gave me the eye more than once.
And a pimp of Albani's to Ostia now tried to lure me,
 Quattro Fontane now, always with notes that had weight.
Did this girl oblige? No, thanks. If there's one thing she's never
 Fancied, it's those who wear gaiters, the purple or red.
For, my father said, "in the end it's you girls who are diddled",
 Though my mother, I think, took a less serious view.

Und so bin ich denn auch am Ende betrogen! Du zürnest
 Nur zum Scheine mit mir, weil du zu fliehen gedenkst.
Geh! Ihr seid der Frauen nicht wert! Wir tragen die Kinder
 Unter dem Herzen, und so tragen die Treue wir auch;
Aber ihr Männer, ihr schüttet mit eurer Kraft und Begierde
 Auch die Liebe zugleich in den Umarmungen aus!»
Also sprach die Geliebte und nahm den Kleinen vom Stuhle,
 Drückt' ihn küssend ans Herz, Tränen entquollen dem Blick.
Und wie saß ich beschämt, daß Reden feindlicher Menschen
 Dieses liebliche Bild mir zu beflecken vermocht!
Dunkel brennt das Feuer nur augenblicklich und dampfet,
 Wenn das Wasser die Glut stürzend und jählings verhüllt;
Aber sie reinigt sich schnell, verjagt die trübenden Dämpfe,
 Neuer und mächtiger dringt leuchtende Flamme hinauf.

VIII

Wenn du mir sagst, du habest als Kind, Geliebte, den Menschen
 Nicht gefallen, und dich habe die Mutter verschmäht,
Bis du größer geworden und still dich entwickelt, ich glaub es:
 Gerne denk ich mir dich als ein besonderes Kind.
Fehlet Bildung und Farbe doch auch der Blüte des Weinstocks,
 Wenn die Beere, gereift, Menschen und Götter entzückt.

X

Alexander und Cäsar und Heinrich und Friedrich, die Großen,
 Gäben die Hälfte mir gern ihres erworbenen Ruhms,
Könnt ich auf Eine Nacht dies Lager jedem vergönnen;
 Aber die armen, sie hält strenge des Orkus Gewalt.
Freue dich also, Lebendger, der lieberwärmeten Stätte,
 Ehe den fliehenden Fuß schauerlich Lethe dir netzt.

XII

Hörest du, Liebchen, das muntre Geschrei den Flaminischen
 Weg her?
 Schnitter sind es; sie ziehn wieder nach Hause zurück,
Weit hinweg. Sie haben des Römers Ernte vollendet,
 Der für Ceres den Kranz selber zu flechten verschmäht.
Keine Feste sind mehr der großen Göttin gewidmet,
 Die, statt Eicheln, zur Kost goldenen Weizen verlieh.
Laß uns beide das Fest im stillen freudig begehen!
 Sind zwei Liebende doch sich ein versammeltes Volk.
Hast du wohl je gehört von jener mystischen Feier,
 Die von Eleusis hieher frühe dem Sieger gefolgt?
Griechen stifteten sie, und immer riefen nur Griechen,

And, in the end, I have been. Diddled by you, when you're only
 Angry with me for show, scheming to jilt me and run.
Do. You men are unworthy of women. We carry the children
 Under our hearts, and there faithfulness also, for two.
But you men, as embracing you spill all your strength and your
 fervor,
 At the same time you lose lovingness, too, in the act!"
So the loved one spoke, and swept up from his chair her one infant
 Son, whom she kissed and hugged, gazed at with tear-misted eyes.
Sitting there, how it shamed me to think that malevolent gossip
 By no fault but my own sullied an image so dear.
Darkly for moments only the fire will be smouldering, smoking,
 Drenched by water that damped, suddenly smothered its glow.
Very soon it revives, dispelling the murk of those vapours,
 And with mightier flames, all the more brightly, flares up.

VIII

When, beloved, you tell me that as a child you were never
 Liked by people, and scorned by your own mother herself
All those years of your quiet growth, till mature, I believe you,
 In my mind's eye enjoy seeing the singular child.
Well, the vine-flower, too, is deficient in shape and in colour,
 Yet to gods and mankind, mellow, the grape yields delight.

X

Alexander and Caesar and Henry and Frederick, the great ones,
 Gladly would give in exchange half of the glory they won
If to each for one night, only one, I could offer such bedding;
 But by strict Hades interned—pity them!—those are held fast,
So rejoice, you that live, in the place that's been warmed by long
 loving,
 Now, before horribly Styx moistens your fugitive foot.

XII

Listen darling: that shouting you hear in the Via Flaminia,
 Reapers it is, on their way back to the country and homes
Far from here, having finished the harvest for them, for the Romans
 Who disdain to wind garlands for Ceres themselves.
Festivals now no more are devoted to her, the great goddess,
 Giver of golden corn, rather than acorns, for fare.
Let the two of us honour that feast-day, rejoicing in private.
 Lovers, at least to themselves, being a nation conjoined.
Have you heard, perhaps, of that mystical celebration
 Which from Eleusis once followed a victor to Rome?
Hellenes founded the rite; and henceforth it has always been
 Hellenes,

Selbst in den Mauern Roms: «Kommt zur geheiligten Nacht!»
 Fern entwich der Profane; da bebte der wartende Neuling,
 Den ein weißes Gewand, Zeichen der Reinheit, umgab.
Wunderlich irrte darauf der Eingeführte durch Kreise
 Seltner Gestalten; im Traum schien er zu wallen: denn hier
Wanden sich Schlangen am Boden umher, verschlossene Kästchen,
 Reich mit Ähren umkränzt, trugen hier Mädchen vorbei,
Vielbedeutend gebärdeten sich die Priester und summten:
 Ungeduldig und bang harrte der Lehrling auf Licht.
Erst nach mancherlei Proben und Prüfungen ward ihm enthüllet,
 Was der geheiligte Kreis seltsam in Bildern verbarg.
Und was war das Geheimnis! als daß Demeter, die große,
 Sich gefällig einmal auch einem Helden bequemt,
Als sie Jasion einst, dem rüstigen König der Kreter,
 Ihres unsterblichen Leibs holdes Verborgne gegönnt.
Da war Kreta beglückt! das Hochzeitbette der Göttin
 Schwoll von Ähren, und reich drückte den Acker die Saat.
Aber die übrige Welt verschmachtete; denn es versäumte
 Über der Liebe Genuß Ceres den schönen Beruf.
Voll Erstaunen vernahm der Eingeweihte das Märchen,
 Winkte der Liebsten—Verstehst du nun, Geliebte, den Wink?
Jene buschige Myrte beschattet ein heiliges Plätzchen!
 Unsre Zufriedenheit bringt keine Gefährde der Welt.

XIVa

Zwei gefährliche Schlangen, vom Chore der Dichter gescholten,
 Grausend nennt sie die Welt Jahre die tausende schon,
Python dich und dich Lernäischer Drache! Doch seid ihr
 Durch die rüstige Hand tätiger Götter gefällt.
Ihr zerstöret nicht mehr mit feurigem Atem und Geifer
 Herde, Wiesen und Wald, goldene Saaten nicht mehr.
Doch welch ein feindlicher Gott hat uns im Zorne die neue
 Ungeheure Geburt giftigen Schlammes gesandt?
Überall schleicht er sich ein, und in den lieblichsten Gärtchen
 Lauert tückisch der Wurm, packt den Genießenden an.
Sei mir, hesperischer Drache, gegrüßt, du zeigtest dich mutig,
 Du verteidigtest kühn goldener Äpfel Besitz!
Aber dieser verteidiget nichts—und wo er sich findet,
 Sind die Gärten, die Frucht keiner Verteidigung wert.
Heimlich krümmet er sich im Busche, besudelt die Quellen,
 Geifert, wandelt in Gift Amors belebenden Tau.

Even in Rome, who called out: "Come into sanctified night!"
Those profane crept away; the expectant novice, though, trembled,
 Wrapped in a garment whose white signified pureness unstained.
Weirdly then the initiate wandered around, within circles
 Formed of strange shapes, in a dream seemed to be moving; for
 here
Serpents wriggled about, a procession of serious virgins
 Carried caskets all locked, garnished with ears of ripe corn.
Meaningfully the priests went about their performances, humming,
 While, impatient and awed, novices waited for light.
Not before many trials and tests were they finally granted
 Clues to the hallowed round's secret and curious signs.
What did the mystery mean, then? No more than this, that Demeter,
 Great though she was, did once yield to a hero's desires,
When to Iasion long since, a vigorous king of the Cretans,
 All her body's occult, inmost delights she vouchsafed.
Overjoyed was all Crete then. The marriage bed of the goddess
 Swelled with new growth, and the corn lushly weighed down all
 the fields.
Yet the rest of the world suffered famine; because in her transports
 Ceres completely forgot cares her high calling imposed.
Full of amazement each novice heard the incredible story,
 Made a sign to his love.—Now do you grasp it, my love?
It's a hallowed small place that bushy-leafed myrtle-tree shadows!
 Our contentedness harms no one, endangers no world.

 XIVa
Two most dangerous serpents, bêtes noires of a chorus of poets,
 For millennia were known, fêted aghast by these names:
Python, you, and you, the Lernaean Hydra! But thanks to
 Capable gods and their strong hands you were beaten and killed.
With your fiery breath and your froth you no longer ravage
 Flocks and meadows and woods, fields newly golden with corn.
Yet what malevolent god in his wrath has more lately afflicted
 Us with the monstrous birth bred out of venomous mire?
Everywhere it intrudes; in the prettiest, neatest of gardens
 Slily the horror lurks, seizes all those who seek joy.
You, hesperian dragon, I hail, for at least you showed courage,
 Boldly defending from theft apples, those golden ones, there!
Nothing this one defends, though; and where it's encountered,
 confronted,
 Garden and fruit will have proved not worth defending at all.
Hidden in shrubs, it proceeds by stealth and pollutes the
 well-springs,
 Frothing, to poison turns Amor's quivering dew.

O! wie glücklich warst du Lucrez! du konntest der Liebe
 Ganz entsagen und dich jeglichem Körper vertraun.
Selig warst du Properz! dir holte der Sklave die Dirnen
 Vom Aventinus herab, aus dem Tarpeischen Hain.
Und wenn Cynthia dich aus jenen Umarmungen schreckte,
 Untreu fand sie dich zwar; aber sie fand dich gesund.
Jetzt wer hütet sich nicht, langweilige Treue zu brechen!
 Wen die Liebe nicht hält, hält die Besorglichkeit auf.
Und auch da, wer weiß! gewagt ist jegliche Freude,
 Nirgend legt man das Haupt ruhig dem Weib in den Schoß.
Sicher ist nicht das Ehbett mehr, nicht sicher der Ehbruch;
 Gatte, Gattin und Freund, eins ist im andern verletzt.
O! der goldenen Zeit! da Jupiter noch, vom Olympus,
 Sich zu Semele bald, bald zu Kallisto begab.
Ihm lag selber daran, die Schwelle des heiligen Tempels
 Rein zu finden, den er liebend und mächtig betrat.
O! wie hätte Juno getobt, wenn im Streite der Liebe
 Gegen sie der Gemahl giftige Waffen gekehrt.
Doch wir sind nicht so ganz, wir alte Heiden, verlassen,
 Immer schwebet ein Gott über der Erde noch hin,
Eilig und geschäftig, ihr kennt ihn alle, verehrt ihn!
 Ihn den Boten des Zeus, Hermes, den heilenden Gott.
Fielen des Vaters Tempel zu Grund, bezeichnen die Säulen
 Paarweis kaum noch den Platz alter verehrender Pracht,
Wird des Sohnes Tempel doch stehn und ewige Zeiten
 Wechselt der Bittende stets dort mit dem Dankenden ab.
Eins nur fleh ich im stillen, an euch ihr Grazien wend ich
 Dieses heiße Gebet tief aus dem Busen herauf.
Schützet immer mein kleines, mein artiges Gärtchen, entfernet
 Jegliches Übel von mir; reichet mir Amor die Hand,
O! so gebet mir stets, sobald ich dem Schelmen vertraue,
 Ohne Sorgen und Furcht, ohne Gefahr den Genuß.

XV

Cäsarn wär ich wohl nie zu fernen Britannen gefolget,
 Florus hätte mich leicht in die Popine geschleppt!
Denn mir bleiben weit mehr die Nebel des traurigen Nordens,
 Als ein geschäftiges Volk südlicher Flöhe verhaßt.
Und noch schöner von heut an seid mir gegrüßet, ihr Schenken,
 Osterien, wie euch schicklich der Römer benennt;
Denn ihr zeigtet mir heute die Liebste, begleitet vom Oheim,
 Den die Gute so oft, mich zu besitzen, betriegt.

Oh, how lucky you were, Lucretius, able to do without passion,
 To renounce it, and yet trust anybody you chose.
And you, Propertius, were blessed. Your slave went out to fetch
 harlots
 Down from the Aventine Hill, out of the Tarpeian Grove,
And if Cynthia surprised you in one of those flagrant embraces
 Unfaithful she found you, true; yet found you healthy at least.
These days, a man will think twice before breaking a faith that's
 grown boring.
 Those whom love does not bind caution as surely deters.
And on home ground, who knows? Any pleasure at all has grown
 risky.
 Nowhere in women's laps heads can be laid without fear.
Marital beds are not safe now, adulterous beds are not safe now.
 Husband, lover and wife, each is a danger to each.
Oh, that golden age! When Jupiter still from Olympus
 Now to Semele went, now with Callisto could meet,
His concern it was also to find that the sanctified temple's
 Threshold was clean when he, loving and potent, came in.
Oh, how would Juno have raged if in love-combat her husband
 Foully against her had used weapons with poisonous tips.
Still not utterly though, have old pagans like us been forsaken,
 Even now there's one god hovering over our earth,
Busy, quick off the mark, so you know him, we all do, and honour
 Him, the herald of Zeus, Mercury, healer of men.
Though the father's temples collapsed, their symmetrical columns
 Scarcely now mark the site glorious once and revered,
Yet the son's will stand, and for ages yet without number
 There will the suppliants come, jostling the ones who give thanks.
One thing only in secret I crave, to the Graces addressing
 This one prayer that wells, fervent and deep, from the heart:
Always protect my own little garden, ward off, I implore you,
 Every evil from me; touched by the hand of the rogue,
Amor, at all times grant me, whenever I trust myself to him,
 Pleasure unmixed with cares, bliss without peril or fear.

<div align="center">XV</div>

Caesar, I think, would never have dragged me to far-away Britons,
 Easily Florus instead into the taverns of Rome!
It's those dismal fogs of the North, still I find them more loathsome
 Than a whole work-team of keen Mediterranean fleas.
And from today more devoutly than ever I'll celebrate wineshops,
 Osterie, as inns aptly by Romans are called;
For today one showed me my darling, her uncle beside her,
 He whom so often the dear hoodwinks to dally with me.

Hier stand unser Tisch, den Deutsche vertraulich umgaben;
 Drüben suchte das Kind neben der Mutter den Platz,
Rückte vielmals die Bank und wußt es artig zu machen,
 Daß ich halb ihr Gesicht, völlig den Nacken gewann.
Lauter sprach sie, als hier die Römerin pfleget, kredenzte,
 Blickte gewendet nach mir, goß und verfehlte das Glas.
Wein floß über den Tisch, und sie, mit zierlichem Finger,
 Zog auf dem hölzernen Blatt Kreise der Feuchtigkeit hin.
Meinen Namen verschlang sie dem ihrigen; immer begierig
 Schaut ich dem Fingerchen nach, und sie bemerkte mich wohl.
Endlich zog sie behende das Zeichen der römischen Fünfe
 Und ein Strichlein davor. Schnell, und sobald ichs gesehn,
Schlang sie Kreise durch Kreise, die Lettern und Ziffern zu löschen;
 Aber die köstliche *Vier* blieb mir ins Auge geprägt.
Stumm war ich sitzen geblieben, und biß die glühende Lippe,
 Halb aus Schalkheit und Lust, halb aus Begierde, mir wund.
Erst noch so lange bis Nacht! dann noch vier Stunden zu warten!
 Hohe Sonne, du weilst, und du beschauest dein Rom!
Größeres sahest du nichts und wirst nichts Größeres sehen,
 Wie es dein Priester Horaz in der Entzückung versprach.
Aber heute verweile mir nicht, und wende die Blicke
 Von dem Siebengebirg früher und williger ab!
Einem Dichter zuliebe verkürze die herrlichen Stunden,
 Die mit begierigem Blick selig der Maler genießt;
Glühend blicke noch schnell zu diesen hohen Fassaden,
 Kuppeln und Säulen zuletzt und Obelisken herauf;
Stürze dich eilig ins Meer, um morgen früher zu sehen,
 Was Jahrhunderte schon göttliche Lust dir gewährt:
Diese feuchten, mit Rohr so lange bewachsnen Gestade,
 Diese mit Bäumen und Busch düster beschatteten Höhn.
Wenig Hütten zeigten sie erst; dann sahst du auf einmal
 Sie vom wimmelnden Volk glücklicher Räuber belebt.
Alles schleppten sie drauf an diese Stätte zusammen;
 Kaum war das übrige Rund deiner Betrachtung noch wert.
Sahst eine Welt hier entstehn, sahst dann eine Welt hier
 in Trümmern,
 Aus den Trümmern aufs neu fast eine größere Welt!
Daß ich diese noch lange von dir beleuchtet erblicke,
 Spinne die Parze mir klug langsam den Faden herab.
Aber sie eile herbei, die schön bezeichnete Stunde!—

Here was our table, the usual circle of Germans around it,
 Next to her mother my love, seating herself over there,
Shifted the bench many times and cleverly managed to turn it
 So that one half of her face, all of her neck was in view.
Raising her voice rather more than do ladies in Rome, she took
 up the
 Bottle, looking at me, poured, when the glass was not there,
Spilling wine on the table, and then with her delicate fingers
 Over the table-top drew circles in liquid, and loops.
With her own she entwined my name; and attentively always
 Those small fingers I watched, she well aware that I did.
Lastly a Roman five she signalled resourcefully, nimbly,
 With an upright in front. Quickly, the signal received,
Circle through circle she wound to erase the letters and symbols,
 Yet that precious F o u r lingered, impressed on my eyes.
Silent I sat there meanwhile, biting my lips that were sore now,
 Partly from mischievous joy, partly from burning desire.
First, the few hours until nightfall; then four long hours of more
 waiting!
 Sun up above, still you keep watch on your city of Rome!
Nothing greater you've seen and never will see a thing greater,
 Just as Horace your priest promised at one time, inspired.
But today, for once, do not stay, but avert your glances
 Soon from the Seven Hills, willing, for once, to depart!
For the sake of one poet curtail that magnificent daylight
 Which with eyes all aflame painters so relish and crave;
Glowing, take one more brief look at the palaces' lofty proportions,
 Cupolas, pillars and, last, up at the obelisks' tops;
Eagerly seek the sea and plunge in, all the sooner tomorrow
 Once again to behold age-old and godlike delight;
All these shores so moist, and so long overgrown with tall rushes,
 All these heights for so long shaded with bushes and trees.
Few small hovels at first they revealed; then all of a sudden
 Peopled you saw them, with crowds, fortunate brigands, they
 teemed.
Every manner of thing then they hauled to these parts and
 assembled;
 Hardly the rest of the globe now you found worthy of note.
Saw a world rise up here and then saw a world here in ruins,
 Out of the ruins once more almost a greater world rise!
So that a long time yet by you I may see it illumined,
 Let the Fate be slow, spinning that life-thread of mine.
All the quicker, however, the hour so invitingly signalled!—

Glücklich! hör ich sie schon? Nein; doch ich höre schon Drei.
So, ihr lieben Musen, betrogt ihr wieder die Länge
 Dieser Weile, die mich von der Geliebten getrennt.
Lebet wohl! Nun eil ich, und fürcht euch nicht zu beleidgen;
 Denn ihr Stolzen, ihr gebt Amorn doch immer den Rang.

XVI

«Warum bist du, Geliebter, nicht heute zur Vigne gekommen?
 Einsam, wie ich versprach, wartet ich oben auf dich.»
Beste, schon war ich hinein; da sah ich zum Glücke den Oheim
 Neben den Stöcken, bemüht, hin sich und her sich zu drehn.
Schleichend eilt ich hinaus!—«O welch ein Irrtum ergriff dich!
 Eine Scheuche nur wars, was dich vertrieb! Die Gestalt
Flickten wir emsig zusammen aus alten Kleidern und Rohren;
 Emsig half ich daran, selbst mir zu schaden bemüht.» —
Nun, des Alten Wunsch ist erfüllt; den losesten Vogel
 Scheucht' er heute, der ihm Gärtchen und Nichte bestiehlt.

XX

Zieret Stärke den Mann und freies mutiges Wesen,
 Oh! so ziemet ihm fast tiefes Geheimnis noch mehr.
Städtebezwingerin du, Verschwiegenheit! Fürstin der Völker!
 Teure Göttin, die mich sicher durchs Leben geführt,
Welches Schicksal erfahr ich! Es löset scherzend die Muse,
 Amor löset, der Schalk, mir den verschlossenen Mund.
Ach, schon wird es so schwer, der Könige Schande verbergen!
 Weder die Krone bedeckt, weder ein phrygischer Bund
Midas' verlängertes Ohr; der nächste Diener entdeckt es,
 Und ihm ängstet und drückt gleich das Geheimnis die Brust.
In die Erde vergrüb er es gern, um sich zu erleichtern:
 Doch die Erde verwahrt solche Geheimnisse nicht;
Rohre sprießen hervor und rauschen und lispeln im Winde:
 Midas! Midas, der Fürst, trägt ein verlängertes Ohr!
Schwerer wird es nun mir, ein schönes Geheimnis zu wahren;
 Ach, den Lippen entquillt Fülle des Herzens so leicht!
Keiner Freundin darf ichs vertraun: sie möchte mich schelten;
 Keinem Freunde: vielleicht brächte der Freund mir Gefahr.
Mein Entzücken dem Hain, dem schallenden Felsen zu sagen,
 Bin ich endlich nicht jung, bin ich nicht einsam genug.
Dir, Hexameter, dir, Pentameter, sei es vertrauet,
 Wie sie des Tags mich erfreut, wie sie des Nachts mich beglückt.
Sie, von vielen Männern gesucht, vermeidet die Schlingen,
 Die ihr der Kühnere frech, heimlich der Listige legt;

Rapt, do I hear it now? No, but the third hour has struck.
So, dear Muses, once more you've beguiled the length of my
 waiting,
 Tedious time-span that kept lover and lover apart.
Now farewell! As I hurry away, not afraid to offend you:
 Proud you are, but to him, Amor, will always defer.

XVI

"Dear one, this morning, why weren't you there as agreed, at the
 vineyard?
 On my own, as I said, there I was waiting for you."—
Love, I was going in; when whom should I see but your uncle
 Prying between the vines, this way and that, as he turned.
Quickly I crept away. "But how foolish of you! What an error!
 To mistake a scarecrow for him! Run for it, too! When the thing
Was a patchwork we made out of canes and old rags, in a hurry,
 Hard I worked at it, too, only to spite my own face."
Well, the old man had his way, and scared off a most feckless
 Bird, for the moment, that steals both from his garden and niece.

XX

Men distinguished by strength, by a frank and courageous nature,
 All the more, it would seem, need to be deeply discreet!
Secrecy, you that subdue a whole city and rule over peoples,
 Tutelar goddess to me, leading me safely through life,—
What a reversal now in my fate! When, all facetious, the Muses,
 Jointly with Amor, the rogue, loosen the lips that were sealed.
Hard enough it's already to cover up royal disgraces!
 Crown or Phrygian cap, neither now serves to conceal
Midas' long pointed ears. Any servant of his will have noticed,
 And at once feels oppressed, awed by the secret within.
Deep he'd like to bury it, and be rid of the worrying knowledge.
 Yet mere earth will not keep secrets like that one intact,
Rushes shoot from the ground and they whisper and sough in the
 breezes:
 "Midas, Midas the king, Midas has long pointed ears!"
Harder now it's for me to preserve my more beautiful secret,
 Given such fullness of heart, easily lips overflow.
To no woman friend I can tell it; for she could reproach me;
 In no male friend confide: danger could come from that source.
To proclaim my rapture to groves and the echoing hillsides
 I'm not young enough now, lonely enough, come to that.
So to you; elegiacs, alone let me tell and entrust it.
 How she delights me by day, fills me with rapture by night.
She, sought after by many men, skilfully shuns all the snares which
 Brashly the bold ones lay, subtly the shame-faced and sly;

Klug und zierlich schlüpft sie vorbei und kennet die Wege,
 Wo sie der Liebste gewiß lauschend begierig empfängt.
Zaudre, Luna, sie kommt! damit sie der Nachbar nicht sehe;
 Rausche, Lüftchen, im Laub! niemand vernehme den Tritt.
Und ihr, wachset und blüht, geliebte Lieder, und wieget
 Euch im leisesten Hauch lauer und liebender Luft,
Und entdeckt den Quiriten, wie jene Rohre geschwätzig,
 Eines glücklichen Paars schönes Geheimnis zuletzt.

Morgenklagen

O du loses, leidigliebes Mädchen,
Sag mir an: womit hab ichs verschuldet,
Daß du mich auf diese Folter spannest,
Daß du dein gegeben Wort gebrochen?
Drucktest doch so freundlich gestern abend
Mir die Hände, lispeltest so lieblich:
Ja, ich komme, komme gegen Morgen
Ganz gewiß, mein Freund, auf deine Stube.

Angelehnet ließ ich meine Türe,
Hatte wohl die Angeln erst geprüfet
Und mich recht gefreut, daß sie nicht knarrten.

Welche Nacht des Wartens ist vergangen!
Wacht ich doch und zählte jedes Viertel;
Schlief ich ein auf wenig Augenblicke,
War mein Herz beständig wach geblieben,
Weckte mich von meinem leisen Schlummer.

Ja, da segnet ich die Finsternisse,
Die so ruhig alles überdeckten,
Freute mich der allgemeinen Stille,
Horchte lauschend immer in die Stille,
Ob sich nicht ein Laut bewegen möchte.

«Hätte sie Gedanken, wie ich denke,
Hätte sie Gefühl, wie ich empfinde,

Lithe and clever, she gives them the slip, for she knows all the
 footpaths
 Where her lover will wait, listening, confident, keen.
Luna, be late, for she comes! And make sure that our neighbour
 won't see her;
 Rustle, leaves, in the shrubs! No one must hear her light step.
And, dear elegies, you, may you flourish and blossom, be cradled
 Warm in the lightest of breaths lovingly wafted by air,
Then give away to all Rome, as they did, those garrulous rushes,
 Secrets one fortunate pair treasured and kept to themselves.

Morning Complaints (1788)

Wicked girl you, loving whom is anguish,
Tell me now, what have I done to merit
Torture on this rack of your devising,
And your breaking of the word you gave me?
You clasped my hands, you whispered very sweetly:
Yes, I'll come, my friend, toward the morning,
To your room, of this you can be certain.

My door, I even left it slightly open,
Tested first the working of the hinges—
Glad indeed to find they were not squeaky.

What a night of waiting I have gone through!
Not a wink, I counted every quarter,
Even if I fell asleep a moment
Now and then, my heart forever wakeful
Roused me from each doze I drifted into.

Yes, and then I blessed the very darkness
Which so quietly enshrouded all things,
Glad I was that all around was silent,
Constantly I listened to the silence
For a sound in it that might be moving.

"If she had the thoughts that I am having,
If she felt the way that I am feeling,

Würde sie den Morgen nicht erwarten,
Würde schon in dieser Stunde kommen,»

Hüpft' ein Kätzchen oben übern Boden,
Knisterte das Mäuschen in der Ecke,
Regte sich, ich weiß nicht was, im Hause,
Immer hofft ich, deinen Schritt zu hören,
Immer glaubt ich, deinen Tritt zu hören.

Und so lag ich lang und immer länger,
Und es fing der Tag schon an zu grauen,
Und es rauschte hier und rauschte dorten.
«Ist es ihre Türe! Wärs die meine!»
Saß ich aufgestemmt in meinem Bette,
Schaute nach der halb erhellten Türe,
Ob sie nicht sich wohl bewegen möchte.
Angelehnet blieben beide Flügel
Auf den leisen Angeln ruhig hangen.

Und der Tag ward immer hell- und heller;
Hört ich schon des Nachbars Türe gehen,
Der das Taglohn zu gewinnen eilet,
Hört ich bald darauf die Wagen rasseln,
War das Tor der Stadt nun auch eröffnet,
Und es regte sich der ganze Plunder
Des bewegten Marktes durcheinander.

Ward nun in dem Haus ein Gehn und Kommen
Auf und ab die Stiegen, hin und wieder
Knarrten Türen, klapperten die Tritte;
Und ich konnte, wie vom schönen Leben,
Mich noch nicht von meiner Hoffnung scheiden.

Endlich, als die ganz verhaßte Sonne
Meine Fenster traf und meine Wände,
Sprang ich auf und eilte nach dem Garten,
Meinen heißen, sehnsuchtsvollen Atem
Mit der kühlen Morgenluft zu mischen,
Dir vielleicht im Garten zu begegnen:
Und nun bist du weder in der Laube
Noch im hohen Lindengang zu finden.

She would never wait until the morning,
She would come to me this very moment."

Say a kitten skittered in the attic,
Say a mouse scratchetted in a corner,
Say in the house I know not what was stirring,
Always I had hopes to hear your footstep,
Always I believed I heard you coming.

There I lay a long, long time, and longer,
And the first gray daylight was apparent,
And from here and there I heard a rustle—
"Can it be her door? If it were mine now!"
Sitting up in bed, propped on my elbows,
I looked across to see the door in half-light,
Might it just be edging wider open?
Both its wings were open very slightly,
Hanging quietly upon their hinges.

And the day grew every moment brighter;
Then I heard my neighbour's door swing open,
As he hurried out to earn a living.
Soon I heard the rattatat of wagons,
For wide open now the city gate was;
All the stuff that throngs the busy market
Now was being rushed in all directions.

Soon the house filled with a coming and going
Up and down the staircase; back and forward
Many doors were banging, footsteps clattered;
Still my hopes I could no more abandon
Than this life that has such beauty in it.

Finally a beam of odious sunlight
Struck my window and the walls around me,
And I rose and hurried to the garden,
There my breath all torrid from such yearning
With the cool and early air to mingle,
And perhaps to meet you in the garden:
And you are not in the arbour either,
Nor on the walk between the lofty lime trees.

Der Besuch

Meine Liebste wollt ich heut beschleichen,
Aber ihre Türe war verschlossen.
Hab ich doch den Schlüssel in der Tasche!
Öffn ich leise die geliebte Türe!

Auf dem Saale fand ich nicht das Mädchen,
Fand das Mädchen nicht in ihrer Stube;
Endlich, da ich leis die Kammer öffne,
Find ich sie gar zierlich eingeschlafen,
Angekleidet, auf dem Sofa liegen.

Bei der Arbeit war sie eingeschlafen:
Das Gestrickte mit den Nadeln ruhte
Zwischen den gefaltnen zarten Händen;
Und ich setzte mich an ihre Seite,
Ging bei mir zu Rat, ob ich sie weckte.

Da betrachtet ich den schönen Frieden,
Der auf ihren Augenlidern ruhte:
Auf den Lippen war die stille Treue,
Auf den Wangen Lieblichkeit zu Hause,
Und die Unschuld eines guten Herzens
Regte sich im Busen hin und wieder.
Jedes ihrer Glieder lag gefällig,
Aufgelöst vom süßen Götterbalsam.

Freudig saß ich da, und die Betrachtung
Hielte die Begierde, sie zu wecken,
Mit geheimen Banden fest und fester.

O du Liebe, dacht ich, kann der Schlummer,
Der Verräter jedes falschen Zuges,
Kann er dir nicht schaden, nichts entdecken,
Was des Freundes zarte Meinung störte?

Deine holden Augen sind geschlossen,
Die mich offen schon allein bezaubern;
Es bewegen deine süßen Lippen
Weder sich zur Rede noch zum Kusse;
Aufgelöst sind diese Zauberbande
Deiner Arme, die mich sonst umschlingen,
Und die Hand, die reizende Gefährtin
Süßer Schmeicheleien, unbeweglich.

The Visit (1788)

Today I wanted to surprise my dearest,
But her door was locked and would not open.
Well, I have the key here in my pocket,
Open up the precious portal, softly.

But I did not find her in the hallway,
Did not find her in her *Stube*, either;
Finally, the bedroom door—and softly
I open it, to find her on the sofa,
Fully clad, and sleeping, very graceful.

She had dropped into a doze while working:
Something she had knitted with her needles
Lay between the tender hands she'd folded;
And I sat myself down there beside her;
Should I wake her up, or not, I wondered.

Fondly, for a time, I contemplated
The lovely peace reposing on her eyelids;
Calm fidelity on her lips was dwelling,
Quite at home, and on her cheeks a sweetness,
And the innocence a kind heart harbours
Rose and fell in the motion of her bosom.
Each and every limb outspread and pleasant
By the gods' sweet balsam had been melted.

Full of joy I sat, my contemplation
Trammelled all my eagerness to wake her,
More and more with secret cords restraining.

O my love, I thought, cannot this slumber,
Revelation of the least false feature,
Can it do no harm, discover nothing
Adverse to your lover's fond opinion?

Now your eyes are shut, which, being open,
Of their own accord alone bewitch me;
Lips that are so sweet, they make no motion,
Either to speak or haply to be kissing;
Melted are your arms, these magic bracelets
Which at other times you put around me;
And your hand is stilled, of sweetest fondlings
Ever the provoker and companion.

Wärs ein Irrtum, wie ich von dir denke,
Wär es Selbstbetrug, wie ich dich liebe,
Müßt ichs jetzt entdecken, da sich Amor
Ohne Binde neben mich gestellet.

Lange saß ich so und freute herzlich
Ihres Wertes mich und meiner Liebe;
Schlafend hatte sie mir so gefallen,
Daß ich mich nicht traute, sie zu wecken.

Leise leg ich ihr zwei Pomeranzen
Und zwei Rosen auf das Tischchen nieder;
Sachte, sachte schleich ich meiner Wege.

Öffnet sie die Augen, meine Gute,
Gleich erblickt sie diese bunte Gabe,
Staunt, wie immer bei verschloßnen Türen
Dieses freundliche Geschenk sich finde.

Seh ich diese Nacht den Engel wieder,
O wie freut sie sich, vergilt mir doppelt
Dieses Opfer meiner zarten Liebe.

Venezianische Epigramme

15

Schüler macht sich der Schwärmer genug, und rühret die Menge,
 Wenn der vernünftige Mann einzelne Liebende zählt.
Wundertätige Bilder sind meist nur schlechte Gemälde:
 Werke des Geists und der Kunst sind für den Pöbel nicht da.

23

Gieße nur, tränke nur fort die rotbemäntelten Frösche,
 Wäßre das durstende Land, daß es uns Broccoli schickt.
Nur durchwäßre mir nicht dies Büchlein; es sei mir ein Fläschchen
 Reinen Arraks, und Punsch mache sich jeder nach Lust.

38

Kehre nicht, liebliches Kind, die Beinchen hinauf zu dem Himmel;
 Jupiter sieht dich, der Schalk, und Ganymed ist besorgt.

If my thoughts about you were mistaken,
And the ways I love you self-deception,
Now and only now I'll know, for Amor
Stands without his blindfold here beside me.

Long I sat there so, my heart with pleasure
Glad with her merits, joyous at my loving;
I liked her so, asleep, I would not venture
Any move that might cause her to waken.

Quietly I set two pomegranates
And two roses on her little table;
Softly, softly on my way I tiptoed.

My good lady, when her eyes shall open,
She'll espy these presents with their colours;
All the doors were locked, so she will wonder
How this friendly gift was placed beside her.

If tonight I see again my angel,
O how glad she'll be, reward me doubly
For this offering of my love so tender.

Venetian Epigrams

15

Phantasts make converts enough and stir a whole crowd into frenzy,
 While the rational man counts on the love of a few.
Miracle-working pictures are usually bungled as painting;
 Works of the mind and of art do not exist for the mob.

23

Let the rain come down with drinks for the redcoated froggies,
 Water the land that is parched, making our broccoli grow!
Keep the water away, however, from my little book now:
 Arak, the purest, it is: anyone's punch it will spice.

38

Careful, my sweet, don't hoist your legs too high in the air now:
 Jupiter's looking, the rogue, Ganymede's anxious and glares.

53

Frankreichs traurig Geschick, die Großen mögens bedenken;
 Aber bedenken fürwahr sollen es Kleine noch mehr.
Große gingen zugrunde: doch wer beschützte die Menge
 Gegen die Menge? Da war Menge der Menge Tyrann.

55

«Sage, tun wir nicht recht? Wir müssen den Pöbel betrügen.
 Sieh nur, wie ungeschickt wild, sieh nur, wie dumm er sich zeigt!»
Ungeschickt scheint er und dumm, weil ihr ihn eben betrüget;
 Seid nur redlich, und er, glaubt mir, ist menschlich und klug.

66

Vieles kann ich ertragen. Die meisten beschwerlichen Dinge
 Duld ich mit ruhigem Mut, wie es ein Gott mir gebeut.
Wenige sind mir jedoch wie Gift und Schlange zuwider,
 Viere: Rauch des Tabaks, Wanzen und Knoblauch und †.

72

Wär ich ein häusliches Weib, und hätte, was ich bedürfte,
 Treu sein wollt ich und froh, herzen und küssen den Mann.
So sang, unter andern, gemeinen Liedern, ein Dirnchen
 Mir in Venedig, und nie hört ich ein frömmer Gebet.

77

Mit Botanik gibst du dich ab? mit Optik? Was tust du?
 Ist es nicht schönrer Gewinn, rühren ein zärtliches Herz?
Ach, die zärtlichen Herzen! ein Pfuscher vermag sie zu rühren;
 Sei es mein einziges Glück, dich zu berühren, Natur!

90

Welch ein lustiges Spiel! Es windet am Faden die Scheibe,
 Die von der Hand entfloh, eilig sich wieder herauf!
Seht, so schein ich mein Herz bald dieser Schönen, bald jener
 Zuzuwerfen; doch gleich kehrt es im Fluge zurück.

53

France's pitiable fate, the great may reflect on its meaning.
 Yet the little still more ought to consider that plight.
True, many great ones perished; but who protected the masses
 From the masses? Then mob proved the oppressor of mob.

55

"Tell us, aren't we right? We've no choice but to hoodwink the
 rabble.
 Only look how uncouth, look how ferocious its ways!"
Crudely hoodwink a man, and uncouth, ferocious you'll make him.
 No, be honest with them. Human they'll grow by degrees.

66

I can put up with a lot. The things that are most of a bother
 Cool and calm I endure, thanks to the gift of a god.
Just one or two are the things I abominate, or, more precisely,
 Four: tobacco (the smoke), bedbugs and garlic and †.

72

"Housewife is what I would like to be and to have what I needed,
 I would be happy and true, hugging and kissing my man."
That's what she sang to me, other songs too, very vulgar, a
 streetgirl
 Somewhere in Venice—a prayer never more pious I heard.

77

So you dabble in botany, optics? How can you, a poet?
 Don't you feel better employed touching a sensitive heart?
Oh, those sensitive hearts. Any charlatan knows how to touch them.
 No, let my one joy be this, Nature, to touch upon you!

90

What an amusing game: the yoyo escapes from a finger,
 Quickly it flies and at once back again winds on the string.
Look, it's the way my heart from one to another goodlooker
 Seems to escape from me, soon back it is flying again.

Nähe des Geliebten

Ich denke dein, wenn mir der Sonne Schimmer
 Vom Meere strahlt;
Ich denke dein, wenn sich des Mondes Flimmer
 In Quellen malt.

Ich sehe dich, wenn auf dem fernen Wege
 Der Staub sich hebt;
In tiefer Nacht, wenn auf dem schmalen Stege
 Der Wandrer bebt.

Ich höre dich, wenn dort mit dumpfem Rauschen
 Die Welle steigt.
Im stillen Haine geh ich oft zu lauschen,
 Wenn alles schweigt.

Ich bin bei dir, du seist auch noch so ferne,
 Du bist mir nah!
Die Sonne sinkt, bald leuchten mir die Sterne.
 O wärst du da!

Die Spinnerin

Als ich still und ruhig spann,
Ohne nur zu stocken,
Trat ein schöner junger Mann
Nahe mir zum Rocken.

Lobte, was zu loben war,
Sollte das was schaden?
Mein dem Flachse gleiches Haar,
Und den gleichen Faden.

Ruhig war er nicht dabei,
Ließ es nicht beim alten;
Und der Faden riß entzwei,
Den ich lang erhalten.

Nearness of the Beloved (c. 1795)

I think of you when from the sea the shimmer
 Of sunlight streams;
I think of you when on the brook the dimmer
 Moon casts her beams.

I see your face when on the distant highway
 Dust whirls and flakes,
In deepest night when on the mountain byway
 The traveller quakes.

I hear your voice when, dully roaring, yonder
 Waves rise and spill;
Listening, in silent woods I often wander
 When all is still.

I walk with you, though miles from you divide me;
 Yet you are near!
The sun goes down, soon stars will shine to guide me.
 Would you were here!

The Spinner (c.1795)

When I was spinning, on and on,
As ever, quiet and good,
A young and handsome gentleman
Came in and by me stood.

Praised this and that, like, he'd compare
—No hurt in what he said!
—To the hank of flax my hair,
Also to the thread.

Him, he made a great to-do,
Altered many things,
And my thread, it snapped in two,
Spite years of cossetings.

Und des Flachses Stein-Gewicht
Gab noch viele Zahlen;
Aber, ach, ich konnte nicht
Mehr mit ihnen prahlen.

Als ich sie zum Weber trug,
Fühlt ich was sich regen,
Und mein armes Herze schlug
Mit geschwindern Schlägen.

Nun, beim heißen Sonnenstich,
Bring ichs auf die Bleiche,
Und mit Mühe bück ich mich
Nach dem nächsten Teiche.

Was ich in dem Kämmerlein
Still und fein gesponnen,
Kommt—wie kann es anders sein?—
Endlich an die Sonnen.

And the stone weight of the flax
Numbered soon fullscore,
Not the kind to fill up sacks
Or boast about, for sure.

Flax then to the loom I brought:
Then felt a little kick;
My poor heart, it didn't ought
To've beat so very quick.

Now the flax, when sun is hot,
I bring to the bleaching ground;
It's difficult to stoop a lot
Across the nearest pond.

What I inside my little room
Spun so soft and bright,
Come it must and very soon
—Can it be helped?—to light.

Mignon

Kennst du das Land, wo die Zitronen blühn,
Im dunkeln Laub die Gold-Orangen glühn,
Ein sanfter Wind vom blauen Himmel weht,
Die Myrte still und hoch der Lorbeer steht,
Kennst du es wohl?
 Dahin! Dahin
Möcht ich mit dir, o mein Geliebter, ziehn.

Kennst du das Haus? Auf Säulen ruht sein Dach,
Es glänzt der Saal, es schimmert das Gemach,
Und Marmorbilder stehn und sehn mich an:
Was hat man dir, du armes Kind, getan?
Kennst du es wohl?
 Dahin! Dahin
Möcht ich mit dir, o mein Beschützer, ziehn.

Kennst du den Berg und seinen Wolkensteg?
Das Maultier sucht im Nebel seinen Weg,
In Höhlen wohnt der Drachen alte Brut,
Es stürzt der Fels und über ihn die Flut;
Kennst du ihn wohl?
 Dahin! Dahin
Geht unser Weg! o Vater, laß uns ziehn!

Die Braut von Korinth

Nach Korinthus von Athen gezogen
Kam ein Jüngling, dort noch unbekannt.
Einen Bürger hofft' er sich gewogen;
Beide Väter waren gastverwandt,
Hatten frühe schon
Töchterchen und Sohn
Braut und Bräutigam voraus genannt.

Mignon

(from *Wilhelm Meisters Lehrjahre*, 1795)

Knowst thou the land of flowering lemon trees?
In leafage dark the golden orange glows,
From azure sky there wafts a gentle breeze,
Calm the myrtle, high the laurel grows,
Knowst thou it still?
 Aiee, aiee,
There would I go, belovèd mine, with thee.

Knowst thou the house? Its column-bedded roof,
The shining hall, the inner room aglow,
The marble statues gaze but do not move:
What have they done, poor child, to hurt thee so?
Knowst thou it still?
 Aiee, aiee,
There would I go, protector mine, with thee.

Knowst thou the mountain, stepping up through cloud?
The mule in mist treads out his path; a cave,
And in it dwells the ancient dragon brood;
The crag swoops down and over it the wave;
Knowst thou it still?
 Aiee, aiee,
There goes the way, father, for thee and me.

*(This translation is dedicated to the memory
of Gérard de Nerval)*

The Bride of Corinth (1797)

To Corinth came a solitary stranger,
Whom none yet knew, a young Athenian;
He sought there to obtain a certain favour
From his father's comrade in the town:
Long had it been planned
For his daughter's hand
To be given to his comrade's son.

Aber wird er auch willkommen scheinen,
Wenn er teuer nicht die Gunst erkauft?
Er ist noch ein Heide mit den Seinen,
Und sie sind schon Christen und getauft.
Keimt ein Glaube neu,
Wird oft Lieb und Treu
Wie ein böses Unkraut ausgerauft.

Und schon lag das ganze Haus im stillen,
Vater, Töchter, nur die Mutter wacht;
Sie empfängt den Gast mit bestem Willen,
Gleich ins Prunkgemach wird er gebracht.
Wein und Essen prangt,
Eh er es verlangt:
So versorgend wünscht sie gute Nacht.

Aber bei dem wohlbestellten Essen
Wird die Lust der Speise nicht erregt;
Müdigkeit läßt Speis und Trank vergessen,
Daß er angekleidet sich aufs Bette legt;
Und er schlummert fast,
Als ein seltner Gast
Sich zur offnen Tür herein bewegt.

Denn er sieht, bei seiner Lampe Schimmer
Tritt, mit weißem Schleier und Gewand,
Sittsam still ein Mädchen in das Zimmer,
Um die Stirn ein schwarz- und goldnes Band.
Wie sie ihn erblickt,
Hebt sie, die erschrickt,
Mit Erstaunen eine weiße Hand.

Bin ich, rief sie aus, so fremd im Hause,
Daß ich von dem Gaste nichts vernahm?
Ach, so hält man mich in meiner Klause!
Und nun überfällt mich hier die Scham.
Ruhe nur so fort
Auf dem Lager dort,
Und ich gehe schnell, so wie ich kam.

Bleibe, schönes Mädchen! ruft der Knabe,
Rafft von seinem Lager sich geschwind:
Hier ist Ceres', hier ist Bacchus' Gabe,
Und du bringst den Amor, liebes Kind!
Bist vor Schrecken blaß!

Might perhaps his welcome there be hindered?
Might the price of it his means exceed?
He is still a pagan, like his kindred;
Baptized the others in the Christian creed.
When new faiths are born,
From the heart are torn,
Sometimes, love and troth like any weed.

All the house was hushed, to rest retiring
Father, daughters—not the mother yet;
Him she welcomed, of his state inquiring,
And to a well-appointed guestroom led.
Wine and food she brought,
Ere of them he thought,
Solicitous, and "Sleep you well," she said.

Yet he felt no hunger and unheeded
Left the wine, and eager for the rest
Which his limbs forspent with travel needed,
Down upon the bed he lay, still dressed;
Drowsing now, when lo,
Gliding forward, slow—
At the door another, wondrous guest.

By his table lamp's unsteady glowing
He sees a girl walk in the room, and stand:
Gentle, modest, veiled in white, a flowing
Snowy robe, a black and gold headband.
As she meets his eyes,
Startled, in surprise,
She has lifted up a snowy hand.

"Is a stranger here, and no-one told me?
Am I then forgotten, just a name?
Ah! Tis thus that in my cell they hold me.
Now I feel quite overcome with shame.
Do not stir," she said,
"Now you are in bed,
I will leave as quickly as I came."

"Do not leave me, lovely one!" and springing
Out of bed he's quickly on his feet.
"Ceres, here, and Bacchus, gifts are bringing,
What you bring is Amor, his delight.
Why are you so pale?

Liebe, komm und laß,
Laß uns sehn, wie froh die Götter sind.

Ferne bleib, o Jüngling! bleibe stehen;
Ich gehöre nicht den Freuden an.
Schon der letzte Schritt ist, ach! geschehen
Durch der guten Mutter kranken Wahn,
Die genesend schwur:
Jugend und Natur
Sei dem Himmel künftig untertan.

Und der alten Götter bunt Gewimmel
Hat sogleich das stille Haus geleert.
Unsichtbar wird Einer nur im Himmel,
Und ein Heiland wird am Kreuz verehrt;
Opfer fallen hier,
Weder Lamm noch Stier,
Aber Menschenopfer unerhört.

Und er fragt und wäget alle Worte,
Deren keines seinem Geist entgeht.
Ist es möglich, daß am stillen Orte
Die geliebte Braut hier vor mir steht?
Sei die Meine nur!
Unsrer Väter Schwur
Hat vom Himmel Segen uns erfleht.

Mich erhältst du nicht, du gute Seele!
Meiner zweiten Schwester gönnt man dich.
Wenn ich mich in stiller Klause quäle,
Ach! in ihren Armen denk an mich,
Die an dich nur denkt,
Die sich liebend kränkt;
In die Erde bald verbirgt sie sich.

Nein! bei dieser Flamme seis geschworen,
Gütig zeigt sie Hymen uns voraus;
Bist der Freude nicht und mir verloren,
Kommst mit mir in meines Vaters Haus.
Liebchen, bleibe hier!
Feire gleich mit mir
Unerwartet unsern Hochzeitschmaus.

Und schon wechseln sie der Treue Zeichen;
Golden reicht sie ihm die Kette dar,

Sweet, now let us hail
The joyous gods, their gifts, with appetite!"

"No, O no, young stranger, come not nigh me.
Joy is not for me, nor festive cheer.
Ah! such bliss may not be tasted by me,
Since my mother, sickened with a fear,
By long illness bowed,
Me to heaven vowed:
Youth and nature I may not come near.

They have left our household, left it lonely,
The jocund gods of old, no more they reign;
One, unseen, in heaven, is worshipped only,
And a saviour crucified and slain.
Sacrifices here—
Neither lamb nor steer,
But man himself in misery and pain."

Weighing all her words, now he must ponder:
Can it be that in this silent spot
He beholds her—what surpassing wonder!—
The belovèd bride that he had sought?
"Be mine only now,
Look, our fathers' vow
Heaven's blessing to us both has brought!"

"No, good heart, not me," she cries in anguish;
Your company is my second sister's place.
When I weep inside my cell and languish,
Think of me, though in her fond embrace.
She who pines for thee
Never shalt thou see:
Soon beneath the earth she'll hide her face."

"No! By this flame I swear between us burning,
Fanned by Hymen, lost thou shalt not be!
Not lost to me or joy, no, but returning
Back to my father's house, come back with me!
Stay, my sweetheart, here,
Taste the bridal cheer,
Spread for us so unexpectedly."

Tokens they exchange, to him she proffers
Her golden necklace now for him to wear,

Und er will ihr eine Schale reichen,
Silbern, künstlich, wie nicht eine war.
Die ist nicht für mich;
Doch, ich bitte dich,
Eine Locke gib von deinem Haar.

Eben schlug die dumpfe Geisterstunde,
Und nun schien es ihr erst wohl zu sein.
Gierig schlürfte sie mit blassem Munde
Nun den dunkel blutgefärbten Wein;
Doch vom Weizenbrot,
Das er freundlich bot,
Nahm sie nicht den kleinsten Bissen ein.

Und dem Jüngling reichte sie die Schale,
Der, wie sie, nun hastig lüstern trank.
Liebe fordert er beim stillen Mahle;
Ach, sein armes Herz war liebekrank.
Doch sie widersteht,
Wie er immer fleht,
Bis er weinend auf das Bette sank.

Und sie kommt und wirft sich zu ihm nieder:
Ach, wie ungern seh ich dich gequält!
Aber, ach! berührst du meine Glieder,
Fühlst du schaudernd, was ich dir verhehlt.
Wie der Schnee so weiß,
Aber kalt wie Eis
Ist das Liebchen, das du dir erwählt.

Heftig faßt er sie mit starken Armen,
Von der Liebe Jugendkraft durchmannt:
Hoffe doch, bei mir noch zu erwarmen,
Wärst du selbst mir aus dem Grab gesandt!
Wechselhauch und Kuß!
Liebesüberfluß!
Brennst du nicht und fühlest mich entbrannt?

Liebe schließet fester sie zusammen,
Tränen mischen sich in ihre Lust;
Gierig saugt sie seines Mundes Flammen,
Eins ist nur im andern sich bewußt.
Seine Liebeswut
Wärmt ihr starres Blut,
Doch es schlägt kein Herz in ihrer Brust.

But she will not touch the cup he offers,
Silver, wrought with skill exceeding rare:
"That is not for me,
All I ask of thee
Is one curly lock of thy own hair."

Dully boomed the ghosting midnight hour;
Only now her eyes take on a shine,
Pallid lips of hers, now they devour,
Gulping it, the bloody-coloured wine,
But of wheaten bread
Offered by the lad
Not a single crumb to take would deign.

Now she gave the cup, and so he drained it,
Impetuous, in haste, he drained it dry;
Love was in his heart, desire pained it,
Till it ached for what she must deny.
Hard as he insists,
She his will resists—
On the bed he flounders with a cry.

She throws herself beside him: "Dearest, still thee!
Ah, how sad I am to see thee so.
But alas, my body would but chill thee,
Thou wouldst find a thing thou mayst not know;
Thou wouldst be afraid,
Finding then the maid
Thou has chosen, cold as ice and snow."

Vehement strong arms the girl emprison
And muscle from the thrill of love acquire:
"Even from the grave wert thou arisen,
I would warm thee well with my desire!"
Breathless kiss on kiss!
Overflowing bliss!
"Dost thou burn and feel my burning fire?"

Closer still they cling and closer, mixing
Tears and cries of love, limbs interlaced,
She sucks his kisses, his with hers transfixing,
Each self aware the other it possessed.
All his passion's flood
Warms her gelid blood—
Yet no heart is beating in her breast.

Unterdessen schleichet auf dem Gange
Häuslich spät die Mutter noch vorbei,
Horchet an der Tür und horchet lange,
Welch ein sonderbarer Ton es sei:
Klag- und Wonnelaut
Bräutigams und Braut,
Und des Liebestammelns Raserei.

Unbeweglich bleibt sie an der Türe,
Weil sie erst sich überzeugen muß,
Und sie hört die höchsten Liebesschwüre,
Lieb- und Schmeichelworte, mit Verdruß —
Still! der Hahn erwacht! —
Aber morgen nacht
Bist du wieder da? —und Kuß auf Kuß.

Länger hält die Mutter nicht das Zürnen,
Öffnet das bekannte Schloß geschwind: —
Gibt es hier im Hause solche Dirnen,
Die dem Fremden gleich zu Willen sind? —
So zur Tür hinein.
Bei der Lampe Schein
Sieht sie —Gott! sie sieht ihr eigen Kind.

Und der Jüngling will im ersten Schrecken
Mit des Mädchens eignem Schleierflor,
Mit dem Teppich die Geliebte decken;
Doch sie windet gleich sich selbst hervor.
Wie mit Geists Gewalt
Hebet die Gestalt
Lang und langsam sich im Bett empor.

Mutter! Mutter! spricht sie hohle Worte,
So mißgönnt Ihr mir die schöne Nacht!
Ihr vertreibt mich von dem warmen Orte.
Bin ich zur Verzweiflung nur erwacht?
Ists Euch nicht genug,
Daß ins Leichentuch,
Daß Ihr früh mich in das Grab gebracht?

Aber aus der schwerbedeckten Enge
Treibet mich ein eigenes Gericht.
Eurer Priester summende Gesänge
Und ihr Segen haben kein Gewicht;
Salz und Wasser kühlt

Meanwhile, down the corridor, the mother
Passes, late, on household tasks intent;
Hears a sound, and listens, then another:
Wonders at the sounds and what they meant.
Who was whispering so?
Voices soft and low,
Rapturous cries and moans of lovers blent.

Ear against the door herself she stations,
Making certain nothing is amiss;
Horrified she hears those protestations
Lovers make, avowals of their bliss:
"The cockerel! Tis light!"
"But tomorrow night
Wilt thou come again?"—and kiss on kiss.

Now she can contain her rage no longer,
Lifts the latch, flings open wide the door:
"Not in my house! Who's this that any stranger
Can slip into his bed, who is this whore?"
Now she's in the room,
By lamplight in the gloom—
God! This girl her daughter was before!

And the youth in terror tried to cover
With her flimsy veil the maiden's head,
Clasped her close; but sliding from her lover,
Back the garment from her face she spread,
As by spirit power
Made longer, straighter, now her
Body slowly rises from the bed.

"Mother! Mother!"—hollow-voiced—"Deprive me
Not of pleasures I this night have known!
From this warm abode why do you drive me?
Do I waken to despair alone?
Are you not content
That in my cerement
To an early grave you forced me down?

Strange is the law that me perforce has brought now
Forth from the dark-heaped chamber where I lay;
The croonings of your priests avail but nought now,
Powerless their blessings were, I say.
Water nor salt in truth

Nicht, wo Jugend fühlt;
Ach! die Erde kühlt die Liebe nicht.

Dieser Jüngling war mir erst versprochen,
Als noch Venus' heitrer Tempel stand.
Mutter, habt Ihr doch das Wort gebrochen,
Weil ein fremd, ein falsch Gelübd Euch band!
Doch kein Gott erhört,
Wenn die Mutter schwört,
Zu versagen ihrer Tochter Hand.

Aus dem Grabe werd ich ausgetrieben,
Noch zu suchen das vermißte Gut,
Noch den schon verlornen Mann zu lieben
Und zu saugen seines Herzens Blut.
Ists um den geschehn,
Muß nach andern gehn,
Und das junge Volk erliegt der Wut.

Schöner Jüngling! kannst nicht länger leben;
Du versiechest nun an diesem Ort.
Meine Kette hab ich dir gegeben;
Deine Locke nehm ich mit mir fort.
Sieh sie an genau!
Morgen bist du grau,
Und nur braun erscheinst du wieder dort.

Höre, Mutter, nun die letzte Bitte:
Einen Scheiterhaufen schichte du;
Öffne meine bange kleine Hütte,
Bring in Flammen Liebende zur Ruh!
Wenn der Funke sprüht,
Wenn die Asche glüht,
Eilen wir den alten Göttern zu.

Can cool the pulse of youth:
Love still burns, though buried under clay.

This young man, to him my troth was plighted,
While yet blithely Venus ruled the land,
Mother!—and that promise you have slighted,
Yielding to an outlandish command.
But no god will hear
If a mother swear
To deny to love her daughter's hand.

From my grave betimes I have been driven,
I seek the good I lost, none shall me thwart,
I seek his love to whom my troth was given,
And I have sucked the lifeblood from his heart.
If he dies, I will
Find me others, still
With my fury tear young folk apart.

Fair young man, thy thread of life is broken,
Human skill can bring no help to thee.
There, thou hast my necklace as a token,
And this curl of thine I take with me.
Soon thou must decay,
Dawn will find thee gray,
In Hades only shalt thou brownhaired be.

Mother! Listen to my last entreaty!
Heap the funeral pyre for us once more;
Open then my little tomb, for pity,
And in flame our souls to peace restore.
Up the sparks will go,
When the embers glow,
To the ancient gods aloft we soar."

Euphrosyne

Auch von des höchsten Gebirgs beeisten zackigen Gipfeln
 Schwindet Purpur und Glanz scheidender Sonne hinweg.
Lange verhüllt schon Nacht das Tal und die Pfade des Wandrers,
 Der, am tosenden Strom, auf zu der Hütte sich sehnt,
Zu dem Ziele des Tags, der stillen hirtlichen Wohnung;
 Und der göttliche Schlaf eilet gefällig voraus,
Dieser holde Geselle des Reisenden. Daß er auch heute
 Segnend kränze das Haupt mir mit dem heiligen Mohn!
Aber was leuchtet mir dort vom Felsen glänzend herüber
 Und erhellet den Duft schäumender Ströme so hold?
Strahlt die Sonne vielleicht durch heimliche Spalten und Klüfte?
 Denn kein irdischer Glanz ist es, der wandelnde, dort.
Näher wälzt sich die Wolke, sie glüht. Ich staune dem Wunder!
 Wird der rosige Strahl nicht ein bewegtes Gebild?
Welche Göttin nahet sich mir? und welche der Musen
 Suchet den treuen Freund, selbst in dem grausen Geklüft?
Schöne Göttin! enthülle dich mir, und täusche, verschwindend,
 Nicht den begeisterten Sinn, nicht das gerührte Gemüt.
Nenne, wenn du es darfst vor einem Sterblichen, deinen
 Göttlichen Namen; wo nicht: rege bedeutend mich auf,
Daß ich fühle, welche du seist von den ewigen Töchtern
 Zeus', und der Dichter sogleich preise dich würdig im Lied.
«Kennst du mich, Guter, nicht mehr? Und käme diese Gestalt dir,
 Die du doch sonst geliebt, schon als ein fremdes Gebild?
Zwar der Erde gehör ich nicht mehr, und trauernd entschwang sich
 Schon der schaudernde Geist jugendlich frohem Genuß;
Aber ich hoffte mein Bild noch fest in des Freundes Erinnrung
 Eingeschrieben, und noch schön durch die Liebe verklärt.
Ja, schon sagt mir gerührt dein Blick, mir sagt es die Träne:
 Euphrosyne, sie ist noch von dem Freunde gekannt.
Sieh, die Scheidende zieht durch Wälder und grause Gebirge,
 Sucht den wandernden Mann, ach! in der Ferne noch auf;
Sucht den Lehrer, den Freund, den Vater und blicket noch einmal
 Nach dem leichten Gerüst irdischer Freuden zurück.
Laß mich der Tage gedenken, da mich, das Kind, du dem Spiele,
 Jener täuschenden Kunst reizender Musen geweiht.
Laß mich der Stunde gedenken und jedes kleineren Umstands;
 Ach, wer ruft nicht so gern Unwiederbringliches an!
Jenes süße Gedränge der leichtesten irdischen Tage,
 Ach, wer schätzt ihn genug, diesen vereilenden Wert!
Klein erscheinet es nun, doch ach! nicht kleinlich dem Herzen;
 Macht die Liebe, die Kunst jegliches Kleine doch groß.

Euphrosyne (1798)

Even the crests of the highest mountain, jagged and icy,
 Gloaming and purple quit, now with the sun going down.
Darkness cloaked the ravine long ago, the wanderer's climbing
 Path by the torrent, he longs soon to arrive at the hut,
Goal of his day, the quiet abode of a mountain shepherd,
 And there is heavenly sleep hurries enticing ahead,
Sleep that sweetly befriends any traveller; may it with sacred
 Poppy garland my head, blessing me also today.
But now what is this gleam from the cliff over yonder, a radiance
 Filling with delicate light vapours that lift from the foam?
Is it the sun, through secret clefts and crevices haply
 Shining? This ambient sheen scarcely belongs to the earth.
Closer it floats, the cloud, it is glowing, I gaze at the marvel;
 Rosy the light, is its ray shaped like a figure that moves?
What goddess is this who comes to me? Which of the Muses
 Might in the chasm so grim search for a trustable friend?
Beautiful goddess, make yourself known to me, do not by vanishing
 Baffle the mind you inspire, thwart all the feelings you touch.
Speak, if you may, your sacred name to a mortal being;
 If that is not to be done, rouse up my passion to feel
Which you may happen to be of Zeus's eternal daughters,
 Then may the poet in song utter your praises at once.
"Do you not know any more, good friend, who I am? This visible
 Form you adored, can it be strange to you now and so soon?
True, I belong to the earth no more, my shuddering spirit,
 Sorrowful, flew from the world's pleasure and gladness and youth;
Yet did I hope that the mind of my friend would carry my image
 Firmly imprinted, and more, make it transfigured by love.
Yes, now I see and feel from your gaze, from your tears I can tell it:
 Well he knows who she is: Euphrosyne I am.
Look you, she who has gone before must walk in the mountain
 Forest, seeking him out, faraway travelling man,
Seeking her teacher, friend, her father, again she is looking
 Back to the joys of the earth, in their provisional frame.
Let me remember when I was a child and the art of dissembling,
 Games of the ravishing Muse, these you tutored me in.
Every moment and tinier detail let me remember;
 Ah, what a pleasure we take; putting a mind to what's lost!
Sweetness of days on earth, the airiest, all in a torrent,
 Ah, who can prize them enough, treasures that trickle away?
Small it may seem to us now, but ah, to the heart never petty;
 Love, to be sure, and art, magnify things that are small.

Denkst du der Stunde noch wohl, wie auf dem Brettergerüste
 Du mich der höheren Kunst ernstere Stufen geführt?
Knabe schien ich, ein rührendes Kind, du nanntest mich Arthur,
 Und belebtest in mir britisches Dichter-Gebild,
Drohtest mit grimmiger Glut den armen Augen und wandtest
 Selbst den tränenden Blick, innig getäuschet, hinweg.
Ach! da warst du so hold und schütztest ein trauriges Leben,
 Das die verwegene Flucht endlich dem Knaben entriß.
Freundlich faßtest du mich, den Zerschmetterten, trugst mich von
 dannen,
 Und ich heuchelte lang, dir an dem Busen, den Tod.
Endlich schlug die Augen ich auf, und sah dich, in ernste,
 Stille Betrachtung versenkt, über den Liebling geneigt.
Kindlich strebt ich empor und küßte dir dankbar die Hände,
 Reiche zum reinen Kuß dir den gefälligen Mund,
Fragte: Warum so ernst, mein Vater? und hab ich gefehlet,
 Oh! so zeige mir an, wie mir das Beßre gelingt.
Keine Mühe verdrießt mich bei dir, und alles und jedes
 Wiederhol ich so gern, wenn du mich leitest und lehrst.
Aber du faßtest mich stark und drücktest mich fester im Arme,
 Und es schauderte mir tief in dem Busen das Herz.
Nein! mein liebliches Kind, so riefst du, alles und jedes,
 Wie du es heute gezeigt, zeig es auch morgen der Stadt.
Rühre sie alle, wie du mich rührst, und es fließen zum Beifall
 Dir von dem trockensten Aug herrliche Tränen herab.
Aber am tiefsten trafst du doch mich, den Freund, der im Arm dich
 Hält, den selber der Schein früherer Leiche geschreckt.
Ach, Natur, wie sicher und groß in allem erscheinst du!
 Himmel und Erde befolgt ewiges, festes Gesetz:
Jahre folgen auf Jahre, dem Frühling reichet der Sommer,
 Und dem reichlichen Herbst traulich der Winter die Hand.
Felsen stehen gegründet, es stürzt sich das ewige Wasser
 Aus der bewölkten Kluft schäumend und brausend hinab.
Fichten grünen so fort, und selbst die entlaubten Gebüsche
 Hegen, im Winter schon, heimliche Knospen am Zweig.
Alles entsteht und vergeht nach Gesetz; doch über des Menschen
 Leben, dem köstlichen Schatz, herrschet ein schwankendes Los.
Nicht dem blühenden nickt der willig scheidende Vater,
 Seinem trefflichen Sohn, freundlich vom Rande der Gruft;
Nicht der Jüngere schließt dem Älteren immer das Auge,
 Das sich willig gesenkt, kräftig dem Schwächeren zu.
Öfter, ach! verkehrt das Geschick die Ordnung der Tage:
 Hilflos klaget ein Greis Kinder und Enkel umsonst,
Steht, ein beschädigter Stamm, dem rings zerschmetterte Zweige
 Um die Seiten umher strömende Schloßen gestreckt.

Do you recall the time when, there on the stage, you taught me
 Serious matters indeed, higher demands of the art?
I appeared as a boy, very winsome, and "Arthur" you called me—
 You were restoring, in me, life to an Englishman's play,
Threatened my eyes with fire you did, with fire, it was terrible,
 Turning away as you wept, under the spell of the scene.
Ah! and then you were kind, protecting a life full of sorrow
 Which precipitate flight finally stole from the boy.
Me, shattered, you took in your friendly arms and away and
 Then for a little I feigned death as I lay on your breast.
Finally, though, I opened my eyes and saw you, so serious,
 Rapt in thought as you gazed down at your darling-in-arms.
Childishly up I reached and kissed your hands, being thankful,
 Offered my charming mouth, chaste was the kiss we exchanged,
Then I asked you: Why so serious? If I'm a failure,
 Tell me, father, I pray, how to do better next time.
Nothing I'll grudge you, gladly rehearse for you, over and over,
 Each and every part, follow your lessons and leads.
But you held me firm in your arms and hugged me more tightly,
 And in my bosom I felt trembling the throb of my heart.
No, my charmingest child, you answered me, people tomorrow—
 Show to them all you have shown, just as you showed it today.
Move them all, as me you have moved, and they will respond with
 Even the driest of eyes weeping their tears of applause.
None will be struck more deeply, yet, than the friend, whom
 corpses
 Horrified once in the past, holding you now in his arms.
Nature, ah, how certain and grand in all things appearing:
 Heaven and Earth must obey firm and immutable laws.
One year follows another, the summer extending to springtime,
 Winter to fullness of fall, a confident helping hand.
Masses of rock stand their ground, and the waters eternal
 Gush from the cloudy cleft, foaming and thundering down.
Firs are green and unleafed bushes, even in winter,
 Tend clandestine buds, ready to sprout from their twigs.
Everything comes to be and perishes lawfully, only
 Human delectable life suffers a wavering fate.
Not to the son who is reaching the flower of youth does a father
 Nod from the brink of the grave, willing to die as he must.
It is not always the young who shut the eyes of the old folk,
 Eyes that are willing to close, frailty yielding to strength.
Fate will reverse, more often, the sequence of days, and a person
 Full of his years must lament children and grandchildren dead,
Stand like a stricken bole, the broken branches around him
 Scattered on every side, ripped by the torrents of hail.

Und so, liebliches Kind, durchdrang mich die tiefe Betrachtung,
 Als du, zur Leiche verstellt, über die Arme mir hingst;
Aber freudig seh ich dich mir in dem Glanze der Jugend,
 Vielgeliebtes Geschöpf, wieder am Herzen belebt.
Springe fröhlich dahin, verstellter Knabe! Das Mädchen
 Wächst zur Freude der Welt, mir zum Entzücken heran.
Immer strebe so fort, und deine natürlichen Gaben
 Bilde, bei jeglichem Schritt steigenden Lebens, die Kunst.
Sei mir lange zur Lust, und eh mein Auge sich schließet,
 Wünsch ich dein schönes Talent glücklich vollendet zu sehn.—
Also sprachst du, und nie vergaß ich der wichtigen Stunde!
 Deutend entwickelt ich mich an dem erhabenen Wort.
O wie sprach ich so gerne zum Volk die rührenden Reden,
 Die du, voller Gehalt, kindlichen Lippen vertraut!
O wie bildet ich mich an deinen Augen, und suchte
 Dich im tiefen Gedräng staunender Hörer heraus!
Doch dort wirst du nun sein, und sitzen, und nimmer bewegt sich
 Euphrosyne hervor, dir zu erheitern den Blick.
Du vernimmst sie nicht mehr, die Töne des wachsenden Zöglings,
 Die du zu liebendem Schmerz frühe, so frühe! gestimmt.
Andere kommen und gehn; es werden dir andre gefallen,
 Selbst dem großen Talent drängt sich ein größeres nach.
Aber du, vergesse mich nicht! Wenn eine dir jemals
 Sich im verworrnen Geschäft heiter entgegen bewegt,
Deinem Winke sich fügt, an deinem Lächeln sich freuet
 Und am Platze sich nur, den du bestimmtest, gefällt,
Wenn sie Mühe nicht spart noch Fleiß, wenn tätig der Kräfte,
 Selbst bis zur Pforte des Grabs, freudiges Opfer sie bringt—
Dann gedenkest du mein, du Guter! und rufest auch spät noch:
 Euphrosyne, sie ist wieder erstanden vor mir!
Vieles sagt ich noch gern; doch ach! die Scheidende weilt nicht,
 Wie sie wollte; mich führt streng ein gebietender Gott.
Lebe wohl! schon zieht michs dahin in schwankendem Eilen.
 Einen Wunsch nur vernimm, freundlich gewähre mir ihn:
Laß nicht ungerühmt mich zu den Schatten hinabgehn!
 Nur die Muse gewährt einiges Leben dem Tod.
Denn gestaltlos schweben umher in Persephoneias
 Reiche, massenweis, Schatten vom Namen getrennt;
Wen der Dichter aber gerühmt, der wandelt, gestaltet,
 Einzeln, gesellet dem Chor aller Heroen sich zu.
Freudig tret ich einher, von deinem Liede verkündet,
 Und der Göttin Blick weilet gefällig auf mir.

Such were the thoughts, my beautiful child, that bore down upon
 me,
 When as a corpse you hung feigning a death in my arms.
But what a joy to see you again, in the glow of your girlhood,
 Creature I love very much, close to my heart and revived.
Off with you now, and be glad, little boy in disguise! For the
 girl will
 Grow to enrapture the world, captivating me quite!
Strive as you strove today; and, as for your natural talent,
 Climbing the ladder of life may it be modelled by art.
Be my delight for years to come, may your beautiful gift be
 Perfect before my eyes finally close on the world.—
Those were your words, an important moment, I'll never forget it,
 Later I grew to be me, thanks to your speech so sublime.
O how I loved to address to people the stirring orations,
 Weighty with meaning, your words, placed on the lips of a child.
When you were watching, O how I grew, I was seeking you always
 Out in the public below, people entirely amazed.
Yet that is where you will be, you will stand there, and Euphrosyne,
 Never again will she step forward to brighten your glance.
You will not hear them again, the sounds of the voice of your pupil,
 Which you so early attuned, early, to passionate grief.
Others come and they go; for others will certainly please you.
 Even a talent that's great fades when a greater one comes.
But don't ever forget me. If anyone ever comes brightly
 Forward to meet you amid vague goings-on of the day,
Follows the signals you give and basks in the smile of your favour,
 Never desiring a place other than that you appoint,
Sparing herself not at all, but working, actively, gladly
 Sacrificing her all, up to the gate of the grave—
Friend, be mindful of me, I ask you, say, sooner or later,
 Euphrosyne again! Back to me she has come!
Much besides I would like to say; but a spirit departing
 Cannot stop as she will; strictly I'm led by a god.
Fare thee well! I am hurried away by a vague commotion.
 Listen, I have one wish: kindly grant it, my friend:
Let me not go down unmagnified into the shadows!
 Only the Muse can endow death with an inkling of life.
For there are floating, in the domain of Persephoneia,
 Multitudes without shape, shadows bereft of all name;
Whomsoever the poet will praise, though, walks with a difference,
 Has an identity, formed, joins in the heroes' choir.
Joy will be winging my step, if a song from you has announced me,
 Gracious upon me will rest, also, the goddess's gaze.

Mild empfängt sie mich dann, und nennt mich; es winken die hohen
 Göttlichen Frauen mich an, immer die nächsten am Thron.
Penelopeia redet zu mir, die treuste der Weiber,
 Auch Euadne, gelehnt auf den geliebten Gemahl.
Jüngere nahen sich dann, zu früh herunter gesandte,
 Und beklagen mit mir unser gemeines Geschick.
Wenn Antigone kommt, die schwesterlichste der Seelen,
 Und Polyxena, trüb noch von dem bräutlichen Tod,
Seh ich als Schwestern sie an und trete würdig zu ihnen;
 Denn der tragischen Kunst holde Geschöpfe sind sie.
Bildete doch ein Dichter auch mich; und seine Gesänge,
 Ja, sie vollenden an mir, was mir das Leben versagt.» —
Also sprach sie, und noch bewegte der liebliche Mund sich,
 Weiter zu reden; allein schwirrend versagte der Ton.
Denn aus dem Purpurgewölk, dem schwebenden, immer bewegten,
 Trat der herrliche Gott Hermes gelassen hervor;
Mild erhob er den Stab und deutete; wallend verschlangen
 Wachsende Wolken, im Zug, beide Gestalten vor mir.
Tiefer liegt die Nacht um mich her; die stürzenden Wasser
 Brausen gewaltiger nun neben dem schlüpfrigen Pfad.
Unbezwingliche Trauer befällt mich, entkräftender Jammer,
 Und ein moosiger Fels stützet den Sinkenden nur.
Wehmut reißt durch die Saiten der Brust, die nächtlichen Tränen
 Fließen; und über dem Wald kündet der Morgen sich an.

Die Musageten

Oft in tiefen Winternächten
Rief ich an die holden Musen:
Keine Morgenröte leuchtet,
Und es will kein Tag erscheinen;
Aber bringt zur rechten Stunde
Mir der Lampe fromm Geleuchte,
Daß es, statt Auror und Phöbus,
Meinen stillen Fleiß belebe!
Doch sie ließen mich im Schlafe,
Dumpf und unerquicklich, liegen,
Und nach jedem späten Morgen
Folgten ungenutzte Tage.

Then she'll receive me with clemency, speaking my name, and the
 others,
 Goddesses, close to the throne, lofty women, will wave.
That most loyal of women, Penelope, she will address me,
 Also Euadne, who clings close to the husband she loves.
Later the others will come who were sent below prematurely,
 Near me there will be girls, grieving with me for our fate.
When Antigone comes, of all the souls most like a sister,
 Also Polýxena, still dark with her death as a bride,
I shall be seeing them all as sisters, joining their number,
 For of the tragical art delicate creatures they are.
Me, too, shaped I was by a poet, and some of his poems,
 Yes, for me, will complete moments denied me in life."—
Thus did she speak and still with her sweet lips open and moving,
 Making as if to speak, only a whirring I heard.
For from the purple cloud as it floated, always in motion,
 Imperturbable strode Hermes the glorious god.
Gently he lifted his staff and pointed: billowing vapours
 Waxed more dense, and the two—swallowed up into them, gone.
Night more darkly presses around me, tumultuous waters
 Thunder now more loud, flanking the slippery path.
Stricken I am, with a sorrow unbearable, shocked with the pity,
 Weak, I lean on a rock, feeling the moss with a hand.
Misery sweeps the strings of my heart, a dark weeping
 Flows; and over the trees comes a first shimmer of dawn.

The Musagetes (1798)

Often in deep nights of winter
I'd be calling to the Muses:
"Dawn the sky does not illumine,
Still there is no hint of daylight;
When the moment is propitious
Bring me, yet, the helping lantern;
If not Phoebus and Aurora,
It may brace my quiet labours."
But they left me in my slumber
Dully sunk and deeply torpid,
And on days beginning lateish
Days ensued that all were wasted.

Da sich nun der Frühling regte,
Sagt ich zu den Nachtigallen:
Liebe Nachtigallen, schlaget
Früh, o früh! vor meinem Fenster,
Weckt mich aus dem vollen Schlafe,
Der den Jüngling mächtig fesselt.
Doch die lieberfüllten Sänger
Dehnten nachts vor meinem Fenster
Ihre süßen Melodien,
Hielten wach die liebe Seele,
Regten zartes neues Sehnen
Aus dem neugerührten Busen.
Und so ging die Nacht vorüber,
Und Aurora fand mich schlafen,
Ja, mich weckte kaum die Sonne.

Endlich ist es Sommer worden,
Und beim ersten Morgenschimmer
Reizt mich aus dem holden Schlummer
Die geschäftig frühe Fliege.
Unbarmherzig kehrt sie wieder,
Wenn auch oft der halb Erwachte
Ungeduldig sie verscheuchet,
Lockt die unverschämten Schwestern,
Und von meinen Augenlidern
Muß der holde Schlaf entweichen.
Rüstig spring ich von dem Lager,
Suche die geliebten Musen,
Finde sie im Buchenhaine,
Mich gefällig zu empfangen,
Und den leidigen Insekten
Dank ich manche goldne Stunde.
Seid mir doch, ihr Unbequemen,
Von dem Dichter hochgepriesen
Als die wahren Musageten.

In the early stir of Springtime
Then to nightingales I pleaded:
"Nightingales, my dears, be singing
Early, early at my window.
Wake this young man from the slumber
Which entangles him entirely."
But all night, those amorous singers,
They deployed before my window
Melodies and songs the sweetest,
Kept the dear soul very wakeful,
Drew a new and tender longing
Out of newly roused emotions.
And so then the night went by me,
And Aurora found me sleeping,
Yes, the sun could hardly wake me.

Now at last is come the summer,
And with light of dawn beginning
I am tickled from my slumber
By a fly that's up and busy.
She returns, quite mercilessly,
Even if, but half awakened,
With impatience I dismiss her,
Brings along outrageous sisters,
And the sleep that was delightful,
Off my eyelids it is lifted.
Out of bed I leap, all buoyant,
Look for the belovèd Muses,
Find them in among the beech trees,
Ready for me and compliant.
And I owe to those vexatious
Insects many a golden moment:
Let the poet, agitators,
Honour now and celebrate you,
Bonafide Musagetes.

Parabase

Freudig war, vor vielen Jahren,
Eifrig so der Geist bestrebt,
Zu erforschen, zu erfahren,
Wie Natur im Schaffen lebt.
Und es ist das ewig Eine,
Das sich vielfach offenbart:
Klein das Große, groß das Kleine,
Alles nach der eignen Art;
Immer wechselnd, fest sich haltend,
Nah und fern und fern und nah,
So gestaltend, umgestaltend—
Zum Erstaunen bin ich da.

Die Metamorphose der Pflanzen

Dich verwirret, Geliebte, die tausendfältige Mischung
 Dieses Blumengewühls über dem Garten umher;
Viele Namen hörest du an, und immer verdränget
 Mit barbarischem Klang einer den andern im Ohr.
Alle Gestalten sind ähnlich, und keine gleichet der andern;
 Und so deutet das Chor auf ein geheimes Gesetz,
Auf ein heiliges Rätsel. O könnt ich dir, liebliche Freundin,
 Überliefern sogleich glücklich das lösende Wort!—
Werdend betrachte sie nun, wie nach und nach sich die Pflanze,
 Stufenweise geführt, bildet zu Blüten und Frucht.
Aus dem Samen entwickelt sie sich, sobald ihn der Erde
 Stille befruchtender Schoß hold in das Leben entläßt
Und dem Reize des Lichts, des heiligen, ewig bewegten,
 Gleich den zärtesten Bau keimender Blätter empfiehlt.
Einfach schlief in dem Samen die Kraft; ein beginnendes Vorbild
 Lag, verschlossen in sich, unter die Hülle gebeugt,
Blatt und Wurzel und Keim, nur halb geformet und farblos;
 Trocken erhält so der Kern ruhiges Leben bewahrt,
Quillet strebend empor, sich milder Feuchte vertrauend,
 Und erhebt sich sogleich aus der umgebenden Nacht.
Aber einfach bleibt die Gestalt der ersten Erscheinung,
 Und so bezeichnet sich auch unter den Pflanzen das Kind.

Parabasis (c. 1820)

Years ago the mind with pleasure
Keenly could investigate,
Could experience the measure
Nature lives by to create.
And it is the One Eternal
Multiply self-manifest:
Small the big is, big the small,
All things to their type attest.
Self-insistent, always changing,
Near and far and far and near,
Birth of shapes, their rearranging—
Wonder of wonders, I am here.

The Metamorphosis of Plants (1798)

Overwhelming, beloved, you find all this mixture of thousands,
 Riot of flowers let loose over the garden's expanse;
Many names you take in, and always the last to be spoken
 Drives out the one heard before, barbarous both to your ear.
All the shapes are akin and none is quite like the other;
 So to a secret law surely that chorus must point,
To a sacred enigma. Dear friend, how I wish I were able
 All at once to pass on, happy, the word that unlocks!
Growing consider the plant and see how by gradual phases,
 Slowly evolved, it forms, rises to blossom and fruit.
From the seed it develops as soon as the quietly fertile
 Womb of earth sends it out, sweetly released into life,
And to the prompting of light, the holy, for ever in motion,
 Like the burgeoning leaves' tenderest build, hands it on.
Single, dormant the power in the seed was; the germ of an image,
 Closed in itself, lay concealed, prototype curled in the husk,
Leaf and root and bud, although colourless yet, half-amorphous;
 Drily the nucleus so safeguards incipient life,
Then, aspiring, springs up, entrusting itself to mild moisture,
 Speedily raises itself out of encompassing night.
Single, simple, however, remains the first visible structure;
 So that what first appears, even in plants, is the child.

Gleich darauf ein folgender Trieb, sich erhebend, erneuet,
 Knoten auf Knoten getürmt, immer das erste Gebild.
Zwar nicht immer das gleiche; denn mannigfaltig erzeugt sich,
 Ausgebildet, du siehsts, immer das folgende Blatt,
Ausgedehnter, gekerbter, getrennter in Spitzen und Teile,
 Die verwachsen vorher ruhten im untern Organ.
Und so erreicht es zuerst die höchst bestimmte Vollendung,
 Die bei manchem Geschlecht dich zum Erstaunen bewegt.
Viel gerippt und gezackt, auf mastig strotzender Fläche,
 Scheinet die Fülle des Triebs frei und unendlich zu sein.
Doch hier hält die Natur, mit mächtigen Händen, die Bildung
 An und lenket sie sanft in das Vollkommnere hin.
Mäßiger leitet sie nun den Saft, verengt die Gefäße,
 Und gleich zeigt die Gestalt zärtere Wirkungen an.
Stille zieht sich der Trieb der strebenden Ränder zurücke,
 Und die Rippe des Stiels bildet sich völliger aus.
Blattlos aber und schnell erhebt sich der zärtere Stengel,
 Und ein Wundergebild zieht den Betrachtenden an.
Rings im Kreise stellet sich nun, gezählet und ohne
 Zahl, das kleinere Blatt neben dem ähnlichen hin.
Um die Achse gedrängt entscheidet der bergende Kelch sich,
 Der zur höchsten Gestalt farbige Kronen entläßt.
Also prangt die Natur in hoher, voller Erscheinung,
 Und sie zeiget, gereiht, Glieder an Glieder gestuft.
Immer staunst du aufs neue, sobald sich am Stengel die Blume
 Über dem schlanken Gerüst wechselnder Blätter bewegt.
Aber die Herrlichkeit wird des neuen Schaffens Verkündung.
 Ja, das farbige Blatt fühlet die göttliche Hand,
Und zusammen zieht es sich schnell; die zärtesten Formen,
 Zwiefach streben sie vor, sich zu vereinen bestimmt.
Traulich stehen sie nun, die holden Paare, beisammen,
 Zahlreich ordnen sie sich um den geweihten Altar.
Hymen schwebet herbei, und herrliche Düfte, gewaltig,
 Strömen süßen Geruch, alles belebend, umher.
Nun vereinzelt schwellen sogleich unzählige Keime,
 Hold in den Mutterschoß schwellender Früchte gehüllt.
Und hier schließt die Natur den Ring der ewigen Kräfte;
 Doch ein neuer sogleich fasset den vorigen an,
Daß die Kette sich fort durch alle Zeiten verlänge,
 Und das Ganze belebt, so wie das Einzelne, sei.
Nun, Geliebte, wende den Blick zum bunten Gewimmel,
 Das verwirrend nicht mehr sich vor dem Geiste bewegt.
Jede Pflanze verkündet dir nun die ewgen Gesetze,
 Jede Blume, sie spricht lauter und lauter mit dir.

Following, rising at once, with one nodule piled on another,
 Always the second renews only the shape of the first.
Not the same, though, for ever; for manifold—you can observe it—
 Mutably fashioned each leaf after the last one unfolds,
More extended, spikier, split into lances or segments
 Which, intergrown before, lay in the organ below.
Only now it attains the complete intended perfection
 Which, in many a kind, moves you to wonder, admire.
Many-jagged and ribbed, on a lusciously, fully fleshed surface,
 Growth so lavishly fed seems without limit and free.
Forcefully here, however, will Nature step in to contain it,
 Curbing rankness here, gently perfecting the shapes.
Now more slowly the sap she conducts, and constricts the vessels,
 And at once the form yields, with diminished effects.
Calmly the outward thrust of the spreading leaf-rims recedes now,
 While, more firmly defined, swells the thin rib of the stalks.
Leafless, though, and swift the more delicate stem rises up now,
 And, a miracle wrought, catches the onlooker's eye.
In a circular cluster, all counted and yet without number,
 Smaller leaves take their place, next to a similar leaf.
Pushed close up to the hub now, the harbouring calyx develops
 Which to the highest of forms rises in colourful crowns.
Thus in fulness of being does Nature now glory, resplendent,
 Limb to limb having joined, all her gradations displayed.
Time after time you wonder as soon as the stalk-crowning blossom
 Sways on its slender support, gamut of mutable leaves.
Yet the splendour becomes an announcement of further creation.
 Yes, to the hand that's divine colourful leaves will respond.
And it quickly furls, contracts; the most delicate structures
 Twofold venture forth, destined to meet and unite.
Wedded now they stand, those delighted couples, together.
 Round the high altar they form multiple, ordered arrays.
Hymen, hovering, nears, and pungent perfumes, exquisite,
 Fill with fragrance and life all the environing air.
One by one now, though numberless, germs are impelled into
 swelling,
 Sweetly wrapped in the womb, likewise swelling, of fruit.
Nature here closes her ring of the energies never-exhausted
 Yet a new one at once links to the circle that's closed,
That the chain may extend into the ages for ever,
 And the whole be infused amply with life, like the part.
Look, beloved, once more on the teeming of so many colours,
 Which no longer may now fill with confusion your mind.
Every plant now declares those eternal designs that have shaped it,
 Ever more clearly to you every flower-head can speak.

Aber entzifferst du hier der Göttin heilige Lettern,
　　Überall siehst du sie dann, auch in verändertem Zug.
Kriechend zaudre die Raupe, der Schmetterling eile geschäftig,
　　Bildsam ändre der Mensch selbst die bestimmte Gestalt.
O, gedenke denn auch, wie aus dem Keim der Bekanntschaft
　　Nach und nach in uns holde Gewohnheit entsproß,
Freundschaft sich mit Macht in unserm Innern enthüllte,
　　Und wie Amor zuletzt Blüten und Früchte gezeugt.
Denke, wie mannigfach bald diese, bald jene Gestalten,
　　Still entfaltend, Natur unsern Gefühlen geliehn!
Freue dich auch des heutigen Tags! Die heilige Liebe
　　Strebt zu der höchsten Frucht gleicher Gesinnungen auf,
Gleicher Ansicht der Dinge, damit in harmonischem Anschaun
　　Sich verbinde das Paar, finde die höhere Welt.

Epirrhema

Müsset im Naturbetrachten
Immer eins wie alles achten:
Nichts ist drinnen, nichts ist draußen;
Denn was innen, das ist außen.
So ergreifet ohne Säumnis
Heilig öffentlich Geheimnis.

Freuet euch des wahren Scheins,
Euch des ernsten Spieles:
Kein Lebendiges ist ein Eins,
Immer ists ein Vieles.

Yet if here you decipher the holy runes of the goddess,
 Everywhere you can read, even though scripts are diverse:
Let the grub drag along, the butterfly busily scurry,
 Imaging man by himself alter the pre-imposed shape.
Oh, and consider then how in us from the germ of acquaintance
 Stage by stage there grew, dear to us, habit's long grace,
Friendship from deep within us burst out of its wrapping,
 And how Amor at last blessed it with blossom and fruit.
Think how variously Nature, the quietly forming, unfolding,
 Lent to our feelings now this, now that so different mode!
Also rejoice in this day. Because love, our holiest blessing
 Looks for the consummate fruit, marriage of minds, in the end,
One perception of things, that together, concerted in seeing,
 Both to the higher world, truly conjoined, find their way.

Epirrhema (c. 1819)

You must, when contemplating nature,
Attend to this, in each and every feature:
There's nought outside and nought within,
For she is inside out and outside in.
Thus will you grasp, with no delay,
The holy secret, clear as day.

Joy in true semblance take, in any
Earnest play:
No living thing is One, I say,
But always Many.

Metamorphose der Tiere

Wagt ihr, also bereitet, die letzte Stufe zu steigen
Dieses Gipfels, so reicht mir die Hand und öffnet den freien
Blick ins weite Feld der Natur. Sie spendet die reichen
Lebensgaben umher, die Göttin; aber empfindet
Keine Sorge wie sterbliche Fraun um ihrer Gebornen
Sichere Nahrung; ihr ziemet es nicht: denn zwiefach bestimmte
Sie das höchste Gesetz, beschränkte jegliches Leben,
Gab ihm gemeßnes Bedürfnis, und ungemessene Gaben,
Leicht zu finden, streute sie aus, und ruhig begünstigt
Sie das muntre Bemühn der vielfach bedürftigen Kinder;
Unerzogen schwärmen sie fort nach ihrer Bestimmung.

Zweck sein selbst ist jegliches Tier, vollkommen entspringt es
Aus dem Schoß der Natur und zeugt vollkommene Kinder.
Alle Glieder bilden sich aus nach ewgen Gesetzen,
Und die seltenste Form bewahrt im geheimen das Urbild.
So ist jeglicher Mund geschickt, die Speise zu fassen,
Welche dem Körper gebührt; es sei nun schwächlich und zahnlos
Oder mächtig der Kiefer gezahnt, in jeglichem Falle
Fördert ein schicklich Organ den übrigen Gliedern die Nahrung.
Auch bewegt sich jeglicher Fuß, der lange, der kurze,
Ganz harmonisch zum Sinne des Tiers und seinem Bedürfnis.

So ist jedem der Kinder die volle, reine Gesundheit
Von der Mutter bestimmt: denn alle lebendigen Glieder
Widersprechen sich nie und wirken alle zum Leben.
Also bestimmt die Gestalt die Lebensweise des Tieres,
Und die Weise, zu leben, sie wirkt auf alle Gestalten
Mächtig zurück. So zeiget sich fest die geordnete Bildung,
Welche zum Wechsel sich neigt durch äußerlich wirkende Wesen.
Doch im Innern befindet die Kraft der edlern Geschöpfe
Sich im heiligen Kreise lebendiger Bildung beschlossen.
Diese Grenzen erweitert kein Gott, es ehrt die Natur sie:
Denn nur also beschränkt war je das Vollkommene möglich.

Doch im Inneren scheint ein Geist gewaltig zu ringen,
Wie er durchbräche den Kreis, Willkür zu schaffen den Formen
Wie dem Wollen; doch was er beginnt, beginnt er vergebens.
Denn zwar drängt er sich vor zu diesen Gliedern, zu jenen,
Stattet mächtig sie aus, jedoch schon darben dagegen
Andere Glieder, die Last des Übergewichtes vernichtet

Metamorphosis of Animals (1806)

Now if your mind is prepared to venture upon the final
Step to this summit, give me your hand and view with an open
Gaze the abundance of Nature before you. Everywhere richly
Gifts she has lavished around, the Goddess, but never she worries
After the manner of mortal women, regarding the nurture
Offspring need in a steady supply, that isn't her wont, for
Doubly she has determined the ultimate law: with a limit,
Set to each life and need in its measure, and then without measure
Gifts she has scattered, easy to find, and she quietly favours
Motley toils for her children, seeing their needs are so many;
So they will flock and yearn, untrained, for the ends that are set
<div align="right">them.</div>

Every animal *is* an end in itself, it issues
Perfect from Nature's womb and its offspring are equally perfect.
All its organs are formed according to laws that are timeless,
Even a form very rare will hold to its type, though in secret.
Every mouth is designed to admit particular foodstuffs,
Such as befit the body; an animal feeble and toothless,
One with jaws that are toothed and massive—a suitable organ
Each will possess for channelling food to the rest of its body.
Also the feet, whether long or short, will always be moving
Tuned to the animal's every need and every intention.

Thus has the Mother ordained the health complete and unbroken
Each of her children enjoys, and the limbs of each, being vital,
Never conflicting the one with the other, have life as their function.
So the shape of an animal patterns its manner of living,
Likewise their manner of living, again, exerts on the animals'
Shapes a massive effect: all organized structures are solid,
Thus, which are prone to change under pressure from outward
<div align="right">conditions.</div>
Deep within the more noble creatures, indeed, a power
Dwells enclosed in the holy ring of vital formation.
Here are the limits no god can alter, honoured by Nature:
Only a limit enables a form to rise to perfection.

Deep within, however, a spirit may seem to be wrestling:
How shall he rupture the ring and cause the forms to be random,
Random the will? Yet all his efforts, they come to nothing;
For, if he burrows his way right through to this organ or that one,
Making it grander by far, then other organs will dwindle,
Disproportionate weight and excess of it quickly destroying

Alle Schöne der Form und alle reine Bewegung.
Siehst du also dem einen Geschöpf besonderen Vorzug
Irgend gegönnt, so frage nur gleich: wo leidet es etwa
Mangel anderswo? und suche mit forschendem Geiste;
Finden wirst du sogleich zu aller Bildung den Schlüssel.

Denn so hat kein Tier, dem sämtliche Zähne den obern
Kiefer umzäunen, ein Horn auf seiner Stirne getragen,
Und daher ist den Löwen gehörnt der ewigen Mutter
Ganz unmöglich zu bilden, und böte sie alle Gewalt auf;
Denn sie hat nicht Masse genug, die Reihen der Zähne
Völlig zu pflanzen und auch Geweih und Hörner zu treiben.

Dieser schöne Begriff von Macht und Schranken, von Willkür
Und Gesetz, von Freiheit und Maß, von beweglicher Ordnung,
Vorzug und Mangel erfreue dich hoch; die heilige Muse
Bringt harmonisch ihn dir, mit sanftem Zwange belehrend.
Keinen höhern Begriff erringt der sittliche Denker,
Keinen der tätige Mann, der dichtende Künstler; der Herrscher,
Der verdient, es zu sein, erfreut nur durch ihn sich der Krone.
Freue dich, höchstes Geschöpf der Natur, du fühlest dich fähig,
Ihr den höchsten Gedanken, zu dem sie schaffend sich aufschwang,
Nachzudenken. Hier stehe nun still und wende die Blicke
Rückwärts, prüfe, vergleiche, und nimm vom Munde der Muse,
Daß du schauest, nicht schwärmst, die liebliche, volle Gewißheit.

Antepirrhema

So schauet mit bescheidnem Blick
Der ewigen Weberin Meisterstück,
Wie *ein* Tritt tausend Fäden regt,
Die Schifflein hinüber herüber schießen,
Die Fäden sich begegnend fließen,
Ein Schlag tausend Verbindungen schlägt!
Das hat sie nicht zusammengebettelt,
Sie hats von Ewigkeit angezettelt;
Damit der ewige Meistermann
Getrost den Einschlag werfen kann.

All the beauty of form and all pure litheness of movement.
So if you see that a creature possesses a certain advantage,
Put the question at once: What is the fault that afflicts it
Elsewhere?—and seek to discover the defect, always inquiring;
Then at once you will find the key to the world of formation.

For there has never existed an animal into whose jawbone
Teeth are pegged that had a horn sprout out of its forehead;
Therefore a lion with a horn the Eternal Mother could never
Possibly make, though she drew on all her potent resources;
For she has not measures sufficient to plant in a being
Rows of teeth, complete, together with horns or with antlers.

May this beautiful concept of power and limit, of random
Venture and law, freedom and measure, of order in motion,
Defect and benefit, bring you high pleasure; gently instructive,
Thus, the sacred Muse in her teaching tells you of harmonies.
Moral philosophers never attained to a concept sublimer,
Nor did men of affairs, nor artists imagining; rulers,
Worthy of power, enjoy their crowns on this account only.
So be glad of it, Nature's loftiest creature, now feeling
Able to follow her loftiest thought on her wings of Creation.
Stand where you are, be still, and looking behind you, backward,
All things consider, compare, and take from the lips of the Muse
 then,
So that you'll see, not dream it, a truth that is sweet and is certain.

Antepirrhema (c. 1819)

Thus view with unassuming eyes
The Weaver Woman's masterpiece:
One pedal shifts a thousand strands,
The shuttles back and forward flying,
Each fluent strand with each complying,
One stroke a thousand links commands;
No patchwork, this, of rag and tatter,
Since time began She plots the matter,
So may the Master, very deft,
Insert with confidence the weft.

Spiegel der Muse

Sich zu schmücken begierig, verfolgte den rinnenden Bach einst
Früh die Muse hinab, sie suchte die ruhigste Stelle.
Eilend und rauschend indes verzog die schwankende Fläche
Stets das bewegliche Bild; die Göttin wandte sich zürnend;
Doch der Bach rief hinter ihr drein und höhnte sie: Freilich
Magst du die Wahrheit nicht sehn, wie rein dir mein Spiegel sie
zeiget!
Aber indessen stand sie schon fern, am Winkel des Seees,
Ihrer Gestalt sich erfreuend, und rückte den Kranz sich zurechte.

Natur und Kunst

Natur und Kunst sie scheinen sich zu fliehen,
Und haben sich, eh man es denkt, gefunden;
Der Widerwille ist auch mir verschwunden,
Und beide scheinen gleich mich anzuziehen.

Es gilt wohl nur ein redliches Bemühen!
Und wenn wir erst in abgemeßnen Stunden
Mit Geist und Fleiß uns an die Kunst gebunden,
Mag frei Natur im Herzen wieder glühen.

So ist's mit aller Bildung auch beschaffen:
Vergebens werden ungebundne Geister
Nach der Vollendung reiner Höhe streben.

Wer Großes will, muß sich zusammenraffen;
In der Beschränkung zeigt sich erst der Meister,
Und das Gesetz nur kann uns Freiheit geben.

The Muse's Mirror (1799)

Early one day, the Muse, when eagerly bent on adornment,
Followed a swift-running streamlet, the quietest nook by it seeking.
Quickly and noisily flowing, the changeful surface distorted
Ever her moving form; the goddess departed in anger.
Yet the stream called mockingly after her, saying: "What, truly!
Wilt thou not view, then, the truth, in my mirror so clearly
depicted?"
But she already was far away, where the lakeshore was angled,
In her figure rejoicing, and duly arranging her garland.

Nature and Art (c. 1800; published 1807)

Nature, it seems, must always clash with Art,
And yet, before we know it, both are one;
I too have learned: Their enmity is none,
Since each compels me, and in equal part.

Hard, honest work counts most! And once we start
To measure out the hours and never shun
Art's daily labor till our task is done,
Freely again may Nature move the heart.

So too all growth and ripening of the mind:
To the pure heights of ultimate consummation
In vain the unbound spirit seeks to flee.

Who seeks great gain leaves easy gain behind.
None proves a master but by limitation
And only law can give us liberty.

Weltseele

Verteilet euch nach allen Regionen
Von diesem heilgen Schmaus!
Begeistert reißt euch durch die nächsten Zonen
Ins All und füllt es aus!

Schon schwebet ihr in ungemeßnen Fernen
Den selgen Göttertraum,
Und leuchtet neu, gesellig, unter Sternen
Im lichtbesäten Raum.

Dann treibt ihr euch, gewaltige Kometen,
Ins Weit und Weitr hinan;
Das Labyrinth der Sonnen und Planeten
Durchschneidet eure Bahn.

Ihr greifet rasch nach ungeformten Erden
Und wirket schöpfrisch jung,
Daß sie belebt und stets belebter werden
Im abgemeßnen Schwung.

Und kreisend führt ihr in bewegten Lüften
Den wandelbaren Flor
Und schreibt dem Stein in allen seinen Grüften
Die festen Formen vor.

Nun alles sich mit göttlichem Erkühnen
Zu übertreffen strebt;
Das Wasser will, das unfruchtbare, grünen,
Und jedes Stäubchen lebt.

Und so verdrängt mit liebevollem Streiten
Der feuchten Qualme Nacht;
Nun glühen schon des Paradieses Weiten
In überbunter Pracht.

Wie regt sich bald, ein holdes Licht zu schauen,
Gestaltenreiche Schar,
Und ihr erstaunt auf den beglückten Auen
Nun als das erste Paar,

Und bald verlischt ein unbegrenztes Streben
Im selgen Wechselblick.
Und so empfangt, mit Dank, das schönste Leben
Vom All ins All zurück.

Universal Soul (1801)

Go forth, now that this holy feast is done,
Into all regions of the world disperse;
Stop not in purlews with your inspiration,
Enter the All, make full the universe!

Vast distances already loft your flight;
Under the stars, together, as you race
You float the dream of gods, and you give light
In light-inseminated outer space.

Urge ever onward then, as mighty comets;
Your course will intersect, as on it runs,
Pressing against the far and farther limits,
The labyrinth of planets and of suns.

Young in your each creative act and bold,
On earths devoid of form, that more and more
Vivid they may become, quickly take hold
As you complete your measured curvature.

And in your orbits through the vibrant air
You guide of cloud the variable skeins;
In all its crypts prescribe to stone the share
Of those abiding forms that it contains.

With godlike courage all things come to mean
A self-surpassing, whither all must strive:
The fruitless water wishes to be green
And every particle of dust is live.

And so with loving contest you put paid
To night with its chaotic dismal dews;
The full expanse of paradise arrayed
Already glows, intense, with many hues.

Now how the crowd of creatures multiform
Is all astir, delicious light to see;
And on a happy meadow the firstborn
Couple you are, in wonder there to be.

And now the boundless striving flickers out,
Becomes the look that you exchange in bliss:
Thankful you turn this gift of life about—
Restored the universe within us is.

Dauer im Wechsel

Hielte diesen frühen Segen
Ach, nur Eine Stunde fest!
Aber vollen Blütenregen
Schüttelt schon der laue West.
Soll ich mich des Grünen freuen,
Dem ich Schatten erst verdankt?
Bald wird Sturm auch das zerstreuen,
Wenn es falb im Herbst geschwankt.

Willst du nach den Früchten greifen,
Eilig nimm dein Teil davon!
Diese fangen an zu reifen,
Und die andern keimen schon;
Gleich mit jedem Regengusse
Ändert sich dein holdes Tal,
Ach, und in demselben Flusse
Schwimmst du nicht zum zweitenmal.

Du nun selbst! Was felsenfeste
Sich vor dir hervorgetan,
Mauern siehst du, siehst Paläste
Stets mit andern Augen an.
Weggeschwunden ist die Lippe,
Die im Kusse sonst genas,
Jener Fuß, der an der Klippe
Sich mit Gemsenfreche maß,

Jene Hand, die gern und milde
Sich bewegte wohlzutun,
Das gegliederte Gebilde,
Alles ist ein andres nun.
Und was sich an jener Stelle
Nun mit deinem Namen nennt,
Kam herbei wie eine Welle,
Und so eilts zum Element.

Laß den Anfang mit dem Ende
Sich in Eins zusammenziehn!
Schneller als die Gegenstände
Selber dich vorüberfliehn.
Danke, daß die Gunst der Musen
Unvergängliches verheißt,
Den Gehalt in deinem Busen
Und die Form in deinem Geist.

Permanence in Change (1803)

Early blossoms—could a single
Hour preserve them just as now!
But the warmer west will scatter
Petals showering from the bough.
How enjoy these leaves, that lately
I was grateful to for shade?
Soon the wind and snow are rolling
What the late Novembers fade.

Fruit—you'd reach a hand and have it?
Better have it then with speed.
These you see about to ripen,
Those already gone to seed.
Half a rainy day, and there's your
Pleasant valley not the same,
None could swim that very river
Twice, so quick the changes came.

You yourself! What all around you
Strong as stonework used to lie
—Castles, battlements—you see them
With an ever-changing eye.
Now the lips are dim and withered
Once the kisses set aglow;
Lame the leg, that on the mountain
Left the mountain goat below.

Or that hand, that knew such loving
Ways, outstretching in caress,
—Cunningly adjusted structure—
Now can function less and less.
All are gone; this substitution
Has your name and nothing more.
Like a wave it lifts and passes,
Back to atoms on the shore.

See in each beginning, ending,
Double aspects of the One;
Here, amid stampeding objects,
Be among the first to run,
Thankful to a muse whose favor
Grants you one unchanging thing:
What the heart can hold to ponder;
What the spirit shape to sing.

Bergschloss

Da droben auf jenem Berge,
Da steht ein altes Schloß,
Wo hinter Toren und Türen
Sonst lauerten Ritter und Roß.

Verbrannt sind Türen und Tore,
Und überall ist es so still;
Das alte verfallne Gemäuer
Durchklettr ich, wie ich nur will.

Hierneben lag ein Keller,
So voll von köstlichem Wein;
Nun steiget nicht mehr mit Krügen
Die Kellnerin heiter hinein.

Sie setzt den Gästen im Saale
Nicht mehr die Becher umher,
Sie füllt zum Heiligen Mahle
Dem Pfaffen das Fläschchen nicht mehr.

Sie reicht dem lüsternen Knappen
Nicht mehr auf dem Gange den Trank,
Und nimmt für flüchtige Gabe
Nicht mehr den flüchtigen Dank.

Denn alle Balken und Decken,
Sie sind schon lange verbrannt,
Und Trepp und Gang und Kapelle
In Schutt und Trümmer verwandt.

Doch als mit Zither und Flasche
Nach diesen felsigen Höhn
Ich an dem heitersten Tage
Mein Liebchen steigen gesehn,

Da drängte sich frohes Behagen
Hervor aus verödeter Ruh,
Da gings wie in alten Tagen
Recht feierlich wieder zu.

Als wären für stattliche Gäste
Die weitesten Räume bereit,

Mountain Castle (1804)
(dedicated to Sylvie von Ziegesar)

There stands an ancient castle
On yonder mountain height,
And once within its portal
Were lurking horse and knight.

But gone is now the portal,
And all is hushed and still;
I clamber in the ruins
Of ramparts as I will.

Abundant wines and noble
Were cellared in this place,
The cellarer no more comes up
With flask and smiling face.

No more she sets the tankards
For guests who come to feast,
Nor does she fill, near time of Mass,
A bottle for the priest.

No longer in the hallway
Gives lusty squires their drinks,
No more for gifts so fleeting
Receives their fleeting thanks.

For every roof and rafter
Long years ago burned down,
And stair and hall and chapel
To dust and wreck are gone.

Yet when with flask and zither,
One day of clear sunlight,
I saw my love go up the slope
To reach that rocky height,

Sprung out of desolation
A zest on me took hold:
It seemed they were about us,
The festive days of old.

As if for splendid visitors
The largest rooms were spread,

Als käm ein Pärchen gegangen
Aus jener tüchtigen Zeit.

Als stünd in seiner Kapelle
Der würdige Pfaffe schon da
Und fragte: Wollt ihr einander?
Wir aber lächelten: Ja!

Und tief bewegten Gesänge
Des Herzens innigsten Grund,
Es zeugte, statt der Menge,
Der Echo schallender Mund.

Und als sich gegen den Abend
Im stillen alles verlor,
Da blickte die glühende Sonne
Zum schroffen Gipfel empor.

Und Knapp und Kellnerin glänzen
Als Herren weit und breit;
Sie nimmt sich zum Kredenzen
Und er zum Danke sich Zeit.

And from that solid age there came
A couple to be wed.

And standing in his chapel,
The worthy priest, he says:
Now take ye one another?
We smile and answer: Yes!

While every heart bore witness
Enraptured songs were sung—
Not by the congregation—
They flew from Echo's tongue.

When, with approach of nightfall
Extinguished, all was hushed,
The glowing sun glanced upward,
Across that peak it flashed:

Now squire and cellarer, shining
As masters through the land,
She takes the time to tilt a jug
And he a grateful hand.

Nachtgesang

O gib, vom weichen Pfühle,
Träumend, ein halb Gehör!
Bei meinem Saitenspiele
Schlafe! was willst du mehr?

Bei meinem Saitenspiele
Segnet der Sterne Heer
Die ewigen Gefühle;
Schlafe! was willst du mehr?

Die ewigen Gefühle
Heben mich, hoch und hehr,
Aus irdischem Gewühle;
Schlafe! was willst du mehr?

Vom irdischen Gewühle
Trennst du mich nur zu sehr,
Bannst mich in diese Kühle;
Schlafe! was willst du mehr!

Bannst mich in diese Kühle,
Gibst nur im Traum Gehör.
Ach, auf dem weichen Pfühle
Schlafe! was willst du mehr?

Freibeuter

Mein Haus hat kein Tür,
Mein Tür hat ke Haus;
Und immer mit Schätzel
Hinein und heraus.

Mei Küch hat ke Herd,
Mei Herd hat ke Küch;
Da bratets und siedets
Für sich und für mich.

Night Song (1804)

Pillowed so soft, dream on,
Half listen, I implore,
To this my zithersong,
Sleep, could you wish for more?

To this my zithersong
Is heart's eternal core
Blessed by the starry throng;
Sleep, could you wish for more?

Blessed by the starry throng,
Out of this world I soar
Endless desires among;
Sleep, could you wish for more?

Endless desires among—
Yet you have shut your door,
Cool is the night and long;
Sleep, could you wish for more?

Cool, ah, the night and long,
Only in dreams, on your
Pillow, you hear my song,
Sleep, could you wish for more?

Buccaneer (c. 1808; published 1827)
(Original in dialect)

My house has no door
My door has no house;
And always my sweetheart
She comes and she goes.

No fire in my kitchen,
No kitchen, you see;
But I fry up and boil for
My pleasure and me.

Mei Bett hat ke G'stell,
Mei G'stell hat ke Bett;
Doch wüßt ich nit enen,
Ders lustiger hett.

Mei Keller is hoch,
Mei Scheuer is tief;
Zuoberst zuunterst —
Da lag ich und schlief.

Und bin ich erwachen,
Da geht es so fort;
Mei Ort hat ke Bleibens,
Mein Bleibens ken Ort.

Mächtiges Überraschen

Ein Strom entrauscht umwölktem Felsensaale,
 Dem Ozean sich eilig zu verbinden;
 Was auch sich spiegeln mag von Grund zu Gründen,
 Er wandelt unaufhaltsam fort zu Tale.

Dämonisch aber stürzt mit einem Male —
 Ihr folgen Berg und Wald in Wirbelwinden —
 Sich Oreas, Behagen dort zu finden,
 Und hemmt den Lauf, begrenzt die weite Schale.

Die Welle sprüht, und staunt zurück und weichet,
 Und schwillt bergan, sich immer selbst zu trinken;
 Gehemmt ist nun zum Vater hin das Streben.

Sie schwankt und ruht, zum See zurückgedeichet;
 Gestirne, spiegelnd sich, beschaun das Blinken
 Des Wellenschlags am Fels, ein neues Leben.

My bed has no trestle
My trestle no bed;
But no man I know rests
A happier head.

My cellar is high,
My barn, it is deep;
All topsy and turvy
I lay down to sleep.

And sharpish, awaking,
I'm off at a pace;
At no place I'm stopping,
My stopping's no place.

Sonnet I: Immense Astonishment (1807–08)

A river from a cloud-wrapped chamber gone,
Of rock, and roaring to be one with ocean,
Much it reflects from deep to deep, its motion
Never relenting valleyward and on.

But with abrupt demoniacal force,
By forest, mountain, whirling wind pursued,
Oreas tumbles down into quietude,
And there she brims the bowl, impedes the course.

The wave breaks into spray, astonished, back
Uphill it washes, drinking itself always;
Its urge to join the Father hindered, too,

It rolls and rests, is dammed into a lake;
The constellations, mirrored, fix their gaze:
The flash of wave on rock, a life made new.

Abschied

War unersättlich nach viel tausend Küssen,
 Und mußt mit Einem Kuß am Ende scheiden.
 Nach herber Trennung tiefempfundnem Leiden
War mir das Ufer, dem ich mich entrissen,

Mit Wohnungen, mit Bergen, Hügeln, Flüssen,
 Solang ichs deutlich sah, ein Schatz der Freuden;
 Zuletzt im Blauen blieb ein Augenweiden
An fernentwichnen, lichten Finsternissen.

Und endlich, als das Meer den Blick umgrenzte,
 Fiel mir zurück ins Herz mein heiß Verlangen;
 Ich suchte mein Verlornes gar verdrossen.

Da war es gleich, als ob der Himmel glänzte;
 Mir schien, als wäre nichts mir, nichts entgangen,
 Als hätt ich alles, was ich je genossen.

~~~~~~~~~~~~~~

Wär nicht das Auge sonnenhaft,
Die Sonne könnt es nie erblicken;
Läg nicht in uns des Gottes eigne Kraft,
Wie könnt uns Göttliches entzücken?

# Sonnet VII: The Farewell (1807–08)

Craved for a thousand kisses, craved for more,
Had finally to say farewell, with one.
Bitter parting, pain felt to the bone,
Yet when I wrenched myself away, the shore

With dwellings, rivers, hill and mountain height
—It was a fund of joy, while I saw clear;
My vision, stopped in the blue hemisphere,
Lay on a dark withdrawn abode of light.

And as at last the ocean ringed my eye,
Back to the heart my hot desires fall;
I fret for what I lost that was my own.

Promptly a shining seemed to fill the sky,
As if—nothing had gone from me at all,
And mine were each and every joy I'd known.

# Something Like the Sun
## (from *Theory of Colours*, 1810)

Something like the sun the eye must be,
Else it no glint of sun could ever see;
Surely God's own powers with us unite,
Else godly things would not compel delight.

# Das Tagebuch

*—aliam tenui, sed iam quum gaudia adirem,*
*Admonuit dominae deseruitque Venus.*

Wir hören's oft und glauben's wohl am Ende:
Das Menschenherz sei ewig unergründlich,
Und wie man auch sich hin und wider wende,
So sei der Christe wie der Heide sündlich.
Das Beste bleibt, wir geben uns die Hände
Und nehmen's mit der Lehre nicht empfindlich;
Denn zeigt sich auch ein Dämon, uns versuchend,
So waltet was, gerettet ist die Tugend.

Von meiner Trauten lange Zeit entfernet,
Wie's öfters geht, nach irdischem Gewinne,
Und was ich auch gewonnen und gelernet,
So hatt ich doch nur immer Sie im Sinne;
Und wie zu Nacht der Himmel erst sich sternet,
Erinnrung uns umleuchtet ferner Minne:
So ward im Federzug des Tags Ereignis
Mit süßen Worten ihr ein freundlich Gleichnis.

Ich eilte nun zurück. Zerbrochen sollte
Mein Wagen mich noch eine Nacht verspäten;
Schon dacht ich mich, wie ich zu Hause rollte,
Allein da war Geduld und Werk vonnöten.
Und wie ich auch mit Schmied und Wagner tollte,
Sie hämmerten, verschmähten viel zu reden.
Ein jedes Handwerk hat nun seine Schnurren.
Was blieb mir nun? Zu weilen und zu murren.

So stand ich nun. Der Stern des nächsten Schildes
Berief mich hin, die Wohnung schien erträglich.
Ein Mädchen kam, des seltensten Gebildes,
Das Licht erleuchtend. Mir ward gleich behäglich.
Hausflur und Treppe sah ich als ein Mildes,
Die Zimmerchen erfreuten mich unsäglich.
Den sündigen Menschen der im Freien schwebet —
Die Schönheit spinnt, sie ist's die ihn umwebet.

Nun setzt ich mich zu meiner Tasch und Briefen
Und meines Tagebuchs Genauigkeiten,
Um so wie sonst, wenn alle Menschen schliefen,

# The Diary (1810)

We've heard and heard, and finally believe:
There's no enigma like the heart of man.
The things we do! No good to twist or weave—
We're human yet, in Rome as Turkestan.
What's my advice? Forget it. Maybe heave
One sigh, and then live with it if you can.
Also, when sins come nudging with that leer,
Count on some Sturdy Virtue to appear.

Once, when I left my love and had to travel
Off on affairs a traveling man transacts,
Collecting facts and figures to unravel
(Thinking of her, *her* figure and its facts),
As always, when the night spread, thick as gravel,
Its load of stars, my mind went starry. Stacks
Of paper (balanced on my solar plexus)
Told of the day, in mostly O's and X's.

Finally I'm rolling homeward, when—you'd know it!—
*Cru-ungk!* and the axle goes. So one less night
Back in the bed I'm dreaming of—but stow it!
There's work now. Cross your fingers and sit tight.
Two blacksmiths come. I'm grumpy, and I show it.
Shrugging, the one spits left, the other right.
"It'll be done when done," they grunt, and batter
*Whang!* at the wheel. Sparks flying. Clang and clatter.

Stuck in the sticks! With just an inn; The Star,
It says outside. Looks bearable. I'm glad
To see a girl with lantern there. So far
So good. She lifts it higher and—not bad!—
Beckons me in: nice lounge, a decent bar.
The bedroom's cozy as a travel ad.
Poor sinners! When they're wandering on the loose,
Nothing like pretty girls to jerk the noose.

I take the room, and shuffle papers out.
My diary—got to keep it up to date
The way I do just every night, about.

Mir und der Trauten Freude zu bereiten;
Doch weiß ich nicht, die Tintenworte liefen
Nicht so wie sonst in alle Kleinigkeiten:
Das Mädchen kam, des Abendessens Bürde
Verteilte sie gewandt mit Gruß und Würde.

Sie geht und kommt; ich spreche, sie erwidert;
Mit jedem Wort erscheint sie mir geschmückter.
Und wie sie leicht mir nun das Huhn zergliedert,
Bewegend Hand und Arm, geschickt, geschickter—
Was auch das tolle Zeug in uns befiedert—
Genug ich bin verworrner, bin verrückter,
Den Stuhl umwerfend spring ich auf und fasse
Das schöne Kind; sie lispelt: «Lasse, lasse!

Die Muhme drunten lauscht, ein alter Drache,
Sie zählt bedächtig des Geschäfts Minute;
Sie denkt sich unten, was ich oben mache,
Bei jedem Zögern schwenkt sie frisch die Rute.
Doch schließe deine Türe nicht und wache,
So kommt die Mitternacht uns wohl zu Gute.»
Rasch meinem Arm entwindet sie die Glieder,
Und eilet fort und kommt nur dienend wieder;

Doch blickend auch! So daß aus jedem Blicke
Sich himmlisches Versprechen mir entfaltet.
Den stillen Seufzer drängt sie nicht zurücke,
Der ihren Busen herrlicher gestaltet.
Ich sehe, daß am Ohr, um Hals und Gnicke
Der flüchtigen Röte Liebesblüte waltet,
Und da sie nichts zu leisten weiter findet,
Geht sie und zögert, sieht sich um, verschwindet.

Der Mitternacht gehören Haus und Straßen,
Mir ist ein weites Lager aufgebreitet,
Wovon den kleinsten Teil mir anzumaßen
Die Liebe rät, die alles wohl bereitet;
Ich zaudre noch, die Kerzen auszublasen,
Nun hör ich sie, wie leise sie auch gleitet,
Mit gierigem Blick die Hochgestalt umschweif ich,
Sie senkt sich her, die Wohlgestalt ergreif ich.

Sie macht sich los: «Vergönne daß ich rede,
Damit ich dir nicht völlig fremd gehöre.
Der Schein ist wider mich, sonst war ich blöde,

I like to write; my darling says I'm great.
But now, though, nothing comes. Some writer's gout?
I seem distracted, somehow. Better wait.
That girl again. She lays the table first,
Hands deft and cool. Nice manners. I'm immersed

In studying her skirt, flung out and in.
I ask. She knows the answers. That's my girl!
Can she disjoint a chicken! Flick the skin!
Those arms! And hands with fingertips in pearl!
I feel that certain stirring-up begin
And dizzy with her, crazy for—I hurl
The chair away; impulsively I twist her
Into my arms, close, closer. "Listen, mister,

Cool it," she cuddles murmuring. "My aunt,
Old hatchet face, is listening all the time.
She's down there guessing what I can or can't
Be up to every minute. Next she'll climb
Up with that cane of hers, sniff, snuffle, pant!
But look, don't lock your door. At midnight I'm
More on my own—" Untwisting (it's delicious!)
She hurries out. And hurries back with dishes.

Dishes—and warmer eyes. I'm in a blur.
The heavens open and the angels sing.
She sighs, and every sigh looks good on her:
It makes the heaving breast a pretty thing.
She loves me, I can tell: Such colors stir
Deeper on neck and ear—she crimsoning!
Then sad, "Well, dinner's over, I suppose."
She goes. She doesn't want to, but she goes.

The chimes at midnight on the sleeping town!
My double bed looks wider by the minute.
"Leave half for her. That's friendlier, you clown!"
I say, and squiggle over. To begin it,
We'll leave the candles lit, I plan—when down
The hall a rustle! Slinky silk—she's in it!
My eyes devour that fully blossomed flesh.
She settles by me and our fingers mesh.

Then sweet and low: "First tell me once or twice
You love me as a person? Say you do.
As girls around here go, I'm rather nice.

Stets gegen Männer setzt ich mich zur Wehre.
Mich nennt die Stadt, mich nennt die Gegend spröde;
Nun aber weiß ich, wie das Herz sich kehre:
Du bist mein Sieger, laß dich's nicht verdrießen,
Ich sah, ich liebte, schwur dich zu genießen.

Du hast mich rein, und wenn ich's besser wüßte,
So gäb ich's dir, ich tue was ich sage.»
So schließt sie mich an ihre süßen Brüste,
Als ob ihr nur an meiner Brust behage.
Und wie ich Mund und Aug und Stirne küßte,
So war ich doch in wunderbarer Lage:
Denn der so hitzig sonst den Meister spielet,
Weicht schülerhaft zurück und abgekühlet.

Ihr scheint ein süßes Wort, ein Kuß zu gnügen,
Als wär es alles was ihr Herz begehrte.
Wie keusch sie mir, mit liebevollem Fügen,
Des süßen Körpers Fülleform gewährte!
Entzückt und froh in allen ihren Zügen
Und ruhig dann, als wenn sie nichts entbehrte.
So ruht ich auch, gefällig sie beschauend,
Noch auf den Meister hoffend und vertrauend.

Doch als ich länger mein Geschick bedachte,
Von tausend Flüchen mir die Seele kochte,
Mich selbst verwünschend, grinsend mich belachte,
Nichts besser ward, wie ich auch zaudern mochte,
Da lag sie schlafend, schöner als sie wachte;
Die Lichter dämmerten mit langem Dochte.
Der Tages-Arbeit, jugendlicher Mühe
Gesellt sich gern der Schlaf und nie zu frühe.

So lag sie himmlisch an bequemer Stelle,
Als wenn das Lager ihr allein gehörte,
Und an die Wand gedrückt, gequetscht zur Hölle,
Ohnmächtig jener, dem sie nichts verwehrte.
Vom Schlangenbisse fällt zunächst der Quelle
Ein Wandrer so, den schon der Durst verzehrte.
Sie atmet lieblich holdem Traum entgegen;
Er hält den Atem, sie nicht aufzuregen.

Gefaßt bei dem, was ihm noch nie begegnet,
Spricht er zu sich: So mußt du doch erfahren,

Said *no* to every man, till I saw you.
Why do you think they call me 'Piece of Ice'?
Of ice, indeed! Just feel! I'm melting through.
You did it to me, darling. So be good.
And let's be lovers, do as lovers should.

"I'm starting out, remember. Make it sweet.
If I had more to give, I'd even dare."
She pressed her cooler breasts against my heat
As if she liked it and felt safer there.
Lips linger on her lips; toes reach and meet,
But—something funny happening elsewhere.
What always strutted in the leading role
Now shrank like some beginner. Bless my soul!

The girl seemed happy with a kiss, a word,
Smiling as if she couldn't ask for more.
So pure a gaze—yet every limb concurred.
So sweet a blossom, and not picked before.
Oh, but she looked ecstatic when she stirred!
And then lay back relaxing, to adore.
Me, I lay back a bit and . . . beamed away.
Nagged at my dragging actor, "Do the play!"

The more I brooded on my situation,
The more I seethed with curses, inwardly.
Laughed at myself, God knows without elation.
It got me down. And sleeping, breathing, she
Lay lovelier yet, a gilt-edged invitation.
The candles stood and burned, derisively.
Young people who work hard to earn their bread
Soon as they hit the hay are turned to lead.

She dreamed—I'd swear, an angel—flushed and snug;
Breathed easily, as if the bed were hers.
I'm scrunched up by the wall—there's *that* to hug!
Can't lift a finger. It's like what occurs
To thirsty travelers in the sands when—glug!—
There's water bubbling. But a rattler whirs!
Her lips stir softly, talking to a dream.
I hold my breath: O honeychild! And beam.

Detached—for you could call it that—I say,
Well, it's a new experience. Now you know

Warum der Bräutigam sich kreuzt und segnet,
Vor Nestelknüpfen scheu sich zu bewahren.
Weit lieber da, wo's Hellebarden regnet,
Als hier im Schimpf! So war es nicht vor Jahren,
Als deine Herrin dir zum ersten Male
Vors Auge trat im prachterhellten Saale.

Da quoll dein Herz, da quollen deine Sinnen,
So daß der ganze Mensch entzückt sich regte.
Zum raschen Tanze trugst du sie von hinnen,
Die kaum der Arm und schon der Busen hegte,
Als wolltest du dir selbst sie abgewinnen;
Vervielfacht war, was sich für sie bewegte:
Verstand und Witz und alle Lebensgeister
Und rascher als die andern jener Meister.

So immerfort wuchs Neigung und Begierde,
Brautleute wurden wir im frühen Jahre,
Sie selbst des Maien schönste Blum und Zierde;
Wie wuchs die Kraft zur Lust im jungen Paare!
Und als ich endlich sie zur Kirche führte,
Gesteh ich's nur, vor Priester und Altare,
Vor deinem Jammerkreuz, blutrünstiger Christe,
Verzeih mir's Gott, es regte sich der Iste.

Und ihr, der Brautnacht reiche Bettgehänge,
Ihr Pfühle, die ihr euch so breit erstrecktet,
Ihr Teppiche, die Lieb und Lustgedränge
Mit euren seidnen Fittichen bedecktet!
Ihr Käfigvögel, die durch Zwitscher-Sänge
Zu neuer Lust und nie zu früh erwecktet!
Ihr kanntet uns, von euerm Schutz umfriedet,
Teilnehmend sie, mich immer unermüdet.

Und wie wir oft sodann im Raub genossen
Nach Buhlenart des Ehstands heilige Rechte,
Von reifer Saat umwogt, vom Rohr umschlossen,
An manchem Unort, wo ich's mich erfrechte,
Wir waren augenblicklich, unverdrossen
Und wiederholt bedient vom braven Knechte!
Verfluchter Knecht, wie unerwecklich liegst du!
Und deinen Herrn ums schönste Glück betriegst du.

Doch Meister Iste hat nun seine Grillen
Und läßt sich nicht befehlen noch verachten,

Why bridegrooms in a panic start to pray
They won't get spooked and see their chances go.
I'd rather be cut up in saberplay
Than in a bind like this. It wasn't so
When first I saw my real love: from the gloom
Stared at her, brilliant in the brilliant room.

Ah, but my heart leaped then, and every sense,
My whole man's-shape a pulsing of delight.
Lord, how I swept her off in a wild dance
Light in my arms, her weight against me tight.
You'd think I fought myself for her. One glance
Would tell how I grew greater, gathered might
For her sake, mind and body, heart and soul.
That was the day my actor lived his role!

Worship and lovely lust—with both in view
I wooed her all that year, until the spring
(Violins, maestro!), when the world was new
And she outflowered, in June, the floweriest thing,
The date was set. So great our passion grew
That even in church (I blush) with heaven's King
Racked on his cross, before the priest and all,
My impudent hero made his curtain call!

And you, four-posters of the wedding night,
You pillows, that were tossed and rumpled soon,
You blankets, drawn around so our delight
Was ours alone, through morning, afternoon;
You parakeets in cages, rose and white,
Whose twitter music perked our deeper tune—
Could even you, who played your minor part,
Tell which of us was which? Or end from start?

The days of make-believe! The "Let's pretend,
Honey, we're sexy tramps!" I'd toss her there
Laughing, among the cornstalks, or we'd bend
Reeds by the river, threshing who knows where?
In public places, nearly. What a friend
My sturdy plowboy then! He wouldn't scare!
But now, with all the virgin field to reap,
Look at the lousy helper sound asleep.

Or was. But now he's rousing. He's the one!
You can't ignore him, and you can't command.

Auf einmal ist er da, und ganz im stillen
Erhebt er sich zu allen seinen Prachten;
So steht es nun dem Wandrer ganz zu Willen,
Nicht lechzend mehr am Quell zu übernachten.
Er neigt sich hin, er will die Schläferin küssen,
Allein er stockt, er fühlt sich weggerissen.

Wer hat zur Kraft ihn wieder aufgestählet,
Als jenes Bild, das ihm auf ewig teuer,
Mit dem er sich in Jugendlust vermählet?
Dort leuchtet her ein frisch erquicklich Feuer,
Und wie er erst in Ohnmacht sich gequälet,
So wird nun hier dem Starken nicht geheuer;
Er schaudert weg, vorsichtig, leise, leise
Entzieht er sich dem holden Zauberkreise,

Sitzt, schreibt: «Ich nahte mich der heimischen Pforte,
Entfernen wollten mich die letzten Stunden,
Da hab ich nun, am sonderbarsten Orte,
Mein treues Herz aufs neue dir verbunden.
Zum Schlusse findest du geheime Worte:
*Die Krankheit erst bewähret den Gesunden.*
Dies Büchlein soll dir manches Gute zeigen,
Das Beste nur muß ich zuletzt verschweigen.»

Da kräht der Hahn. Das Mädchen schnell entwindet
Der Decke sich und wirft sich rasch ins Mieder.
Und da sie sich so seltsam wiederfindet,
So stutzt sie, blickt und schlägt die Augen nieder;
Und da sie ihm zum letzten Mal verschwindet,
Im Auge bleiben ihm die schönen Glieder:
Das Posthorn tönt, er wirft sich in den Wagen
Und läßt getrost sich zu der Liebsten tragen.

Und weil zuletzt bei jeder Dichtungsweise
Moralien uns ernstlich fördern sollen,
So will auch ich in so beliebtem Gleise
Euch gern bekennen, was die Verse wollen:
Wir stolpern wohl auf unsrer Lebensreise,
Und doch vermögen in der Welt, der tollen,
Zwei Hebel viel aufs irdische Getriebe:
Sehr viel die *Pflicht*, unendlich mehr die *Liebe!*

He's suddenly himself. And like the sun,
Is soaring full of splendor. Suave and bland.
You mean the long thirst's over with and done?
The desert traveler's at the promised land?
I lean across to kiss my sleeping girl
And—hey!—the glorious banner starts to furl!

What made him tough and proud a moment? She,
His only idol now, as long ago;
The one he took in church exultantly.
From worlds away it comes, that rosy glow.
And, as before it worried him to be
Meager, so now he's vexed at swelling so
With her afar. Soft, soft, he shrinks away
Out of the magic circle, all dismay.

That's that. I'm up and scribbling, "Close to home,
I almost thought I wouldn't make it there.
Honey, I'm yours, in Turkestan or Rome.
I'm writing you in bed, and by a bare
—Well, call it piece of luck or something, hmmmm!
Impotence proved I'm superman. Now where
'S a prettier riddle? Leave it; read the rest.
Dearest, I've told you all. Except the best."

Then *cock-a-doodle-doo!* At once the girl's
Thrown off a bed sheet and thrown on a slip;
She rubs her eyes, shakes out her tousled curls,
Looks blushing at bare feet and bites her lip.
Without a word she's vanishing in swirls
Of underpretties over breast and hip.
She's dear, I murmur—rushing from above
Down to my coach. And on the road for love!

I'll tell you what, we writers like to bumble
Onto a moral somewhere, forehead glowing
Over a Noble Truth. Some readers grumble
Unless they feel improved. My moral's showing:
Look, it's a crazy world. We slip and stumble,
But two things, Love and Duty, keep us going.
I couldn't rightly call them hand in glove.
Duty?—who really needs it? Trust your Love.

# Fliegentod

Sie saugt mit Gier verrätrisches Getränke
Unabgesetzt, vom ersten Zug verführt;
Sie fühlt sich wohl, und längst sind die Gelenke
Der zarten Beinchen schon paralysiert,
Nicht mehr gewandt, die Flügelchen zu putzen,
Nicht mehr geschickt, das Köpfchen aufzustutzen—
Das Leben so sich im Genuß verliert.
Zum Stehen kaum wird noch das Füßchen taugen;
So schlürft sie fort, und mitten unterm Saugen
Umnebelt ihr der Tod die tausend Augen.

# Sizilianisches Lied

Ihr schwarzen Äugelein!
Wenn ihr nur winket,
Es fallen Häuser ein,
Es fallen Städte;
Und diese Leimenwand
Vor meinem Herzen—
Bedenk doch nur einmal—
Die sollt nicht fallen!

# Gefunden

Ich ging im Walde
So für mich hin,
Und nichts zu suchen,
Das war mein Sinn.

Im Schatten sah ich
Ein Blümchen stehn,

# Death of a Fly
## (1810, from 'Sixteen Parables')

With greed she quaffs and quaffs the traitorous drink,
Unceasing, from the start wholly enticed,
She feels so far so good, and every link
In her delicate little legs is paralyzed—
No longer deft they are, to groom her wings,
No longer dexterous, to preen her head;
Her life expended, thus, in pleasurings,
Her little feet soon have nowhere to tread;
So does she drink and drink, and while she does,
Comes misty death her myriad eyes to close.

# Sicilian Song (1811)

Eyes bright and cherry-black,
If you but blink
The tallest houses crack,
Whole cities fall;
And do you think perhaps
This cob wall of my heart,
Mere straw and clay and gravel,
Will not collapse?

# Found (1813)

Once in the forest
I strolled content,
To look for nothing
My sole intent.

I saw a flower,
Shaded and shy,

Wie Sterne leuchtend,
Wie Äuglein schön.

Ich wollt es brechen,
Da sagt' es fein:
Soll ich zum Welken
Gebrochen sein?

Ich grubs mit allen
Den Würzlein aus,
Zum Garten trug ichs
Am hübschen Haus.

Und pflanzt es wieder
Am stillen Ort;
Nun zweigt es immer
Und blüht so fort.

Shining like starlight,
Bright as an eye.

I went to pluck it;
Gently it said:
Must I be broken,
Wilt and be dead?

Then whole I dug it
Out of the loam
And to my garden
Carried it home,

There to replant it
Where no wind blows.
More bright than ever
It blooms and grows.

# Gegenwart

Alles kündet dich an!
Erscheinet die herrliche Sonne,
Folgst du, so hoff ich es, bald.

Trittst du im Garten hervor,
So bist du die Rose der Rosen,
Lilie der Lilien zugleich.

Wenn du im Tanze dich regst,
So regen sich alle Gestirne
Mit dir und um dich umher.

Nacht! und so wär es denn Nacht!
Nun überscheinst du des Mondes
Lieblichen, ladenden Glanz.

Ladend und lieblich bist du,
Und Blumen, Mond und Gestirne
Huldigen, Sonne, nur dir.

Sonne! so sei du auch mir
Die Schöpferin herrlicher Tage;
Leben und Ewigkeit ists.

# Den Originalen

Ein Quidam sagt: «Ich bin von keiner Schule;
Kein Meister lebt, mit dem ich buhle;
Auch bin ich weit davon entfernt,
Daß ich von Toten was gelernt.»
Das heißt, wenn ich ihn recht verstand:
Ich bin ein Narr auf eigne Hand.

# Presence (1813)

All's a foretelling of you.
Sun in its glory ascending,
Soon you will follow, I hope.

Into the garden you walk,
Rose of the roses you are,
Lily of lilies as well.

When you but move in the dance,
All of the stars are in motion
With you and round where you move.

Night! just let the night come!
Now you outshine the attractive
Delicate glow of the moon.

Delicate, fetching you are,
Flowers, the moon, and the stars
Celebrate, sun, only you.

Sun! be such to me too,
Creator of days in a glory;
Life and eternity—thus.

---

# On Originality (1812)

I

Somebody says: "Of no school I am part,
Never to living master lost my heart;
Nor any more can I be said
To have learned anything from the dead."
That statement—subject to appeal—
Means: "I'm a self-made imbecile."

Vom Vater hab ich die Statur,
Des Lebens ernstes Führen,
Vom Mütterchen die Frohnatur
Und Lust zu fabulieren.
Urahnherr war der Schönsten hold,
Das spukt so hin und wieder;
Urahnfrau liebte Schmuck und Gold,
Das zuckt wohl durch die Glieder.
Sind nun die Elemente nicht
Aus dem Komplex zu trennen,
Was ist denn an dem ganzen Wicht
Original zu nennen?

## Eigentum

Ich weiß, daß mir nichts angehört
Als der Gedanke, der ungestört
Aus meiner Seele will fließen,
Und jeder günstige Augenblick,
Den mich ein liebendes Geschick
Von Grund aus läßt genießen.

## Landschaft

Das alles sieht so lustig aus,
So wohl gewaschen das Bauerhaus,
So morgentaulich Gras und Baum,
So herrlich blau der Berge Saum!
Seht nur das Wölkchen, wie es spielt
Und sich im reinen Äther kühlt!
Fände sich ein Niederländer hier,
Er nähme wahrlich gleich Quartier,
Und was er sieht und was er malt,
Wird hundert Jahre nachgezahlt.

II

My build from Father I inherit,
His neat and serious ways;
Combined with Mother's cheerful spirit,
Her love of telling stories.
Great-grandfather courted the loveliest,
His ghost won't leave me alone;
Great-grandmother liked fine jewels best,
This twitch I've also known.
If, then, no mortal chemist can
Divide the components from the whole,
What is there in the entire man
You could call original?

(c. 1812–14)

## Possessions (1813)

I know that Nought
Is mine but thought that flows
Straight from the soul
And every twinkling of
The moment favoured
A kindly fate on me bestows
To be wholly savoured.

## Landscape (c. 1813)

So blithe, the whole depicted scene,
The farmer's house, washed bright and clean,
Grass and tree as in morning dew,
The hem of hills a splendid blue.
Look now, the little cloud up there
At play and cooling in pure air!
A Netherlander, if he came
And set up house inside the frame,
Would see and paint what could be sold
As if it were a century old.

Wie kommt dir denn das alles vor?
Es glänzt als wie durch Silberflor,
Durchscheinend ists, es steht ein Licht
Dahinter, lieblichstes Gesicht.
Durch solcher holden Lampe Schein
Wird alles klar und überrein,
Was sonst ein garstig Ungefähr,
Tagtäglich, ein Gemeines wär.
Fehlts dir an Geist und Kunst-Gebühr,
Die Liebe weiß schon Rat dafür.

# Die Jahre

Die Jahre sind allerliebste Leut:
Sie brachten gestern, sie bringen heut,
Und so verbringen wir Jüngern eben
Das allerliebste Schlaraffen-Leben.
Und dann fällts den Jahren auf einmal ein,
Nicht mehr, wie sonst, bequem zu sein;
Wollen nicht mehr schenken, wollen nicht mehr borgen,
Sie nehmen heute, sie nehmen morgen.

How does it all look to you?
Transparent, as if shining through
A skein of silver, or lamplight
Behind the picture charms the sight:
Whatever was ugly and vague before
Such delicate light makes ultrapure,
A limpid ray illumining
Any quotidian humdrum thing.
If you lack the mind or entrance fee
For art, love lets you in for free.

---

# The Years (1814)

The years? A charming lot, I say.
Brought presents yesterday, bring presents today,
And so we younger ones maintain
The charming life that's led in Cockayne.
Then all of a sudden the years change their mind,
Are no longer obliging, no longer kind;
Won't give you presents, won't let you borrow,
Dun you today, and rob you tomorrow.

# IV

# Gedichte aus dem
# *West-Östlichen Diwan*
# Poems 1814–18 from
# *The Parliament of West and East*

# Hegire

Nord und West und Süd zersplittern,
Throne bersten, Reiche zittern,
Flüchte du, im reinen Osten
Patriarchenluft zu kosten,
Unter Lieben, Trinken, Singen
Soll dich Chisers Quell verjüngen.

Dort im Reinen und im Rechten
Will ich menschlichen Geschlechten
In des Ursprungs Tiefe dringen,
Wo sie noch von Gott empfingen
Himmelslehr in Erdesprachen,
Und sich nicht den Kopf zerbrachen.

Wo sie Väter hoch verehrten,
Jeden fremden Dienst verwehrten;
Will mich freun der Jugendschranke:
Glaube weit, eng der Gedanke,
Wie das Wort so wichtig dort war,
Weil es ein gesprochen Wort war.

Will mich unter Hirten mischen,
An Oasen mich erfrischen,
Wenn mit Karawanen wandle,
Schal, Kaffee und Moschus handle;
Jeden Pfad will ich betreten
Von der Wüste zu den Städten.

Bösen Felsweg auf und nieder
Trösten, Hafis, deine Lieder,
Wenn der Führer mit Entzücken
Von des Maultiers hohem Rücken
Singt, die Sterne zu erwecken
Und die Räuber zu erschrecken.

Will in Bädern und in Schenken,
Heilger Hafis, dein gedenken;

# Hegira (1814)

North and West and South are breaking,
Thrones are bursting, kingdoms shaking:
Flee, then, to the essential East,
Where on patriarch's air you'll feast!
There to love and drink and sing,
Drawing youth from Khizr's spring.

Pure and righteous there I'll trace
To its source the human race,
Prime of nations, when to each
Heavenly truth in earthly speech
Still by God himself was given,
Human brains not racked and riven.

When they honored ancestors,
To strange doctrine closed their doors;
Youthful bounds shall be my pride,
My thought narrow, my faith wide.
And I'll find the token word,
Dear because a spoken word.

Mix with goatherds in dry places,
Seek refreshment in oases
When with caravans I fare,
Coffee, shawls, and musk my ware;
Every road and path explore,
Desert, cities and seashore;

Dangerous track, through rock and scree:
Hafiz, there you'll comfort me
When the guide, enchanted, tells
On the mule's back, your ghazels,
Sings them for the stars to hear,
Robber bands to quail with fear.

Holy Hafiz, you in all
Baths and taverns I'll recall,

Wenn den Schleier Liebchen lüftet,
Schüttelnd Ambralocken düftet.
Ja des Dichters Liebeflüstern
Mache selbst die Huris lüstern.

Wolltet ihr ihm dies beneiden,
Oder etwa gar verleiden;
Wisset nur, daß Dichterworte
Um des Paradieses Pforte
Immer leise klopfend schweben
Sich erbittend ewges Leben.

# Unbegrenzt

Daß du nicht enden kannst, das macht dich groß,
Und daß du nie beginnst, das ist dein Los.
Dein Lied ist drehend wie das Sterngewölbe,
Anfang und Ende immerfort dasselbe,
Und was die Mitte bringt ist offenbar
Das was zu Ende bleibt und anfangs war.

Du bist der Freuden echte Dichterquelle,
Und ungezählt entfließt dir Well auf Welle.
Zum Küssen stets bereiter Mund,
Ein Brustgesang der lieblich fließet,
Zum Trinken stets gereizter Schlund,
Ein gutes Herz das sich ergießet.

Und mag die ganze Welt versinken!
Hafis, mit dir, mit dir allein
Will ich wetteifern! Lust und Pein
Sei uns den Zwillingen gemein!
Wie du zu lieben und zu trinken,
Das soll mein Stolz, mein Leben sein.

Nun töne Lied mit eignem Feuer!
Denn du bist älter, du bist neuer.

When the loved one lifts her veil,
Ambergris her locks exhale.
More: the poet's love song must
Melt the houris, move their lust.

Now, should you begrudge him this,
Even long to spoil such bliss,
Poets' words, I'd have you know,
Round the gate of Eden flow,
Gently knocking without rest,
Everlasting life their quest.

# Unbounded (1814–15)

What makes you great is that you cannot end,
And never to begin you are predestined
Your song revolves as does the starry dome,
Beginning, end for ever more the same;
And what the middle brings will prove to be
What last remains and was initially.

Of poets' joys you are the one true source,
Wave after numberless wave you give to verse.
Lips that of kissing never tire,
Song from the breast that sweetly wells,
A throat that's never quenched, on fire,
An honest heart that freely tells.

And though the whole world were to sink,
Hafiz, with you, with you alone
I will compete! Delight, despair,
Let us, the twins, entirely share!
Like you to love, like you to drink
My life and pride I here declare.

Self-fuelled now, my song, ring truer!
For you are older, you are newer.

# Selige Sehnsucht

Sagt es niemand, nur den Weisen,
Weil die Menge gleich verhöhnet,
Das Lebendge will ich preisen
Das nach Flammentod sich sehnet.

In der Liebesnächte Kühlung,
Die dich zeugte, wo du zeugtest,
Überfällt dich fremde Fühlung
Wenn die stille Kerze leuchtet.

Nicht mehr bleibest du umfangen
In der Finsternis Beschattung,
Und dich reißet neu Verlangen
Auf zu höherer Begattung.

Keine Ferne macht dich schwierig,
Kommst geflogen und gebannt,
Und zuletzt, des Lichts begierig,
Bist du Schmetterling verbrannt.

Und so lang du das nicht hast,
Dieses: Stirb und werde!
Bist du nur ein trüber Gast
Auf der dunklen Erde.

# Blessed Longing (1814)

Tell it only to the wise,
For the crowd at once will jeer:
That which is alive I praise,
That which longs for death by fire.

Cooled by passionate love at night,
Procreated, procreating,
You have known the alien feeling
In the calm of candlelight;

Gloom-embraced will lie no more,
By the flickering shades obscured,
But are seized by new desire,
To a higher union lured.

Then no distance holds you fast;
Winged, enchanted, on you fly,
Light your longing, and at last,
Moth, you meet the flame and die.

Never prompted to that quest:
Die and dare rebirth!
You remain a dreary guest
On our gloomy earth.

# Versunken

Voll Locken kraus ein Haupt so rund!—
Und darf ich dann in solchen reichen Haaren
Mit vollen Händen hin und wider fahren,
Da fühl ich mich von Herzensgrund gesund.
Und küß ich Stirne, Bogen, Auge, Mund,
Dann bin ich frisch und immer wieder wund.
Der fünfgezackte Kamm wo sollt er stocken?
Er kehrt schon wieder zu den Locken.
Das Ohr versagt sich nicht dem Spiel,
Hier ist nicht Fleisch, hier ist nicht Haut,
So zart zum Scherz, so liebeviel!
Doch wie man auf dem Köpfchen kraut,
Man wird in solchen reichen Haaren
Für ewig auf und nieder fahren.
So hast du, Hafis, auch getan,
Wir fangen es von vornen an.

# Gingo Biloba

Dieses Baums Blatt, der von Osten
Meinem Garten anvertraut,
Gibt geheimen Sinn zu kosten,
Wie's den Wissenden erbaut.

Ist es ein lebendig Wesen,
Das sich in sich selbst getrennt?
Sind es zwei, die sich erlesen,
Daß man sie als eines kennt?

Solche Frage zu erwidern
Fand ich wohl den rechten Sinn:
Fühlst du nicht an meinen Liedern,
Daß ich eins und doppelt bin?

# Submerged (1815)

Full of crisp curls, a head so round!—
And if in such abundant hair I may
With full hands travel, or return to stay,
Down to my inmost being I feel sound.
If forehead, eyebrow, eye and lips I kiss,
Ever again renewed, I'm sore with bliss.
The five comb-fingers, where should their roaming end?
Already to those curls again they bend.
Nor do the ears refuse their part.
They are not flesh, they are not skin,
Such a love-gamut for tenderly bantering art!
No matter how fondled, here, within
One little head's abundant hair,
For ever forth and back you'll fare.
So, Hafiz, once you used to do,
And we embark on it anew.

# Gingo Biloba (1815)

This tree's leaf that from the East
To my garden's been entrusted
Holds a secret sense, and grist
To a man intent on knowledge.

Is it *one*, this thing alive,
By and in itself divided,
Or two beings who connive
That as *one* the world shall see them?

Fitly now I can reveal
What the pondered question taught me;
In my songs do you not feel
That at once I'm one and double?

# An vollen Büschelzweigen

An vollen Büschelzweigen,
Geliebte, sieh nur hin!
Laß dir die Früchte zeigen
Umschalet stachlig grün.

Sie hängen längst geballet,
Still, unbekannt mit sich,
Ein Ast, der schaukelnd wallet
Wiegt sie geduldiglich.

Doch immer reift von innen
Und schwillt der braune Kern,
Er möchte Luft gewinnen
Und säh die Sonne gern.

Die Schale platzt und nieder
Macht er sich freudig los;
So fallen meine Lieder
Gehäuft in deinen Schoß.

Behandelt die Frauen mit Nachsicht!
Aus krummer Rippe ward sie erschaffen,
Gott konnte sie nicht ganz grade machen.
Willst du sie biegen, sie bricht;
Läßt du sie ruhig, sie wird noch krümmer;
Du guter Adam, was ist denn schlimmer?—
Behandelt die Frauen mit Nachsicht:
Es ist nicht gut, daß euch eine Rippe bricht.

# On Laden Twigs (1815)

On laden twigs of bushes,
There, loved one, to be seen,
The fruit let this uncover,
Spiky, encased and green.

Long clenched they have been hanging
Self-unacquaintedly.
A bough that swaying wanders
Cradles them patiently.

Yet always from within them
The swelling seed has matured,
Longs to be out in the open,
Of sun and air assured.

The casing bursts, and joyful
Each one breaks loose from its trap;
So too my songs are dropping
Profusely into your lap.

---

# Be Lenient

Be lenient when handling womankind,
She's made, you see, out of a curving rib,
God could not make her straighter than he did,
Don't try to bend her, or she breaks, you'll find.
And if you let her be, her curve grows greater;
Poor goodman Adam, that is worse a matter.
Be lenient when handling womankind:
A broken rib does you no good, you'll find.

# Hatem

Locken, haltet mich gefangen
In dem Kreise des Gesichts!
Euch geliebten braunen Schlangen
Zu erwidern hab ich nichts.

Nur dies Herz, es ist von Dauer,
Schwillt in jugendlichstem Flor;
Unter Schnee und Nebelschauer
Rast ein Ätna dir hervor.

Du beschämst wie Morgenröte
Jener Gipfel ernste Wand,
Und noch einmal fühlet Hatem
Frühlingshauch und Sommerbrand.

Schenke her! Noch eine Flasche!
Diesen Becher bring ich ihr!
Findet sie ein Häufchen Asche,
Sagt sie: «Der verbrannte mir.»

# Wiederfinden

Ist es möglich! Stern der Sterne,
Drück ich wieder dich ans Herz!
Ach, was ist die Nacht der Ferne
Für ein Abgrund, für ein Schmerz!
Ja, du bist es, meiner Freuden
Süßer, lieber Widerpart;
Eingedenk vergangner Leiden,
Schaudr ich vor der Gegenwart.

Als die Welt im tiefsten Grunde
Lag an Gottes ewger Brust,
Ordnet' er die erste Stunde
Mit erhabner Schöpfungslust,
Und er sprach das Wort: Es werde!
Da erklang ein schmerzlich Ach!

# Hatem (1815)

Hold me, curls, securely caught,
To the circle of her face—
Belovèd tawny snakes, with nought
Can I reward your act of grace.

Except this heart, which does persist,
Blooming in youth, as flowers do;
Underneath the snow and mist
An Etna gushes forth to you.

That volcano's earnest brow
You put like blush of dawn to shame:
Hatem feels, resurgent now,
The breath of Spring and Summer's flame.

Another bottle, publican!
I drink to her! Happen she'll say,
Finding a heap of ash anon:
"For me he burned his life away."

# Reunion (1815)

Star of stars, O can it be,
I press you to my heart again!
What a chasm is the night
Of being far apart, what pain!
Yes, it is you, of all my joys
The dearest image, sweetest rhyme.
Bygone suffering I recall
And shudder at the present time.

When the world lay in the depths
Utmost of God's eternal breast,
Creative with delight sublime
He willed a moment to be first;
As he spoke the word "Become!",
An anguished "Ah!" rang out, the All

Als das All mit Machtgebärde
In die Wirklichkeiten brach.

Auf tat sich das Licht: so trennte
Scheu sich Finsternis von ihm,
Und sogleich die Elemente
Scheidend auseinanderfliehn.
Rasch, in wilden, wüsten Träumen
Jedes nach der Weite rang,
Starr, in ungemeßnen Räumen,
Ohne Sehnsucht, ohne Klang.

Stumm war alles, still und öde,
Einsam Gott zum erstenmal!
Da erschuf er Morgenröte,
Die erbarmte sich der Qual;
Sie entwickelte dem Trüben
Ein erklingend Farbenspiel,
Und nun konnte wieder lieben,
Was erst auseinanderfiel.

Und mit eiligem Bestreben
Sucht sich, was sich angehört;
Und zu ungemeßnem Leben
Ist Gefühl und Blick gekehrt.
Seis Ergreifen, sei es Raffen,
Wenn es nur sich faßt und hält!
Allah braucht nicht mehr zu schaffen,
Wir erschaffen seine Welt.

So, mit morgenroten Flügeln,
Riß es mich an deinen Mund,
Und die Nacht mit tausend Siegeln
Kräftigt sternenhell den Bund.
Beide sind wir auf der Erde
Musterhaft in Freud und Qual,
Und ein zweites Wort: Es werde!
Trennt uns nicht zum zweitenmal.

Exploded with a motion vast
Into being actual.

Light was opened wide: the dark
Withdrew from it with diffidence;
Separation, scattering
Clove then apart the elements.
Quickly each in savage dreams
And desolate its distance found,
Stiffened in unmeasured space
Without longing, without sound.

All was void, and mute, and still,
God's first taste of solitude.
Then he made the rose of dawn,
Pity on the pain she strewed,
So inventing for the dark,
Of hues and harmonies a game,
And everything that fell apart
Now could fall in love again.

Beings, if they do belong,
Each seeks the other in its place;
Sight and feeling hurtle them
Back to life that's measureless.
Grasp or snatch, no matter how,
Take hold they must, if they're to be:
Allah's work for now is done,
Creators of his world are we.

Thus on wings of rosy dawn
To your lips I flew and fly,
Starbright with a thousand seals
Night the bond will ratify.
Together on the earth we stand,
Exemplars both, in joy and pain,
And a second word "Become!"
Shall not tear us apart again.

# In Tausend Formen

In tausend Formen magst du dich verstecken,
Doch, Allerliebste, gleich erkenn ich dich;
Du magst mit Zauberschleiern dich bedecken,
Allgegenwärtge, gleich erkenn ich dich.

An der Zypresse reinstem, jungem Streben,
Allschöngewachsne, gleich erkenn ich dich,
In des Kanales reinem Wellenleben,
Allschmeichelhafte, wohl erkenn ich dich.

Wenn steigend sich der Wasserstrahl entfaltet,
Allspielende, wie froh erkenn ich dich;
Wenn Wolke sich gestaltend umgestaltet,
Allmannigfaltge, dort erkenn ich dich.

An des geblümten Schleiers Wiesenteppich,
Allbuntbesternte, schön erkenn ich dich;
Und greift umher ein tausendarmger Eppich,
O Allumklammernde, da kenn ich dich.

Wenn am Gebirg der Morgen sich entzündet,
Gleich, Allerheiternde, begrüß ich dich,
Dann über mir der Himmel rein sich ründet,
Allherzerweiternde, dann atm ich dich.

Was ich mit äußerm Sinn, mit innerm kenne,
Du Allbelehrende, kenn ich durch dich;
Und wenn ich Allahs Namenhundert nenne,
Mit jedem klingt ein Name nach für dich.

# A Thousand Forms (1815)

Take on a thousand forms, hide as you will,
O Most-Beloved, at once I know tis you;
Conceal yourself in magic veils, and still,
Presence-in-All, at once I know tis you.

The cypress thrusting artless up and young,
Beauty-in-Every-Limb, I know tis you;
The channelled crystal wave life flows along,
All-Gentling-Tender-One, I know tis you.

You in the fountain plume's unfolding tip,
All-Playful-One, what joy to know tis you;
Where cloud assumes a shape and changes it,
One-Manifold-in-All, I know tis you.

I know, when flowers veil the meadow ground,
O Starry-Twinkle-Hued, in beauty you;
When thousand-armed the ivy gropes around,
Environer-of-All, I know tis you.

When on a mountain sparks of dawn appear,
At once, Great Gladdener, I welcome you;
Then with a sky above rotund and clear,
Then, Opener-of-the-Heart, do I breathe you.

What with bodily sense and soul I know,
Teacher-of-All, I know alone through you;
All hundred names on Allah I bestow,
With each will echo then a name for you.

# Höheres und Höchstes

Daß wir solche Dinge lehren
Möge man uns nicht bestrafen:
Wie das alles zu erklären,
Dürft ihr euer Tiefstes fragen.

Und so werdet ihr vernehmen:
Daß der Mensch, mit sich zufrieden,
Gern sein Ich gerettet sähe,
So da droben wie hienieden.

Und mein liebes Ich bedürfte
Mancherlei Bequemlichkeiten,
Freuden wie ich hier sie schlürfte
Wünscht ich auch für ewge Zeiten.

So gefallen schöne Gärten,
Blum und Frucht und hübsche Kinder,
Die uns allen hier gefielen,
Auch verjüngtem Geist nicht minder.

Und so möcht ich alle Freunde,
Jung und alt, in eins versammeln,
Gar zu gern in deutscher Sprache
Paradiesesworte stammeln.

Doch man horcht nun Dialekten
Wie sich Mensch und Engel kosen,
Der Grammatik, der versteckten,
Deklinierend Mohn und Rosen.

Mag man ferner auch in Blicken
Sich rhetorisch gern ergehen
Und zu himmlischem Entzücken
Ohne Klang und Ton erhöhen.

Ton und Klang jedoch entwindet
Sich dem Worte selbstverständlich,
Und entschiedener empfindet
Der Verklärte sich unendlich.

Ist somit dem Fünf der Sinne
Vorgesehn im Paradiese,

# Sublimer and Sublimest (1818)

Let our teachings not be thought
A reprehensible offence:
Reasons for them can be sought
In nether grounds of common sense.

So it is you learn that man,
At peace with self in thought and act,
Would keep his being, if he can,
In heaven, as on earth, intact.

As for me, my *ich* has hugged
On earth a need for *tout confort*,
Pleasures such as I have glugged
I'll want hereafter, evermore.

A garden, thus, or fruit, may so
Delight, a flower, a pretty lass
Appeal to us down here below—
To spirits young again, no less.

Friends I'd gather round, likewise,
And be with them, the old, the young,
We'd stammer words of Paradise,
Jubilant, in the German tongue.

Angel and man, when *tête-à-tête*,
Albeit, dialects compose:
A secret grammar, delicate
Declensions of poppy and the rose.

Glad we are when looks of bliss
We interchange as rhetoric;
We rise to heavenly ecstasies,
No sound, no voice in what we speak.

Self-evidently sound abates,
Voice its every word repeals;
In Glory, no one hesitates,
Intensely infinite one feels.

If Paradise provide, again,
For Senses Five the wherewithal,

Sicher ist es, ich gewinne
Einen Sinn für alle diese.

Und nun dring ich aller Orten
Leichter durch die ewgen Kreise,
Die durchdrungen sind vom Worte
Gottes rein-lebendger Weise.

Ungehemmt mit heißem Triebe
Läßt sich da kein Ende finden,
Bis im Anschaun ewger Liebe
Wir verschweben, wir verschwinden.

---

Schwarzer Schatten ist über dem Staub der Geliebten Gefährte;
Ich machte mich zum Staube, aber der Schatten ging über mich hin.

---

Certain it is I shall obtain
A Single Sense embracing all.

Now lighter through the eternal rings
I pass, no matter where I be —
The Word that penetrates them sings
God's artless living melody.

There unimpeded urges burn
With never an end or latterday,
Till face to face with Love we turn
To floating air and drift away.

# Two Untitled Texts Omitted from the *Diwan* of 1819

Black is the shadow goes over the dust beside my belovèd;
Me I changed into dust: shadow walked over and on.

Mit der Deutschen Freundschaft
Hat's keine Not,
Ärgerlichster Feindschaft
Steht Höflichkeit zu Gebot;
Je sanfter sie sich erwiesen,
Hab ich immer frisch gedroht,
Ließ mich nicht verdrießen
Trübes Morgen- und Abendrot;
Ließ die Wasser fließen,
Fließen zu Freud und Not.
Aber mit allem diesem
Blieb ich mir selbst zu Gebot:
Sie alle wollten genießen
Was ihnen die Stunde bot;
Ihnen hab ich's nicht verwiesen,
Jeder hat seine Not.
Sie lassen mich alle grüßen
Und hassen mich bis in Tod.

With a German, amity
Is easy to attain,
To his bitterest enmity
A *politesse* gives rein;
The gentler they made out to be
I always flashed a fist,
It never got the best of me,
Their late and early mist;
I always let the water flow
Through profit or through loss,
As far as my supply would go
And I was my own boss:
Each one his instant bliss enjoys,
No prudent ifs and buts;
I never said Do Otherwise,
We all have our weak spots—
Goodwill no German me denies,
All hate my very guts.

V
# Spätere Gedichte
# Later Poems
# 1815–30

# Prooemion

Im Namen dessen, der sich Selbst erschuf!
Von Ewigkeit in schaffendem Beruf;
In Seinem Namen, der den Glauben schafft,
Vertrauen, Liebe, Tätigkeit und Kraft;
In Jenes Namen, der, so oft genannt,
Dem Wesen nach blieb immer unbekannt:

Soweit das Ohr, soweit das Auge reicht,
Du findest nur Bekanntes, das Ihm gleicht,
Und deines Geistes höchster Feuerflug
Hat schon am Gleichnis, hat am Bild genug;
Es zieht dich an, es reißt dich heiter fort,
Und wo du wandelst, schmückt sich Weg und Ort;
Du zählst nicht mehr, berechnest keine Zeit,
Und jeder Schritt ist Unermeßlichkeit.

\*

Was wär ein Gott, der nur von außen stieße,
Im Kreis das All am Finger laufen ließe!
Ihm ziemts, die Welt im Innern zu bewegen,
Natur in Sich, Sich in Natur zu hegen,
So daß, was in Ihm lebt und webt und ist,
Nie Seine Kraft, nie Seinen Geist vermißt.

\*

Im Innern ist ein Universum auch;
Daher der Völker löblicher Gebrauch,
Daß jeglicher das Beste, was er kennt,
Er Gott, ja seinen Gott benennt,
Ihm Himmel und Erden übergibt,
Ihn fürchtet, und womöglich liebt.

# Prooemion (first half 1816, the rest 1815)

Now in his name who made himself creation,
Eternal act his single occupation;
In his name, who created all belief,
Confidence, strength, activity, and love;
In that one's name who, named and named again,
Ever in essence lay beyond our ken:

You find as far as ear and eye can go
Semblances of him, the things you know;
Your spirit catching fire, high as it flies,
Itself with semblance, symbol, satisfies;
Symbols attract, and blithely onward borne
Go as you will, pathway and place adorn;
You cease to calculate, count time nor tide,
Immeasurable each and every stride.

*

What would he be, a God from outside prodding,
Who spun the spheres around a finger, nodding?
The world to move from inside suits his pleasure,
Himself in nature, nature in self to treasure,
So that the life in him that weaves and is
May never lack his Mind, his Energies.

*

In us a universe has being, too:
Commendably from this the peoples drew
The way a person naming him bestows
On God, his God, the highest good he knows,
Heaven and Earth to him makes over,
In fear of him, if possible his lover.

# Entoptische Farben
*An Julien*

Laß dir von den Spiegeleien
Unsrer Physiker erzählen,
Die am Phänomen sich freuen,
Mehr sich mit Gedanken quälen.

Spiegel hüben, Spiegel drüben,
Doppelstellung, auserlesen;
Und dazwischen ruht im Trüben
Als Kristall das Erdewesen.

Dieses zeigt, wenn jene blicken,
Allerschönste Farbenspiele;
Dämmerlicht, das beide schicken,
Offenbart sich dem Gefühle.

Schwarz wie Kreuze wirst du sehen,
Pfauenaugen kann man finden;
Tag und Abendlicht vergehen,
Bis zusammen beide schwinden.

Und der Name wird ein Zeichen,
Tief ist der Kristall durchdrungen:
Aug in Auge sieht dergleichen
Wundersame Spiegelungen.

Laß den Makrokosmus gelten,
Seine spenstischen Gestalten!
Da die lieben kleinen Welten
Wirklich Herrlichstes enthalten.

# Entoptic Colours (1817)
*for Julie*

Let me tell you what with mirrors
Physicists of ours have wrought:
Some find phenomena delightful,
More torment themselves with thought.

Mirror facing facing mirror,
Doubles—exquisite effect;
Between them in the shadow stands a
Crystal cube which will reflect,

Analogue of earth, when mirrors
Glance their light across, the loveliest
Play of colours; and their twilight
Touches feeling, manifest.

Black you'll see, as black as crosses,
Peacock eyes you'll surely find,
Fades the light of day and nightfall,
Leaving not a trace behind.

And the word becomes a symbol:
Soaked with hues the crystal is;
Eye to eye we see like marvels—
That mirroring resembles this.

Let it be, the macrocosm,
With its phantom figurings!
Worlds we love and which are little
Harbour the most glorious things.

# Urworte · Orphisch

## ΔΑΙΜΩΝ, Dämon

Wie an dem Tag, der dich der Welt verliehen,
Die Sonne stand zum Gruße der Planeten,
Bist alsobald und fort und fort gediehen
Nach dem Gesetz, wonach du angetreten.
So mußt du sein, dir kannst du nicht entfliehen,
So sagten schon Sibyllen, so Propheten;
Und keine Zeit und keine Macht zerstückelt
Geprägte Form, die lebend sich entwickelt.

## TYXH, das Zufällige

Die strenge Grenze doch umgeht gefällig
Ein Wandelndes, das mit und um uns wandelt;
Nicht einsam bleibst du, bildest dich gesellig,
Und handelst wohl so, wie ein andrer handelt:
Im Leben ists bald hin-, bald widerfällig,
Es ist ein Tand und wird so durchgetandelt.
Schon hat sich still der Jahre Kreis geründet,
Die Lampe harrt der Flamme, die entzündet.

## ΕΡΩΣ, Liebe

Die bleibt nicht aus!—Er stürzt vom Himmel nieder,
Wohin er sich aus alter Öde schwang,
Er schwebt heran auf luftigem Gefieder
Um Stirn und Brust den Frühlingstag entlang,
Scheint jetzt zu fliehn, vom Fliehen kehrt er wieder:
Da wird ein Wohl im Weh, so süß und bang.
Gar manches Herz verschwebt im Allgemeinen,
Doch widmet sich das edelste dem Einen.

## ΑΝΑΓΚΗ, Nötigung

Da ists denn wieder, wie die Sterne wollten:
Bedingung und Gesetz; und aller Wille
Ist nur ein Wollen, weil wir eben sollten,
Und vor dem Willen schweigt die Willkür stille;

# Primal Words · Orphic (1817–18)

## ΔΑΙΜΩΝ, Daemon

As stood the sun to the salute of planets
Upon the day that gave you to the earth,
You grew forthwith, and prospered, in your growing
Heeded the law presiding at your birth.
Sibyls and prophets told it: You must be
None but yourself, from self you cannot flee.
No time there is, no power, can decompose
The minted form that lives and living grows.

## ΤΥΧΗ, Chance

Strict the limit, yet a drifting, pleasant,
Moves around it, with us, circling us;
You are not long alone, you learn decorum,
And likely act as any manjack does:
It comes and goes, in life, you lose or win,
It is a trinket, toyed with, wearing thin.
Full circle come the years, the end is sighted,
The lamp awaits the flame, to be ignited.

## ΕΡΩΣ, Love

Love is not absent! Down from heaven swooping,
Whither from ancient emptiness he flew,
This way he flutters, borne by airy feathers,
Round heart and head the day of Springtime through,
Apparently escapes, returns anon,
So sweet and nervous, pain to pleasure gone.
Some hearts away in general loving float,
The noblest, yet, their all to one devote.

## ΑΝΑΓΚΗ, Necessity

Then back it comes, what in the stars was written;
Law and circumstance; each will is tried,
All willing simply forced, by obligation:
In face of it, the free will's tongue is tied.

Das Liebste wird vom Herzen weggescholten,
Dem harten Muß bequemt sich Will und Grille.
So sind wir scheinfrei denn nach manchen Jahren
Nur enger dran, als wir am Anfang waren.

## ΕΛΠΙΣ, Hoffnung

Doch solcher Grenze, solcher ehrnen Mauer
Höchst widerwärtge Pforte wird entriegelt,
Sie stehe nur mit alter Felsendauer!
Ein Wesen regt sich leicht und ungezügelt:
Aus Wolkendecke, Nebel, Regenschauer
Erhebt sie uns, mit ihr, durch sie beflügelt,
Ihr kennt sie wohl, sie schwärmt durch alle Zonen —
Ein Flügelschlag — und hinter uns Äonen!

# Um Mitternacht

Um Mitternacht ging ich, nicht eben gerne,
Klein, kleiner Knabe, jenen Kirchhof hin
Zu Vaters Haus, des Pfarrers; Stern am Sterne,
Sie leuchteten doch alle gar zu schön;
    Um Mitternacht.

Wenn ich dann ferner in des Lebens Weite
Zur Liebsten mußte, mußte, weil sie zog,
Gestirn und Nordschein über mir im Streite,
Ich gehend, kommend Seligkeiten sog;
    Um Mitternacht.

Bis dann zuletzt des vollen Mondes Helle
So klar und deutlich mir ins Finstere drang,
Auch der Gedanke willig, sinnig, schnelle
Sich ums Vergangne wie ums Künftige schlang;
    Um Mitternacht.

Man's heart forswears what most was loved by him,
To iron "Must" comply both will and whim.
It only seems we're free, years hem us in,
Constraining more than at our origin.

## ΕΛΠΙΣ, Hope

Yet the repulsive gate can be unbolted
Within such bounds, their adamantine wall,
Though it may stand, that gate, like rock for ever;
One being moves, unchecked, ethereal:
From heavy cloud, from fog, from squall of rain
She lifts us to herself, we're winged again,
You know her well, to nowhere she's confined—
A wingbeat—aeons vanish far behind.

# At Midnight (1818)

At midnight, far from gladly at that hour,
A small, small boy along the churchyard I
Walked to my father's vicarage; star on star,
Oh how they shone, too richly lit the sky;
                    At midnight.

When later I, moved farther though not far,
Must see the loved one, must because she drew me,
Above me stars and northern lights at war,
Going and coming I felt bliss flow through me;
                    At midnight.

Until at last the full moon made a rift
So bright, so clear within the dark of me,
And even thought, grown willing, limber, swift
Embraced both past and future easily;
                    At midnight.

# Von Krüdener
## Jena, den 4. April 1818

Junge Huren, alte Nonnen
Hatten sonst schon viel gewonnen,
Wenn, von Pfaffen wohlberaten,
Sie im Kloster Wunder taten.
Jetzt geht's über Land und Leute
Durch Europens edle Weite!
Hofgemäße Löwen schranzen,
Affen, Hund und Bären tanzen—
Neue leidge Zauberflöten—
Hurenpack, zuletzt Propheten!

# Sankt Nepomuks Vorabend
## Karlsbad, den 15. Mai 1820

Lichtlein schwimmen auf dem Strome,
Kinder singen auf der Brücken,
Glocke, Glöckchen fügt vom Dome
Sich der Andacht, dem Entzücken.

Lichtlein schwinden, Sterne schwinden;
Also löste sich die Seele
Unsres Heilgen, nicht verkünden
Durft er anvertraute Fehle.

Lichtlein, schwimmet! Spielt, ihr Kinder!
Kinder-Chor, o! singe, singe!
Und verkündiget nicht minder,
Was den Stern zu Sternen bringe.

# Von Krüdener (1818)

Young whores and old nuns
Would do us all a few good turns,
If, by priests put through their paces,
They'd work miracles in monastic places.
Now they're sweeping hand in hand
Through every fine old European land!
Royal Household Lions cringe,
Apes, Dogs, and Bears go on the binge:
Modern miserable Magic Flutes—
Prophesying prostitutes!

# Saint Nepomuk's Eve
## (1820)

Children sing upon the bridge,
Tapers float upon the stream,
From the dome small bell and big
Ring for worship and the dream.

Stars and little tapers dwindle;
From our saint who would not say
What fault to him had been confided,
Thus the soul did flit away.

Tapers, float! Play on, you children!
Choir of children, sing, but sing!
And reveal, no less, what may
That star to all the others bring.

# Allerdings: *Dem Physiker*

*«Ins Innre der Natur»* —
O du Philister! —
*«Dringt kein erschaffner Geist.»*
Mich und Geschwister
Mögt ihr an solches Wort
Nur nicht erinnern!
Wir denken: Ort für Ort
Sind wir im Innern.
*«Glückselig, wem sie nur*
*Die äußre Schale weist!»*
Das hör ich sechzig Jahre wiederholen,
Ich fluche drauf, aber verstohlen;
Sage mir tausend tausendmale:
Alles gibt sie reichlich und gern;
Natur hat weder Kern
Noch Schale,
Alles ist sie mit einem Male.
Dich prüfe du nur allermeist,
Ob du Kern oder Schale seist.

# Auf den Kauf

Wo ist einer, der sich quälet
Mit der Last, die wir getragen?
Wenn es an Gestalten fehlet,
Ist ein Kreuz geschwind geschlagen.

# True Enough: *To the Physicist* (1820)

"Into the core of Nature"—
O Philistine—
"No earthly mind can enter."
The maxim is fine;
But have the grace
To spare the dissenter,
Me and my kind.
We think: in every place
We're at the center.
"Happy the mortal creature
To whom she shows no more
Than the outer rind,"
For sixty years I've heard your sort announce.
It makes me swear, though quietly;
To myself a thousand times I say:
All things she grants, gladly and lavishly;
Nature has neither core
Nor outer rind,
Being all things at once.
It's yourself you should scrutinize to see
Whether you're center or periphery.

# (FOUR EPIGRAMS ON LITERARY MATTERS, 1814–1820s)

# Shopping (1814)

Who is there now to tell the pain
Of our prolonged oppression?
If character you can't sustain,
Try beads and quick confession.

Pfaffenhelden singen sie,
Frauen wohl empfohlen;
Oberleder bringen sie,
Aber keine Sohlen.

Jung und Alte, Groß und Klein,
Gräßliches Gelichter!
Niemand will ein Schuster sein,
Jedermann ein Dichter.

Alle kommen sie gerennt,
Möchtens gerne treiben;
Doch wer keinen Leisten kennt,
Wird ein Pfuscher bleiben.

Willst du das verfluchte Zeug
Auf dem Markte kaufen,
Wirst du, eh es möglich deucht,
Wirst du barfuß laufen.

# Demut

Seh ich die Werke der Meister an,
So seh ich das, was sie getan;
Betracht ich meine Siebensachen,
Seh ich, was ich hätt sollen machen.

They sing of heroes who are priests,
They eulogize their ladies,
They bring us uppers, two apiece,
But bootsoles? No, just maybes.

What a frightful potpourri,
Callow, senile, tall, or slighter:
Cobbler no-one wants to be,
Everyone a writer.

All come rushing up so fast
To crash the writing party;
A shoemaker sticks to his last,
These bunglers don't—they're arty.

You want to buy their trash, perhaps?
Go to the market, choose:
You'll soon enough pick up your traps
And hobble off—no shoes!

# Humility (1815)

The masters' works I look upon,
And I can see what they have done;
When looking upon this or that by me,
What I should have done is what I see.

# Kronos als Kunstrichter

Saturnus eigne Kinder frißt,
Hat irgend kein Gewissen;
Ohne Senf und Salz, und wie ihr wißt,
Verschlingt er euch den Bissen.

Shakespearen sollt es auch ergehn
Nach hergebrachter Weise:—
Den hebt mir auf, sagt Polyphem,
Daß ich zuletzt ihn speise.

# Ins Weite

Das geht so fröhlich
Ins Allgemeine!
Ist leicht und selig,
Als wärs auch reine.
Sie wissen gar nichts
Von stillen Riffen;
Und wie sie schiffen,
Die lieben Heitern,
Sie werden wie gar nichts
Zusammen scheitern.

# Eins und Alles

Im Grenzenlosen sich zu finden,
Wird gern der einzelne verschwinden,
Da löst sich aller Überdruß;
Statt heißem Wünschen, wildem Wollen,
Statt lästgem Fordern, strengem Sollen
Sich aufzugeben ist Genuß.

# Kronos As Art-Critic (1820)

Saturn eats his own offspring,
Doesn't give a cuss;
Gobbles without seasoning
What else might nourish us.

Should even Shakespeare then comply
With custom hard and fast?
Says Polyphemus: Put him by,
So I can eat him last.

# Into the Blue (1820s)

Off they chase
Into the wide blue yonder—
Hilarious!
But real? I wonder:
Of placid reefs
They've no idea,
The way they steer—
Fond heads-in-air—
They'll come to grief,
And all go under.

# One and All (1821)

In boundlessness, itself discovering there,
The singular would gladly disappear,
Satiety is then absolvèd quite;
Ardent wishing, savage will abate,
Strict obligation, coping, ah, with Fate:
In self-abandon is delight.

Weltseele, komm, uns zu durchdringen!
Dann mit dem Weltgeist selbst zu ringen,
Wird unsrer Kräfte Hochberuf.
Teilnehmend führen gute Geister,
Gelinde leitend höchste Meister
Zu dem, der alles schafft und schuf.

Und umzuschaffen das Geschaffne,
Damit sichs nicht zum Starren waffne,
Wirkt ewiges, lebendiges Tun.
Und was nicht war, nun will es werden
Zu reinen Sonnen, farbigen Erden;
In keinem Falle darf es ruhn.

Es soll sich regen, schaffend handeln,
Erst sich gestalten, dann verwandeln;
Nur scheinbar stehts Momente still.
Das Ewige regt sich fort in allen:
Denn alles muß in Nichts zerfallen,
Wenn es im Sein beharren will.

# Trilogie der Leidenschaft

### AN WERTHER

Noch einmal wagst du, vielbeweinter Schatten,
Hervor dich an das Tageslicht,
Begegnest mir auf neu beblümten Matten,
Und meinen Anblick scheust du nicht.
Es ist, als ob du lebtest in der Frühe,
Wo uns der Tau auf Einem Feld erquickt
Und nach des Tages unwillkommner Mühe
Der Scheidesonne letzter Strahl entzückt;
Zum Bleiben ich, zum Scheiden du erkoren,
Gingst du voran—und hast nicht viel verloren.

Des Menschen Leben scheint ein herrlich Los:
Der Tag wie lieblich, so die Nacht wie groß!
Und wir, gepflanzt in Paradieses Wonne,

Soul of the world, soak into us, descend,
Then with the very *Weltgeist* to contend
Our finest faculties contract;
Spirits benign will guide and sympathize,
Sublimest masters gently ways devise
To the perpetual Creative Act.

And with effect to make creation new,
Its weaponed rigour soon enough undo,
Action eternal, vivid, rose;
And what was not, now wishes to unfold,
Become unsullied suns, a coloured world;
No circumstance permits repose.

It has to move, to be creating deed,
First make its form, then, changing it, proceed;
All stopping, short—illusion's twist.
For the Eternal onward moves in all,
And into nothing everything must fall,
If it in being would persist.

# Trilogy of Passion (1823–24)

### TO WERTHER

So once again, poor much-lamented shadow.
You venture in the light of day?
And here, in blossoms of the fresher meadow,
Confront me and not turn away?
Alive as in the early dawn, when tender
Chill of a misty field bestirred the two,
When both were dazzled by the west in splendor
After the drudging summer days were through.
My doom: endure. And yours: depart forlorn.
Is early death, we wonder, much to mourn?

In theory how magnificent, man's fate!
The day agreeable, the night so great.
Yet we, in such a paradise begun,

Genießen kaum der hocherlauchten Sonne,
Da kämpft sogleich verworrene Bestrebung
Bald mit uns selbst und bald mit der Umgebung;
Keins wird vom andern wünschenswert ergänzt,
Von außen düsterts, wenn es innen glänzt,
Ein glänzend Äußres deckt ein trüber Blick,
Da steht es nah—und man verkennt das Glück.

Nun glauben wirs zu kennen! Mit Gewalt
Ergreift uns Liebreiz weiblicher Gestalt:
Der Jüngling, froh wie in der Kindheit Flor,
Im Frühling tritt als Frühling selbst hervor,
Entzückt, erstaunt, wer dies ihm angetan?
Er schaut umher, die Welt gehört ihm an.
Ins Weite zieht ihn unbefangne Hast,
Nichts engt ihn ein, nicht Mauer, nicht Palast;
Wie Vögelschar an Wäldergipfeln streift,
So schwebt auch er, der um die Liebste schweift,
Er sucht vom Äther, den er gern verläßt,
Den treuen Blick, und dieser hält ihn fest.

Doch erst zu früh und dann zu spät gewarnt,
Fühlt er den Flug gehemmt, fühlt sich umgarnt.
Das Wiedersehn ist froh, das Scheiden schwer,
Das Wieder-Wiedersehn beglückt noch mehr,
Und Jahre sind im Augenblick ersetzt;
Doch tückisch harrt das Lebewohl zuletzt.

Du lächelst, Freund, gefühlvoll, wie sich ziemt:
Ein gräßlich Scheiden machte dich berühmt;
Wir feierten dein kläglich Mißgeschick,
Du ließest uns zu Wohl und Weh zurück.
Dann zog uns wieder ungewisse Bahn
Der Leidenschaften labyrinthisch an;
Und wir, verschlungen wiederholter Not,
Dem Scheiden endlich—Scheiden ist der Tod!
Wie klingt es rührend, wenn der Dichter singt,
Den Tod zu meiden, den das Scheiden bringt!
Verstrickt in solche Qualen, halbverschuldet,
Geb ihm ein Gott zu sagen, was er duldet.

Enjoy but briefly the amazing sun,
And then the battle's on: vague causes found
To struggle with ourself, the world around.
Neither completes the other as it should:
The skies are gloomy when our humor's good;
The vista glitters and we're glum enough.
Joy near at hand, but we—at blindman's buff.

At times we think it ours: some darling girl!
Borne on a fragrant whirlwind, off we whirl.
The young man, breezy as in boyhood's prime,
Like spring itself goes strutting in springtime.
Astounded, charmed, "Who's doing this, all for me?"
Claims like a cocky heir the land and sea.
Goes footloose anywhere, without a thought;
No wall, no palace holds him, even if caught.
As swallows skim the treetops in a blur,
He hovers round, in rings, that certain her,
Scans, from the height he means to leave at last,
Earth for an answering gaze, that holds him fast.

First warned too soon, and then too late, he'll swear
His feet are bound, traps planted everywhere.
Sweet meetings are a joy, departure's pain.
Meeting again—what hopes we entertain!
Moments with her make good the years away.
Yet there's a treacherous parting, come the day.

You smile, my friend, eyes welling. Still the same!
Yours, what a ghastly avenue to fame.
We dressed in mourning when your luck ran out
And you deserted, leaving ours in doubt.
For us, the road resuming God knows where,
Through labyrinths of passion, heavy air,
Still drew us on, bone-tired, with desperate breath
Up to a final parting. Parting's death!
True: it's affecting when the poet sings
To wish away the death that parting brings.
Some god—though man's half guilty, hurt past cure—
Grant him a tongue to murmur: I endure.

## Elegie

*Und wenn der Mensch in seiner Qual verstummt,*
*Gab mir ein Gott zu sagen, was ich leide.*

Was soll ich nun vom Wiedersehen hoffen,
Von dieses Tages noch geschloßner Blüte?
Das Paradies, die Hölle steht dir offen;
Wie wankelsinnig regt sichs im Gemüte!—
Kein Zweifeln mehr! Sie tritt ans Himmelstor,
Zu ihren Armen hebt sie dich empor.

So warst du denn im Paradies empfangen,
Als wärst du wert des ewig schönen Lebens;
Dir blieb kein Wunsch, kein Hoffen, kein Verlangen,
Hier war das Ziel des innigsten Bestrebens,
Und in dem Anschaun dieses einzig Schönen
Versiegte gleich der Quell sehnsüchtiger Tränen.

Wie regte nicht der Tag die raschen Flügel,
Schien die Minuten vor sich her zu treiben!
Der Abendkuß, ein treu verbindlich Siegel:
So wird es auch der nächsten Sonne bleiben.
Die Stunden glichen sich in zartem Wandern
Wie Schwestern zwar, doch keine ganz den andern.

Der Kuß, der letzte, grausam süß, zerschneidend
Ein herrliches Geflecht verschlungner Minnen.
Nun eilt, nun stockt der Fuß, die Schwelle meidend,
Als trieb' ein Cherub flammend ihn von hinnen;
Das Auge starrt auf düstrem Pfad verdrossen,
Es blickt zurück, die Pforte steht verschlossen.

Und nun verschlossen in sich selbst, als hätte
Dies Herz sich nie geöffnet, selige Stunden
Mit jedem Stern des Himmels um die Wette
An ihrer Seite leuchtend nicht empfunden;
Und Mißmut, Reue, Vorwurf, Sorgenschwere
Belastens nun in schwüler Atmosphäre.

Ist denn die Welt nicht übrig? Felsenwände,
Sind sie nicht mehr gekrönt von heiligen Schatten?
Die Ernte, reift sie nicht? Ein grün Gelände,
Zieht sichs nicht hin am Fluß durch Busch und Matten?
Und wölbt sich nicht das überweltlich Große,
Gestaltenreiche, bald Gestaltenlose?

## ELEGY

*Though most men suffer dumbly, yet a god*
*Gave me a tongue to utter all my pain.*

What's to be hoped from seeing her again?
Hoped from the still-shut blossoms of today?
Which opens, heaven or hell, around me? When
I guess, my thoughts go wandering every way.
But steady—there! She's there, at heaven's door;
Her arms enfold and raise me, as before.

So then the heavens are open, take me in
As if deserving life forever blest.
No wish, no longing, and no might-have-been
Stinted: the very goal of all my quest.
Eyes well delighted on that loveliest thing,
Their tears subsiding at the passionate spring.

Didn't the day go by on flashing feathers!
Didn't it send the minutes skimming there!
Our sign, the kiss at evening—and what weathers
It promised: fair tonight, tomorrow fair.
Hours were like sisters, lingering as they passed,
Each face alike, each different from the last.

Our final kiss, so shuddering sweet, it tore
The sheerest of all fiber, heart's desire.
My foot, abrupt or dragging, dodged her door
As if an angel waved that sword of fire.
Eyes frozen on the dusky ruts go glum.
Turn, and her door's a darkness, shut and dumb.

My soul's a darkness, shut and dumb—as though
This heart had never opened, never found
Hours of delight beside her, such a glow
As all the stars of heaven let dance around.
Now gloom, remorse, self-mockery—clouds of care
Clutch at it, sluggish, in the sluggish air.

What of the world—it's done for? Cliffs of granite
Crowned shadowy with the sacred grove—they're vapor?
No harvest-moon? Green delta country (can it?)
Turn with its trees to ash, like burning paper?
That grandeur curved above us—all undone?—
Now with its thousand clouds, and now with none.

Wie leicht und zierlich, klar und zart gewoben
Schwebt, seraphgleich, aus ernster Wolken Chor,
Als glich' es ihr, am blauen Äther droben
Ein schlank Gebild aus lichtem Duft empor!
So sahst du sie in frohem Tanze walten,
Die lieblichste der lieblichsten Gestalten.

Doch nur Momente darfst dich unterwinden,
Ein Luftgebild statt ihrer festzuhalten;
Ins Herz zurück! dort wirst dus besser finden,
Dort regt sie sich in wechselnden Gestalten:
Zu Vielen bildet Eine sich hinüber,
So tausendfach, und immer, immer lieber.

Wie zum Empfang sie an den Pforten weilte
Und mich von dannauf stufenweis beglückte,
Selbst nach dem letzten Kuß mich noch ereilte,
Den letztesten mir auf die Lippen drückte:
So klar beweglich bleibt das Bild der Lieben
Mit Flammenschrift ins treue Herz geschrieben.

Ins Herz, das fest, wie zinnenhohe Mauer,
Sich ihr bewahrt und sie in sich bewahret,
Für sie sich freut an seiner eignen Dauer,
Nur weiß von sich, wenn sie sich offenbaret,
Sich freier fühlt in so geliebten Schranken
Und nur noch schlägt, für alles ihr zu danken.

War Fähigkeit zu lieben, war Bedürfen
Von Gegenliebe weggelöscht, verschwunden,
Ist Hoffnungslust zu freudigen Entwürfen,
Entschlüssen, rascher Tat sogleich gefunden!
Wenn Liebe je den Liebenden begeistet,
Ward es an mir aufs lieblichste geleistet;

Und zwar durch sie!—Wie lag ein innres Bangen
Auf Geist und Körper, unwillkommner Schwere:
Von Schauerbildern rings der Blick umfangen
Im wüsten Raum beklommner Herzensleere;
Nun dämmert Hoffnung von bekannter Schwelle,
Sie selbst erscheint in milder Sonnenhelle.

Dem Frieden Gottes, welcher euch hienieden
Mehr als Vernunft beseliget—wir lesens—
Vergleich ich wohl der Liebe heitern Frieden

A form there!—rare and airy, silken, bright,
Floats forth, among the clouds in grave ballet,
An angel in blue noon, or—? No, a white
Slim body—hers!—inclining far away.
You saw her lean so at the gala ball;
Among the loveliest, lovelier far than all.

A ruse for moments only. Don't suppose
The empty air a match for her embraces.
Back to your heart of hearts, that better knows
Her and the changing miracle her face is.
In every guise she's greater. Like a flame,
Forever varying and the very same.

Once by the gate she waited; in she brought me;
Onward from joy to keener joy we passed.
The last last kiss—but how she ran and caught me,
Pressed to my mouth an even laster last.
Still that indelible image of desire
Burns on my heart in script of living fire—

My heart (its battlement a height securing
Her for itself alone, itself for her)
Only for her is happy in enduring;
Knows it has life by stirring if she stir.
Confined in love, is free and on its own;
Praising, with each pulsation, her alone,

Because: when dead to love, and hardly caring
Whether another's love could sink or save it
—She came. And my old verve in dreaming, daring,
Resolving, up-and-doing—this she gave it.
If ever love restored a human soul,
It took my shrunken self and made it whole.

And all through her! In mind and body's gloom
I mooned lugubrious, lurching and agrope.
Look where I would, saw shuddering visions loom
Over the heart's eroded acres. Hope
—Suddenly, out of hopelessness—was there:
A girl with the light of morning on her hair.

To God's own peace, the peace that here below
Passeth all understanding (so the preacher)
I'm minded to compare that heady glow

In Gegenwart des allgeliebten Wesens;
Da ruht das Herz, und nichts vermag zu stören
Den tiefsten Sinn, den Sinn: ihr zu gehören.

In unsers Busens Reine wogt ein Streben,
Sich einem Höhern, Reinern, Unbekannten
Aus Dankbarkeit freiwillig hinzugeben,
Enträtselnd sich den ewig Ungenannten;
Wir heißens: fromm sein!—Solcher seligen Höhe
Fühl ich mich teilhaft, wenn ich vor ihr stehe.

Vor ihrem Blick, wie vor der Sonne Walten,
Vor ihrem Atem, wie vor Frühlingslüften,
Zerschmilzt, so längst sich eisig starr gehalten,
Der Selbstsinn tief in winterlichen Grüften;
Kein Eigennutz, kein Eigenwille dauert,
Vor ihrem Kommen sind sie weggeschauert.

Es ist, als wenn sie sagte: «Stund um Stunde
Wird uns das Leben freundlich dargeboten.
Das Gestrige ließ uns geringe Kunde,
Das Morgende—zu wissen ists verboten;
Und wenn ich je mich vor dem Abend scheute,
Die Sonne sank und sah noch, was mich freute.

Drum tu wie ich und schaue, froh verständig,
Dem Augenblick ins Auge! Kein Verschieben!
Begegn ihm schnell, wohlwollend wie lebendig,
Im Handeln seis, zur Freude seis dem Lieben.
Nur wo du bist, sei alles, immer kindlich,
So bist du alles, bist unüberwindlich.»

Du hast gut reden, dacht ich: zum Geleite
Gab dir ein Gott die Gunst des Augenblickes,
Und jeder fühlt an deiner holden Seite
Sich augenblicks den Günstling des Geschickes;
Mich schreckt der Wink, von dir mich zu entfernen—
Was hilft es mir, so hohe Weisheit lernen!

Nun bin ich fern! Der jetzigen Minute,
Was ziemt denn der? Ich wüßt es nicht zu sagen;
Sie bietet mir zum Schönen manches Gute,
Das lastet nur, ich muß mich ihm entschlagen.
Mich treibt umher ein unbezwinglich Sehnen,
Da bleibt kein Rat als grenzenlose Tränen.

Of fervor, being near a certain creature.
The heart's at ease; not one distraction blurs
That deepest sense, the sense of *wholly hers*.

In the pure ocean of the soul, a comber
Flings itself, out of thankfulness, self-giving,
Toward something Purer, Higher—Grand Misnomer
However named—to approach the ever-living.
We call it, *being reverent*. And its flight
Sweeps me, when I'm beside her, height to height.

Before her gaze, like sun where winter lingers,
Before her breathing, like the stir of May,
Self-love, that steely ice that digs its fingers
Deep in our rigid psyche, melts away.
No self-concern, no self-importance where
She sets a foot. They squirm away, that pair.

As if I heard her, urgent: "Hour by hour
Life gives itself, exuberant, unbidden.
Yesterday's meaning is a withered flower;
Tomorrow!—who can live there? Where's it hidden?
Today though—if I quailed with sunset near
Never a sun but showed me something dear.

"Then do as I do: Look with knowing pride
Each moment in the face. But no evasion!
Keep every nerve a-tingle! Open-eyed
Rush to it all: day's effort, love's elation.
But where you are, be wholly. Be a child.
You're *all* then. Undefeatable," she smiled.

Easy, I thought, for you to say! Some grace
Shows you forever as the moment's friend.
Anyone near you for a moment's space
Is fortune's favorite—till the moment end.
As end it does! In panic I depart:
You and your pretty wisdom break the heart!

Now miles and miles between us. If I could,
How should I live this minute? Who's to say?
It offers much desirable and good
—All like a shabby pack to shrug away.
Invincible longing dogs me as I go.
Tears are the one philosophy I know.

So quellt denn fort! und fließet unaufhaltsam;
Doch nie gelängs, die innre Glut zu dämpfen!
Schon rasts und reißt in meiner Brust gewaltsam,
Wo Tod und Leben grausend sich bekämpfen.
Wohl Kräuter gäbs, des Körpers Qual zu stillen;
Allein dem Geist fehlts am Entschluß und Willen,

Fehlts am Begriff: wie sollt er sie vermissen?
Er wiederholt ihr Bild zu tausendmalen.
Das zaudert bald, bald wird es weggerissen,
Undeutlich jetzt und jetzt im reinsten Strahlen;
Wie könnte dies geringstem Troste frommen,
Die Ebb und Flut, das Gehen wie das Kommen?

\*

Verlaßt mich hier, getreue Weggenossen!
Laßt mich allein am Fels, in Moor und Moos;
Nur immer zu! euch ist die Welt erschlossen,
Die Erde weit, der Himmel hehr und groß;
Betrachtet, forscht, die Einzelnheiten sammelt,
Naturgeheimnis werde nachgestammelt.

Mir ist das All, ich bin mir selbst verloren,
Der ich noch erst den Göttern Liebling war;
Sie prüften mich, verliehen mir Pandoren,
So reich an Gütern, reicher an Gefahr;
Sie drängten mich zum gabeseligen Munde,
Sie trennen mich, und richten mich zugrunde.

\*

### AUSSÖHNUNG

Die Leidenschaft bringt Leiden!—Wer beschwichtigt,
Beklommnes Herz, dich, das zu viel verloren?
Wo sind die Stunden, überschnell verflüchtigt?

So let them have their way now, unrepressed.
No chance they'll damp the furnaces within.
Embattled there, all's berserk in my breast
With life and death locked grisly. Which to win?
Herbs dull our suffering when the body's ill,
But if the soul lack nerve, lack even will—?

Or worse, lack understanding? Years without her!
Whose image haunts me in a thousand ways.
Sun on her hair, the falling dusk about her—
The memories lag, or dwindle off in haze.
What good's all this? What comfort? shaken so
By all this coming, going, ebb and flow?

*

Well, leave me, good companions to endure it
Here on the moor alone, with rocks and moss.
But you, the world's before you. On. Explore it,
The whole wide earth, the heaven so broad across!
Make your investigations, scour and scout.
Nature has clues to shuffle and sort out.

I've lost it all, earth, heaven, self. Ignore a
Man the gods coddled with a "lucky star"!
They put me to the proof with that Pandora
So rich in gifts, in havoc richer far.
They pressed me to sweet lips that gave and gave;
Then crushed and flung me headlong. Toward the grave.

*

RECONCILIATION

Passion, and then the anguish. And with whom
To soothe you, heavy heart that lost so much?
Love's hour escaped, unstoppered like perfume?

Vergebens war das Schönste dir erkoren!
Trüb ist der Geist, verworren das Beginnen;
Die hehre Welt, wie schwindet sie den Sinnen!

Da schwebt hervor Musik mit Engelsschwingen,
Verflicht zu Millionen Tön um Töne,
Des Menschen Wesen durch und durch zu dringen,
Zu überfüllen ihn mit ewger Schöne:
Das Auge netzt sich, fühlt im höhern Sehnen
Den Götter-Wert der Töne wie der Tränen.

Und so das Herz erleichtert merkt behende,
Daß es noch lebt und schlägt und möchte schlagen,
Zum reinsten Dank der überreichen Spende
Sich selbst erwidernd willig darzutragen.
Da fühlte sich—o daß es ewig bliebe!
Das Doppel-Glück der Töne wie der Liebe.

# Ein Gleichnis

Jüngst pflückt ich einen Wiesenstrauß,
Trug ihn gedankenvoll nach Haus,
Da hatten von der warmen Hand
Die Kronen sich alle zur Erde gewandt.
Ich setzte sie in frisches Glas,
Und welch ein Wunder war mir das!
Die Köpfchen hoben sich empor,
Die Blätterstengel im grünen Flor,
Und allzusammen so gesund
Als stünden sie noch auf Muttergrund.

So war mir's als ich wundersam
Mein Lied in fremder Sprache vernahm.

The loveliest—all for nothing—within touch?
Cloudy the mind; mere muddle all it tries.
And the great world adrift before the eyes.

Then music to the fore like angels swarming,
A million tones in galaxy. We surrender
All of our inner fort to forces storming
—Irresistibly overrun with splendor.
The eye goes damp: in longings past tomorrow
We guess at the infinite worth of song and sorrow.

And so the heart, disburdened, in a flash
Knows: I endure, and beat, and pound with pleasure!
Gives itself over utterly, in rash
Thanks for the windfall, life. No common treasure.
Then came—could it only last!—that feeling of
Double delight from music and from love.

## A Likeness (c. 1825–28)

I picked some flowers that I saw bloom
In a field, and thoughtfully carried them home;
But soon their heads, in the warm hand bound,
Had fallen, and limply hung to the ground.
I put them in water, in a fresh glass;
Next, what a wonder came to pass!
The little heads rose up straightway,
And the stems of the leaves in green display;
And altogether so healthy and sound
As if they still stood on their mother-ground.

So it was with me when miracle-sprung
I heard my song in a foreign tongue.

# Beruf des Storches

Der Storch, der sich von Frosch und Wurm
An unserm Teiche nähret,
Was nistet er auf dem Kirchenturm
Wo er nicht hingehöret?

Dort klappt und klappert er genung,
Verdrießlich anzuhören;
Doch wagt es weder alt noch jung
Ihm in das Nest zu stören.

Wodurch—gesagt mit Reverenz—
Kann er sein Recht beweisen,
Als durch die löbliche Tendenz,
Aufs Kirchendach zu . . . . . . . .

# Im Ernsten Beinhaus

Im ernsten Beinhaus wars, wo ich beschaute,
    Wie Schädel Schädeln angeordnet paßten;
    Die alte Zeit gedacht ich, die ergraute.
Sie stehn in Reih geklemmt, die sonst sich haßten,
    Und derbe Knochen, die sich tödlich schlugen,
    Sie liegen kreuzweis, zahm allhier zu rasten.
Entrenkte Schulterblätter! was sie trugen,
    Fragt niemand mehr, und zierlich tätge Glieder,
    Die Hand, der Fuß, zerstreut aus Lebensfugen.
Ihr Müden also lagt vergebens nieder,
    Nicht Ruh im Grabe ließ man euch, vertrieben
    Seid ihr herauf zum lichten Tage wieder,
Und niemand kann die dürre Schale lieben,
    Welch herrlich edlen Kern sie auch bewahrte.
    Doch mir Adepten war die Schrift geschrieben,

# The Stork's Profession (1820s)

The stork that feeds on frog and worm
Beside our pond, so free,
Why does he nest on the *Kirchenturm*
Where he has no right to be?

He clatters about and snaps enough,
Sounds we all detest;
But young and old folks lack the guff
To plague him in his nest.

What squatting rights—all due respects—
Entitle him to it,
Save that he pleasingly elects
On the church's roof to . . . ?

# Lines Written upon the Contemplation of Schiller's Skull (1826)

Skull upon skull arranged in fit array
In solemn vault of burial I beheld
And thought of bygone years and times turned grey.

Near neighbours now, in rows they stand tight-held:
Rough bones that clashed in deadly strife before
Lie crosswise here, their rage to quiet quelled.

Unjointed shoulderblades! what once they bore
None now will ask; and limbs once full of grace,
Hands, feet, lie scattered and will move no more.

So all in vain you sought this resting-place,
Poor weary ones! they would not let you lie,
Whom daywards from your shadowy grave they chase,

And none cares now for husks that have gone dry
Though glorious kernels they did once contain.
Yet here was written what my adept's eye,

Die heilgen Sinn nicht jedem offenbarte,
  Als ich inmitten solcher starren Menge
  Unschätzbar herrlich ein Gebild gewahrte,
Daß in des Raumes Moderkält und Enge
  Ich frei und wärmefühlend mich erquickte,
  Als ob ein Lebensquell dem Tod entspränge.
Wie mich geheimnisvoll die Form entzückte!
  Die gottgedachte Spur, die sich erhalten!
  Ein Blick, der mich an jenes Meer entrückte,
Das flutend strömt gesteigerte Gestalten.
  Geheim Gefäß! Orakelsprüche spendend,
  Wie bin ich wert, dich in der Hand zu halten?
Dich höchsten Schatz aus Moder fromm entwendend
  Und in die freie Luft, zu freiem Sinnen,
  Zum Sonnenlicht andächtig hin mich wendend.
Was kann der Mensch im Leben mehr gewinnen,
  Als daß sich Gott-Natur ihm offenbare?
  Wie sie das Feste läßt zu Geist verrinnen,
  Wie sie das Geisterzeugte fest bewahre.

# Begeisterung

Fassest du die Muse nur beim Zipfel,
Hast du wenig nur getan;
Geist und Kunst, auf ihrem höchsten Gipfel,
Muten alle Menschen an.

Though few would guess its sacred sense, read plain:
Amid the rigid throng one shape I saw
Of rare nobility—and at once again

In this cold mouldering chamber's narrow maw
I felt refreshed and warmed, alive and free:
What welling life-spring here outleapt death's law?

O outline traced by God, still clear to see!
O lineaments enchanting to my eyes,
Transporting me to that mysterious sea

Whence transformed forms perpetually rise!
Strange vessel, fountainhead of sapience,
How dares my hand to hold you? Previous prize

Which from decay I snatch with reverence
And into free air, freely there to muse,
Out into sunlight, piously bear hence.

To what more noble end our life we use
Than knowing God-and-Nature, which are one?
Firm matter melts which She as Mind renews,
And She makes firm what fertile Mind has done.

———————

# Being Inspired (before 1827)

To catch a braid the Muse may trail behind
Is not much to have done;
The highest peaks of art and mind
Brace and strengthen everyone.

# Dämmerung senkte sich von oben

Dämmrung senkte sich von oben,
Schon ist alle Nähe fern;
Doch zuerst emporgehoben
Holden Lichts der Abendstern!
Alles schwankt ins Ungewisse
Nebel schleichen in die Höh;
Schwarzvertiefte Finsternisse
Widerspiegelnd ruht der See.

Nun am östlichen Bereiche
Ahn ich Mondenglanz und -glut,
Schlanker Weiden Haargezweige
Scherzen auf der nächsten Flut.
Durch bewegter Schatten Spiele
Zittert Lunas Zauberschein,
Und durchs Auge schleicht die Kühle
Sänftigend ins Herz hinein.

# War schöner als der schönste Tag

War schöner als der schönste Tag,
Drum muß man mir verzeihen,
Daß ich sie nicht vergessen mag,
Am wenigsten im Freien.
Im Garten war's, sie kam heran,
Mir ihre Gunst zu zeigen;
Das fühl ich noch und denke dran,
Und bleib' ihr ganz zu eigen.

# Twilight down from Heaven (1827)

Twilight down from heaven wafted,
What was near, now it is far;
Gentle, though, and firstly lofted
Lustre of the evening star.
Off all things the contours shiver,
Sliding mist, way up it goes;
Mirrored deeps more black than ever
Darken the lake in its repose.

Now a hint of moon, I wonder,
From the east, a silver glow,
Boughs of hair the willow slender
Dandles in the flood below.
Through the sport of shadows gliding
Luna's unsteady auras dart,
Through the eye the coolness sliding
Touches with a calm the heart.

# Lovelier She (1827)

Lovelier she than the loveliest day;
Others me will pardon
That the memory never goes away,
Least of all in a garden.
In a garden it was she came along
To offer me her favour,
I feel it still, to her belong,
Thinking of it, for ever.

# Dem aufgehenden Vollmonde
### Dornburg, den 25. August 1828

Willst du mich sogleich verlassen?
Warst im Augenblick so nah!
Dich umfinstern Wolkenmassen,
Und nun bist du gar nicht da.

Doch du fühlst, wie ich betrübt bin,
Blickt dein Rand herauf als Stern!
Zeugest mir, daß ich geliebt bin,
Sei das Liebchen noch so fern.

So hinan denn! hell und heller,
Reiner Bahn, in voller Pracht!
Schlägt mein Herz auch schmerzlich schneller,
Überselig ist die Nacht.

# Früh, wenn Tal, Gebirg und Garten
### Dornburg, September 1828

Früh, wenn Tal, Gebirg und Garten
Nebelschleiern sich enthüllen,
Und dem sehnlichsten Erwarten
Blumenkelche bunt sich füllen;

Wenn der Äther, Wolken tragend,
Mit dem klaren Tage streitet,
Und ein Ostwind, sie verjagend,
Blaue Sonnenbahn bereitet;

Dankst du dann, am Blick dich weidend,
Reiner Brust der Großen, Holden,
Wird die Sonne, rötlich scheidend,
Rings den Horizont vergolden.

# To the Full Moon Rising (1828)

Must you now so soon be leaving?
Moments gone, so close you were.
Sombre clouds around you cleaving,
Now you are not even there.

Yet you feel my feeling darken,
Show a single edge, as star,
Testify that love will hearken:
I am loved, though from afar.

Go your way, in purest splendour,
More and more intensely bright.
Let my heart race and ache, so tender—
Rapturous it is, the night.

# Garden, Valley, Hill (1828)

To veils of mist in morning light
Disclosed are garden, valley, hill,
And cups of flowers with colours bright
To the most ardent longing fill.

Ether, in the clouds it bears,
Quarrels with the candid day,
And east wind, for the sun, prepares
A blue path, chasing them away.

With pure heart thank the mild great one,
With moving gaze the scene behold,
Then will the reddish setting sun
Ring the horizon round with gold.

Es spricht sich aus der stumme Schmerz,
Der Äther klärt sich blau und bläuer,
Da schwebt sie ja die goldne Leier,
Komm, alte Freundin, komm ans Herz.

Note: the Artemis reading "alte Freude" is corrected here to "alte Freundin,"
following the Hamburg and Manesse texts.

# Der Bräutigam

Um Mitternacht, ich schlief, im Busen wachte
Das liebevolle Herz als wär es Tag;
Der Tag erschien, mir war, als ob es nachte,
Was ist es mir, so viel er bringen mag.

Sie fehlte ja, mein emsig Tun und Streben
Für sie allein ertrug ich's durch die Glut
Der heißen Stunde; welch erquicktes Leben
Am kühlen Abend! lohnend war's und gut.

# Pain, Dumb (1828)

Pain, dumb,
Has the word: air
Clears,

Blue, bluer;
From there
Come

She must, and does
Descend,
Floating, the golden

Lyre, I'll
Hold you now to my heart,
Old ladyfriend.

---

# The Bridegroom (1828)

At midnight, I was sleeping, in my breast
My fond heart lay awake, as though it were day;
Day broke: as though by falling night oppressed
I thought: what's day to me, bring what it may?

Since she was lacking; all my toil and strife
For her alone patiently I'd withstood
Throughout the hot noon hours. What quickening life
In the cool evening! Blessed it was, and good.

Die Sonne sank und Hand in Hand verpflichtet
Begrüßten wir den letzten Segensblick,
Und Auge sprach, ins Auge klar gerichtet:
Von Osten, hoffe nur, sie kommt zurück.

Um Mitternacht, der Sterne Glanz geleitet
Im holden Traum zur Schwelle, wo sie ruht.
O sei auch mir dort auszuruhn bereitet,
Wie es auch sei, das Leben, es ist gut.

# Vermächtnis

Kein Wesen kann zu nichts zerfallen!
Das Ewge regt sich fort in allen,
Am Sein erhalte dich beglückt!
Das Sein ist ewig: denn Gesetze
Bewahren die lebendgen Schätze,
Aus welchen sich das All geschmückt.

Das Wahre war schon längst gefunden,
Hat edle Geisterschaft verbunden;
Das alte Wahre, faß es an!
Verdank es, Erdensohn, dem Weisen,
Der ihr, die Sonne zu umkreisen,
Und dem Geschwister wies die Bahn.

Sofort nun wende dich nach innen:
Das Zentrum findest du da drinnen,
Woran kein Edler zweifeln mag.
Wirst keine Regel da vermissen:
Denn das selbständige Gewissen
Ist Sonne deinem Sittentag.

Den Sinnen hast du dann zu trauen,
Kein Falsches lassen sie dich schauen,
Wenn dein Verstand dich wach erhält.

The sun went down; and hand to dear hand wedded
We took our leave of him, watched the last ray burn,
And the eye said, eye to clear eye threaded:
But hope, and from the East he will return.

At midnight! Led by starlight through the gloom,
Dream-wrapt, I go to where she lies at rest.
Oh, may I lie at last in that same room!
Life's good, though worst befall us, life is blessed.

# Testament (1829)

No thing on earth to nought can fall,
The Eternal onward moves in all;
Rejoice, by being be sustained.
Being is deathless: living wealth,
With which the All adorns itself,
By laws abides and is maintained.

Long since, the true was found and could
Spirits join in brotherhood;
The ancient truth set hand upon.
Thank now the sage, O child of earth,
Who showed her and her kin the path
For circuiting about the sun.

Now turn yourself about, within:
Your centre you will find therein,
No noble soul can this gainsay.
No principle within you'll miss,
For independent conscience is
The sun that rules your moral day.

The senses next you must believe;
With nothing false will they deceive
If intellect keeps you awake.

Mit frischem Blick bemerke freudig
Und wandle, sicher wie geschmeidig,
Durch Auen reichbegabter Welt.

Genieße mäßig Füll und Segen;
Vernunft sei überall zugegen,
Wo Leben sich des Lebens freut.
Dann ist Vergangenheit beständig,
Das Künftige voraus lebendig,
Der Augenblick ist Ewigkeit.

Und war es endlich dir gelungen,
Und bist du vom Gefühl durchdrungen:
Was fruchtbar ist, allein ist wahr—
Du prüfst das allgemeine Walten,
Es wird nach seiner Weise schalten,
Geselle dich zur kleinsten Schar.

Und wie von alters her, im stillen,
Ein Liebewerk nach eignem Willen
Der Philosoph, der Dichter schuf,
So wirst du schönste Gunst erzielen:
Denn edlen Seelen vorzufühlen
Ist wünschenswertester Beruf.

Be fresh of eye, with joy attend;
A way, footsure and supple, wend,
A walk in worlds of pasture take.

Be moderate when blessings flow,
Good sense in every detail show
Where life is in its ecstasies;
Then bygone time gives permanence,
The future lives, and in advance:
Eternity the moment is.

Should you at last your end attain,
The feeling flow in every vein
That fruitfulness alone is true,
You'll scrutinize the common round,
Its general habit having found
You'll be advised to join the few.

And as in secret down the years
The poets, the philosophers
Shape works of love, each to his will,
The finest favour you'll assay:
For noble souls, feel out the way—
No task is more desirable.

# Parabel

Ich trat in meine Gartentür,
Drei Freunde kamen, auch wohl vier,
Ich bat sie höflich zu mir ein
Und sagte: sie sollten willkommen sein;
Da in der Mitte, im heitern Saal,
Stünd grade ein hübsches Frühstücksmahl.
Wollt jedem der Garten wohl Gefallen,
Darin nach seiner Art zu wallen.
Der eine schlich in dichte Lauben,
Der andre kletterte nach Trauben,
Sein Bruder nach hohen Äpfeln schielt,
Die er für ganz vortrefflich hielt.
Ich sagte: die stünden alle frisch
Zusammen drin auf rundem Tisch,
Und wären ihnen gar schön empfohlen.
Sie aber wollten sie selber holen;
Auch war der letzte, wie eine Maus,
Fort! wohl zur Hintertür hinaus.
Ich aber ging zum Saal hinein,
Verzehrte mein Frühstück ganz allein.

# Parable (1830)

Went to open my garden door,
Three friends are standing there, or four—
Told them come in (all politesse),
Bid them welcome at my place;
Folks, here it is, the table's laid
For breakfast, we'll go shares, I said.
They certainly like the garden a lot:
One slinks off to a shady spot,
One gawks at apples high in the trees,
They're nosing around just as they please,
Another reaches for a bunch of grapes—
Aha, says he, *what cultured shapes.*
Take all you want, said I, from the dish
On the round table—and I wish
One and all *guten Appetit.*
Rascals, they preferred to eat
What they could steal. The fourth, I think,
Snuck through the house and out in a wink.
So I stumped off back inside, and broke
My fast alone, without those folk.

# Anhang
# Paralipomena
# zu den Gedichten
# (Auswahl)

# Appendix
# A Selection of Texts
# from Paralipomena

UND Freude schwebt wie Sternenklang
Uns nur im Traume vor.

In goldnen Frühlingssonnenstunden
Lag ich gebunden
An dies Gesicht;
In holder Dunkelheit der Sinnen
Konnt ich wohl diesen Traum beginnen
Vollenden nicht.

# Jussieus Klassen der Pflanzen

Zum bequemen Gedächtnis der fünfzehn natürlichen Klassen,
Wie sie uns Jussieu gibt, versucht ich folgende Verse.
Ohne Samenstück keimen: die Schwämme, die Algen, die Leber-
Und die übrigen Moose, die Farren und die Najaden.
Einfach ist der Samenkern und die Stamina
Stehen über der Frucht in einfach blühender Blume
Als der Arums, der Typhen, der Cyperos und die Gräser.
Um die Frucht sind die Faden gestellt bei Palmen und Spargeln,
Rohren, Lilien und Bromelien, auch Asphodelen,
Bei Narzissen und Iris, und unterfrüchtig die Faden
Bei den Musen und Cannen, bei Orchis und Wassererfreuten.
Groß ist die Zahl der Pflanzen mit doppeltem Kernstück, sie folgen
Ohne Blumen Blatt unter der Frucht die Fäden, sie heißen
Aristolochien allein, und nur die

And joy like a star sound
Floats only in a dream before us.

In golden moments of the springtime sun
This vision held me
Spellbound; sweet
That darkness of the senses,
This dream I could begin
But not complete.

# Jussieu's Classes of Plants

To memorize conveniently the fifteen natural classes
Proposed by Jussieu, I tried the following lines:
Without seed the fungi grow, algae, hepaticas
And other kinds of moss, ferns, and naiads.
Simple is the seed, with stamens over the fruit
In simple blooms, for instance
Arums, typhas, cyperi, and grasses.
Round the fruit the filaments are placed in palms,
Asparagus, reeds, lilies, bromelias, likewise asphodel,
Daffodil, iris; and beneath the fruit
In moulds and canes, in orchids and waterparsleys.
Great is the number of plants with a double seed, as follows
Flowerless the leaf and filaments beneath the fruit,
They are called Aristolochias only, and only the

EINST wendeten im [?] Verdruß [?] die Grazien sich nach Norden
   Schaudernd kamen durch Schnee die zierlichen Dirnen[?]
Eine Türe fanden sie offen, sie eilten und wollten
   sich der Gastfreundschaft erfreuen
Trunken [?] tritt ein Mann in die Türe: wer seid ihr
   Fort riß er          Schleier[?] mit h. . . . nicht auf

Bitter ist Schnee uns, doch bittrer der Anblick des Mannes

~~~~~~~~~~~~~~~~~~~

WAS ich geschrieben habe das hab ich vertraulich den Deutschen[?]
 Hingelegt und nun steht es die ewige Zeit.
Manches hab ich gefehlt in meinem Leben, doch keinen
 Hab ich belistet.

~~~~~~~~~~~~~~~~~~~

MASTEN stehen gedrängt an Masten, es trocknet die Segel
   In dem Sonnenschein ruhig der Schiffer an dem Gestade der
                                        Stadt.

~~~~~~~~~~~~~~~~~~~

Alles verschwindet dem Blicke Bettine wenn du kleine
Tische und Leuchter besteigst [oben dich zeigst] und Masten und
 zwischen Hin. .
Du Bettina dich zeigst alles verschwindet dem Blick

Once in annoyance the Graces turned to the north,
Through snow they came shivering, the delicate lasses,
One door open they found, hurried and hoped for a welcome.
Drunk, a man stood in the door—"Who are you?"
Tore away their veils (. . .)

Bitter the snow to us, bitterer still that man, the sight of him

What I have written I set before the Germans
In confidence and now it stands for ever.
In my life I have made mistakes but not once ever
Tricked anyone.

Thronged masts, the sailor calmly drying
Sails in the sun on the shore of the city.

Everything vanishes Bettina little one when you
Climb over tables and candlesticks and masts and between
(. . .)
When you appear Bettina everything vanishes

WÄR ich ein Maler mit lauter Bettinen
Wollt ich den Himmel mit lauter Bettinen bevölkern
.
Das Christkindchen wünschte sich keinen schöneren Pagen [?]
Und der Prinz in Stroh [?]

Was ist oben was unten an dir was vorne was hinten?

Voller Gefahr scheint jede Bewegung Sorge
 Und so zierlich du's machst wünscht die Gefahr man erneut.

LEBEN hab ich gelernt, fristet mir Götter die Zeit.

If I were a painter with only Bettinas
I'd people the heavens with only Bettinas

No better pageboy could the Christ Child ask for
And the Prince in the hay

━━━━━━━━━━━━━━━

What is above with you and below, what before and behind?

Perilous every motion you make, it seems,
Yet so graceful one's left wanting the danger anew.

━━━━━━━━━━━━━━━

I have learned how to live, let me gods live out my time

Pfaffe möcht ich sein im Glauben und Götter verzehren
 Die ich mit eigener Hand einmal[?] mir täglich erzeugt
Pilger möcht ich sein und glauben daß Schritte nach Schritten
 Der v

Nur nicht Lavater sein und Sinn mit Unsinn vermischen
 Denn so glauben das heißt sündgen am heiligen Geist

Zwiespalt wenn man dich sieht

Ein ander Handwerk und doch wer möchte dich nicht hier am
 Strande sehen
Genießen und doch
Glücklich wer einst dich genießt wenn du das Wachstum vollendet
dem du die Schenkelchen zart über den Körper legst
Aber laß andre Weiber Freuden geben und gebären[?]
du gib einstweilen [?] Vergnügen[?] was keine geben kann
Die Segel[?] die Riva der Sciavoni
das Kind mit den Beinchen in die Höhe
Farben blau weiß rot gold
Wär ich ein Maler du solltest als Engelchen überall sein

Vom Nil Hylas Hiazynth Chilon[?] Antinous

I'd like to be a priest believing and eat the gods
I'd make day after day by my own handiwork
I'd like to be a pilgrim and believe that step by step
(. . .)

But not be Lavater mixing sense with nonsense
That manner of belief is a sin against the Holy Ghost

Mind split on seeing you

Another métier, but who would miss
The sight of you here on the beach
Enjoy and yet
Happy the man who will enjoy you when you are fullgrown
Over whose body you'll tenderly place your little thighs
But let other women give joy and give birth
Meanwhile give pleasures no other can
The sails the Riva dei Sciavoni
the child with her legs in the air
Colours blue white red gold
If I were a painter you would be everywhere an angel

From the Nile, Hylas Hyacinth Chilon Antinous

Mir bescheidnem Christ
Wäre schon köstlich indessen[?] wenn mir das Kind in den Armen
 ruhte
Alles fällt mir wieder bei diesem Kind ein

So seht nur wie gefährlich es ist unser[?] Büchlein zu lesen

Die Mühen und Tränen die dichs gekostet

Wenn du dich überschlägst dein Köpfchen mit den Füßen in Eins
Auf den Ellenbogen gehst Es wird ein . . . [unleserliches Wort]
Da wenn du auf ein[mal] wieder auf den Füßen stehst
sieht man dich immer[?] lieber

So führt der Tonkünstler uns durch viele Töne bis er uns wieder
zurück mit dem Grundton befriedigt

Ich wär auch gern e'mal dumm gewesen
Hätten nur die Dummen nit so viel gelesen.

Unassuming Christian as I am
It would be delicious to have the child lying in my arms

Everything returns to my mind when I see this child

—————————————

Notice how dangerous it is to read our little book

—————————————

The troubles and tears it has cost you

When all of a sudden you somersault, head over heels
Walk on your elbows then there's a (. . .)
Suddenly stand on your feet again
Each time seen, lovelier than before

Thus will a composer lead us through many notes before
He finally brings us back to the keynote gratified

—————————————

For once I'd like to be an idiot, too,
If the others would only read less than they do.

WOLKEN Massen Wolken Ballen
Steigen düster aus dem Meere
Kl. . . . E. . . [Erz?] und Hörner [?] schallen
Wie von aufgeregtem Heere
Dreht sichs da und wirbelt heftig
Bl. [Bläst?] und s. [saust?] [oder Blasend sausend]

DES Alten Schatten war noch was,
Des Sohnes Körper was ist das?

EIN dürres Blatt im Wind getrieben,
Sieht öfters einem Vogel gleich.

WEIL er da recht war wo er war
Und nicht von Zephiretten [?] Traumge
Von nichts zu nichts getragen ward.

Erbe,
Wo nicht des Weltreichs, Erbe großen Mißgeschicks.

Clouds masses clouds globes
Rise crepuscular from the sea
Small bronze (?) and horns clamour
It's like an army on the move
Sweeping around a violent whirl
(. . .)

⌒⌒⌒⌒⌒⌒⌒⌒⌒⌒

The shadow of the Ancient One was something still.
The body of the Son, now is that real?

⌒⌒⌒⌒⌒⌒⌒⌒⌒⌒

A dry leaf driven by the wind
Often looks like a bird.

⌒⌒⌒⌒⌒⌒⌒⌒⌒⌒

Because he was exactly where he was
And not blown by dreamy zephyrlings
From nought to nought.

⌒⌒⌒⌒⌒⌒⌒⌒⌒⌒

Inheritor
If not a world empire, inheritor of a great misfortune.

ICH weiß zwar nicht woher wir kommen

Aber ins Teufels Namen
Rechtet mit Byron und dem Talent
 seinem

DIE Dämonen spotten meiner
Das weiß ich recht gut

KEIN umrollender Kräusel kein Haspel wirkt in dem Orkus

NACHTGESPENSTER ziehen nicht mehr die garstigen langen;
 Neumond kündest du an! Almanac, redest du Wahr?
Leuchtet mir doch das Gemach von holdem mondlichem Schimmer
 Wohl das Mondengesicht, senkte vom Himmel sich her.

Truly I don't know where we come from

But in the devil's name
Pick a bone with Byron and his expertise

~~~~~~~~~~~~~~~~~

The demons make fun of me,
No doubt about it

~~~~~~~~~~~~~~~~~

A spinning top and a windlass won't work in Orcus

~~~~~~~~~~~~~~~~~

No more ghosts will walk in the night, the horrible tall ones,
New is the moon you announce, Almanac, can it be true?
Yes, my room is aglow with delicate shimmering moonlight
Shed by the face of the moon, floating from heaven above.

MIRABELLEN pflanz ich in meinem Garten in Reihen
Daß nun die Wunderschöne wandelnd in Gesellschaft sei.

~~~~~~~~~~~~~~~~~~~~

GOLDSTAUB wirf in das Wasser er wird zum Grunde sich senken
Bärlappsamen er deckt leicht wie ein Häutchen das Naß.

Rows of mirabelles I shall plant in my garden,
Then my beauty shall have company there on her walks.

<div align="center">~~~~~~~~~~~~~~~~~~~</div>

Toss gold dust into water and straight it sinks to the bottom,
Lightly the clubmoss seed covers the surface like skin.

Notes

I. *Early Poems, 1768–75* (written in Leipzig, Strasbourg, Frankfurt). The first twelve poems illustrate G.'s emergence from playful (not often so audacious) Rococo conventions, to create a style all his own, marked by unprecedented *brio*, velocity, vocal aptitude, and directness. The verse is formal, but the tempi are quick, emotions violent and volatile. "Willkommen und Abschied" and "Mailied": two of a series of lyrics provoked by G.'s love for Friederike Brion of Sesenheim (near Strasbourg). "Heidenröslein," "Der König in Thule"; encouraged by Herder, G. is here grafting the newly revaluated folksong idiom on to his own motifs: eruptive passion, with nature or artifact as symbols of Self. (The latter poem is sung by Gretchen at a turningpoint in G.'s *Urfaust.*) "Wandrers Sturmlied": an extempore, of "Pindaric" inspiration, ending with an irony seldom recognized: the poem hovers between heaven and mud. Jupiter Pluvius = Jupiter as Raingod; Bromius = Bacchus (Dionysus); allusions to Greek poets do not rupture the frame of immediate sensory experience. "Mahomets Gesang": relic of a projected drama, with Mahomet as exemplary religious genius, here transformed into the "nature-symbol" of the river as artifex of human community. Rhapsodic mode: the text dates from G.'s early Frankfurt Storm and Stress period. "Prometheus": also a relic from a proposed play, figuring the Greek proto-hero, much esteemed by Storm and Stress writers (G.'s poem is less a critique of deity as such, than an attack on authority and injustice). "Ganymed": the obverse of "Prometheus," here the compliant shepherd boy of Greek myth is lifted invisibly (not by an eagle, as in the myth) up to Olympus. "Auf dem See": written during a journey in Switzerland (the lake was the Zürichsee); "golden dreams"—of Lili Schönemann, the heiress whom G. almost married in Frankfurt: but really the poem concerns passionate perception of relations between features in space, an immediate world of primal phenomena, cosmic germinations. Likewise: "Herbstgefühl" (also from Switzerland).

II. *The First Weimar Years.* "Erklärung eines alten Holzschnittes": Hans Sachs, great 16th century South German folk poet, whom G. rediscovered. The poem contains numerous allusions to Sachs's plays and the verse-form imitates Sachs's "Knittelvers". No original "woodcut" has been identified, but G. is imagining a large folio with a series of images, of the kind commonly hawked in markets ("popular iconography"). The following four poems and "Nachtgedanken" (below) are eloquent of G.'s inexplicable passion for Charlotte von Stein, who undertook to civilize him in Weimar. "Ein Gleiches" was scratched in pencil on a wall-plank in a mountain hut. "Harzreise im Winter": another sublime extempore, in "free rhythms," of Pindaric inspiration, tracking (as hereafter in German poetry) intuitions of divine-human contact. The poem was probably composed on horseback, during a prospecting expedition (minerals) in the Harz Mountains. The person whom G. had in mind ("Aber abseits, wer ist's?") was called Plessing: he had written to G. in Weimar; G. visited him, but incognito, during the journey. The peak viewed at the end is the Brocken, celebrated as a gathering place of witches on Walpurgisnacht. Cudgels: peasant vegetable gardens were ravaged by wild boars that might only be hunted in sea-

son by the gentry (an historic grievance, which motivated many onslaughts on landowners, or their agents, a generation later during the French Revolution). "Zueignung": originally written to preface the long stanzaic narrative poem "Die Geheimnisse," which was never completed. The record of psychic contact and communication here matches in many details that of shaman-initiation documented the world over. Rhymes in translation do not accord with the German *ottava rima*.

III. *"Klassik" and the Turn of the Century.* "Amor als Landschaftsmaler": written in Italy, remarkable for its modern self-reflexivity, the poem is about *poiesis*. It also reflects G.'s intense interest in painting, and voices his belief in the interdependence of productive imagination and Eros. "Römische Elegien" (for scansion, see below—"Euphrosyne"): written after G.'s return from Italy (1786–88), and nuanced also by his new love, Christiane Vulpius (1765–1816), who is also the recipient of "Morgenklagen" and "Der Besuch" (like "Amor als Landschaftsmaler," those two poems are written in trochaic pentameters). In March–June 1790, G. was in Venice, whence came (along with the intermaxillary bone he discovered) the 100-odd "Venezianische Epigramme": see 'Paralipomena' for more details of the little street-acrobat girl (perhaps a Gipsy) evoked in epigram 38. "Nähe des Geliebten", "Die Spinnerin", "Mignon": all three are songlike texts for feminine voices (respectively: bourgeois, working class, and unplaceable). Mignon figures as a major character in *Wilhelm Meisters Lehrjahre* (1795), an enigmatic child associated with the ancient "Harpist" —but the "father" in her song could also be Wilhelm. Her song spans three primal "spaces": culture, nature, and legend (or the unconscious). "Die Braut von Korinth": based on a tale collected for the Emperor Hadrian by Phlegon of Tralles (2nd century A.D.). Collision between contending value-systems (here Pagan and Christian) is the gist in several of G.'s ballads. This one, in which Transsylvanian and Japanese motifs (at least for a modern reader) seem to mix, is dated at a crucial point in the emergence of Weimar Classicism—the enterprise by which Schiller and G. sought to rescue values they saw threatened by the consequences of the French Revolution (cf. G.'s narrative poem *Hermann und Dorothea*, 1798). "Euphrosyne": elegy for the young actress Christiane Neumann, news of whose death, at the age of 19, reached G. in Switzerland in 1797. "Euphrosyne" (Greek) means "Gaiety". Scansion (as for "Roman Elegies"): the second line in each distich must have a pause (cesura) at the third beat of six (*dum-didi dum-didi dum/dum-didi dum-didi dum* = two dactyls and one beat, followed by two more dactyls and another beat, though trochees (*dumdi*) may be substituted for certain dactyls. The first line, also a hexameter (six beats), should be more rapidly dactylic (too many trochaic substitutions make the line sluggish), and it must have a (disyllabic) feminine ending (*dumdi*). Greek and Latin models were greatly modified in German, where accent, not quantity or "length" of any given syllable, sets the measure. The reader is invited to consider lines 13–14, or 21–22, as a "model," to acquire therefrom the formal feel of the metrical movement, and thence, while holding strictly in mind that formal feel, to read continuously along with the "natural" word-accent (German or English). German poets were fascinated by the contrastive relations which could be generated between natural word-accent and the formally

regulated beat they inherited from the classics (Homer to Ovid; G. had great respect for the translations by J.H. Voss). "Die Musageten": "Musagetes" (Greek) = "Bringers of the Muses". The next five poems, including the two "Metamorphoses", epitomize G.'s unmatched synthesis of poetic and scientific modes of inquiry. His botany and anatomy have little scientific value now; but his vision of phenomena in organic-dynamic configurations, for all its apparent animism, marked an advance in its time, has been most fruitful, and still has distinct value. "Weltseele": for a time, weekly discussions, on scientific, literary, and philosophical matters, were held in G.'s house in Weimar ("The Wednesday Circle"). This poem is a mock-heroic, but still earnest, coda to such a meeting. To conclude the meeting, participants formed pairs, male and female, in a ritual miming of the cosmogonic combining of opposites—hence the penultimate stanza. "Nachtgesang": based on the refrain to a popular Italian song, *Dormi, che vuoi di più*. "Mächtiges Überraschen" and "Abschied": both sonnets come from the cycle of 17 (1807–8) which resulted from G.'s love affair with Minna Herzlieb, and from another, it would seem, with Silvie von Ziegesaar, for whom he wrote "Bergschloss". In "Das Tagebuch", however, the inexpungable beloved is Christiane Vulpius, whom G. had finally married in 1806 (she had shown great courage when French troops swarmed into Weimar after the Battle of Jena). "Landschaft": according to G.'s friend Riemer, the poem refers to a watercolor copy of a Dutch painting in Dresden.

IV. *Poems 1814–18 from The Parliament of West and East* (1819). The collection of twelve cycles, or "books," with numerous Orientalist and other notes, is an intricate fusion of personal, literary, social, philosophical, and religious themes. In this most secret of books (400 copies of the original edition were still unsold in 1914) G. speaks in his own person sometimes, at other times as the Persian Sufic poet Hafiz, or as "Hatem," while his interlocutor—"Suleika"— is identifiable as his adored Marianne von Willemer. "Gingo Biloba": the tree bears a double leaf. "Höheres und Höchstes": voices the unifying theme—poetic ecstasy as participation in continuous cosmogonic process. (The English version is nuanced by the translator's knowledge that the *Diwan* influenced Heine.)

V. *Later Poems, 1815–30*. "Prooemion": the title is the Greek word for "foresong". "Urworte. Orphisch": To his friend Knebel G. wrote: "Through Hermann, Creuzer, Zoega and Welcker, I have become involved in Greek mythology, indeed, in the Orphic obscurities . . ." (letter of October 9, 1817). He called the poem "a recapitulation of the age-old condensed representation of human fate" (as found in Orphism, its Mysteries, and in some pre-Socratic philosophers) (letter to Boisserée, May 15, 1818). In 1820, G. published a commentary of his own in the journal *Kunst und Altertum*. "Von Krüdener" (original title was VR): Julie von Krüdener was a religious enthusiast with a large itinerant following during the last years of Napoleon. She lobbied for the formation of the reactionary Holy Alliance (see J. Christopher Herold's brilliant and entertaining book *Mistress to an Age: A Life of Madame de Staël*, 1958). "Sankt Nepomuks Vorabend": in Karlsbad the nocturnal feast of St. Nepomuk was celebrated with a candlelight procession and singing by children.

By order of King Wenzel of Bohemia, the saint was drowned in the Moldau, because he had refused to divulge secrets told to him at confession by Wenzel's queen. "Ins Weite": a squib aimed at Romantic Absolutists. "Trilogie der Leidenschaft": the triptych was the outcome of a devastating love-affair with Ulrike von Levetzow. G. had first met her at Marienbad (the spa) in 1821, when she was 17 and he 72. Their mutual attraction reached its peak during the 1823 season. In September 1823, traveling in his coach back to Weimar from Karlsbad, G. wrote the "Elegy:" within hours of Ulrike's mother's declining to consider him as a suitable husband for Ulrike. The "Reconciliation" (part 3) was written a little earlier, in August 1823, inspired by music played on the piano by the Polish virtuoso Marie Szymanowska. The first part, 'To Werther,' was written in 1824 (March 24–25), originally to preface a new edition of the novel *Werther*. To Eckermann's remark that the "Elegy" was unlike any other poem of his, G. replied: "That might be due to the fact that I was gambling (*ich setzte*) on the present, and then tried to raise the stakes as high as possible, without exaggerating" (October 27, 1823). In the "Elegy," it is Ulrike, innocent and unencumbered, who can seize the moment and live its full intensity. The poem is certainly one of the most desperately ardent documents of love in Western literature, and to the bittersweet end it is sustained by perfectly balanced formal movement. "Beruf des Storches": supposedly a squib against critics, or, *mutatis mutandis,* against the Church. "Im ernsten Beinhaus war's": Schiller had been buried (1805) in the Weimar general cemetery (of the St. Jakobskirche). In 1826 the terrain was cleared: the putative skull and assorted bones were brought to G.'s house on September 24, to be re-interred several months later in the Royal Crypt. Verse-form: terza rima (G. was reading Dante at the time). "Dämmerung senkte sich von oben:" one of G.'s most dense— and ethereally objective—lyrics, written when he was 78, the poem gently deals with death-in-life, while it also alludes (as does "Wiederfinden") to his *Theory of Colors (Farbenlehre)*; like the earlier "Auf dem See," it dramatizes perceptions, too, of relations between features in space, as reflections of time. "Dem aufgehenden Vollmonde": this and the next two poems were written in Dornburg, where G. was absorbed in meteorological studies (he associated clouds with protean Indian gods). "Früh, wenn Tal . . .": a floating puzzle —serial perceptions of change in the time of day, a world disclosed, as Universe, and enclosed, with thanksgiving. "Parabel": supposedly a satire against critics.

Appendix: Paralipomena. These were notes and drafts for poems and they do not appear in standard editions, though the complete Artemis edition includes them. The selection here (less than a quarter of the whole) includes several curious notes from Venice. The absence of finish, confinement of utterance to a few bold but groping strokes, bring a reader as close as may be to the first movement of G.'s poetic conception.

Index of German Titles and First Lines